inspiration

Judy

Student's Book 3

MACMILLAN

CONTENTS

UNIT 1 — TEEN LIFE

		Grammar	Functions and Skills	Pronunciation	Vocabulary
Learning Styles	6	Present simple and present continous	Talking about language learning		Language learning Classroom activities
1 How are you feeling?	8	Present tense review Adverbial phrases of frequency	Talking about states and routines Talking about what's happening now Talking about future arrangements Writing a personal profile	/ɒ/ j<u>o</u>b /ʌ/ cl<u>u</u>b	Leisure activities School subjects Clothes
2 I wanted to go home	10	Past simple review	Describing past events Listening to a phone conversation Role play: a phone conversation Writing a diary entry	/θ/ b<u>o</u>th /ð/ to<u>ge</u>ther	Family members Adjectives for feelings
3 Everyone was cheering	12	Past simple and past continuous	Describing what happened and what was happening Writing a newspaper article about a dramatic event Listening to a radio broadcast	/ʃ/ cra<u>sh</u> /tʃ/ bea<u>ch</u>	Water Parts of the body Phrasal verbs with *get*
4 Integrated Skills Describing 'first times'	14	Revision	**Reading** Connecting ideas: Martin Scorsese interview **Listening** Identifying speakers and noting details: personal anecdotes **Speaking** Interviewing **Writing** Describing an important 'first time' **Learner Independence** Learning Diary; Word creation: prefixes *dis-* and *un-*		Music Feelings Useful expressions
Inspiration *Extra!*	16	**Project** Special Day File	**Sketch** The Mirror	**Revision & Extension**	**Your Choice!**
Culture	18	Identity			

UNIT 2 — ARTS

		Grammar	Functions and Skills	Pronunciation	Vocabulary
1 You can't help laughing	20	Verb/Preposition + gerund *so/nor* + auxiliary verbs	Talking about likes and dislikes Agreeing and disagreeing Writing a film review	Syllable stress	Films Adjectives for opinions
2 Promise to work together	22	Verb (+ object) + infinitive	Talking about plans and abilities Completing a questionnaire Listening to an interview	Syllable stress	Music and dance Skills
3 Books are left in public places	24	Present simple passive	Describing a system Doing a quiz Writing a book review	Linking: consonant sound + vowel	Books World records Phrasal verbs with *up*
4 Integrated Skills Describing a picture	26	Linking words: *which* and *who*	**Reading** Matching texts with pictures: What's your favourite picture? **Listening** Listening for details in a description **Speaking** Interviewing **Writing** Description of a picture **Learner Independence** Classroom English; Word creation: adjective suffixes *-ful* and *-less*		Feelings Useful expressions
Inspiration *Extra!*	28	**Project** Two-Minute Talks	**Song** You've Got a Friend	**Revision & Extension**	**Your Choice!**
Review Units 1–2	30	**Grammar & Vocabulary**	**Progress Check**		

CONTENTS

UNIT 3 — OPINIONS

		Grammar	Functions and Skills	Pronunciation	Vocabulary
1	It can't be her — 32	*must* and *can't* *could*, *may* and *might* Verbs of perception	Making logical deductions and discussing possibility Describing sensations (1) Listening to a TV game show Writing definitions	Silent letters	Food
2	You can't take a lion to the cinema — 34	*must* and *mustn't/can't* *have to* and *don't have to* Reflexive pronouns	Expressing obligation and prohibition Listening to information about UK laws	Syllable stress	Rules and regulations Age limit laws
3	You should calm down! — 36	*should/ought to* and *shouldn't* *had better* Adjective + infinitive	Giving advice Reading an online problem page Writing notes about problems, and giving advice	/æ/ s<u>a</u>d /e/ s<u>ai</u>d	School life Teenage problems Adjectives for opinions Phrasal verbs with *down*
4	Integrated Skills Discussing facts and opinions — 38	Linking words: *however* and *and*	**Reading** Distinguishing between fact and opinion: *World Poverty* and *The Aid Debate* articles **Listening** Noting details about saving energy **Speaking** Interview/Discussion **Writing** Report/Dialogue **Learner Independence** Learning contracts; Word creation: adjective prefixes *il-*, *im-* and *in-*		Poverty and aid Energy-saving Useful expressions

Inspiration Extra! — 40 **Project** Debate   **Sketch** Sign Language   **Revision & Extension**   **Your Choice!**

Culture — 42 Great Novels

UNIT 4 — MIND OVER MATTER

		Grammar	Functions and Skills	Pronunciation	Vocabulary
1	They hear him singing — 44	Verbs of perception + present participle *can/could* + verbs of perception	Describing sensations (2) Describing a picture Listening to a story	/eə/ h<u>air</u> /ɪə/ h<u>ear</u>	Sensations and sounds Parts of the body
2	I'll keep my fingers crossed! — 46	Future review: *will/won't*, *shall* and *going to*	Making predictions, promises and offers Talking about plans and intentions Completing a questionnaire Listening and predicting what happens in a story	Word stress in sentences	Superstitions Phrasal verbs with *out*
3	If you fly in a small plane … — 48	First conditional	Talking about future possibility Completing a questionnaire	Syllable stress	Flight School life
4	Integrated Skills Telling a story — 50	Revision	**Reading** *Rebecca* story **Speaking** Continuing the story based on pictures, and predicting outcomes **Listening** Listening to check predictions **Writing** Retelling the end of the story **Learner Independence** Guessing the meaning; Word creation: noun → adjective, verb → noun		Useful expressions

Inspiration Extra! — 52 **Project** Mystery File   **Song** Celebrate The Future   **Revision & Extension**   **Your Choice!**

Review Units 3–4 — 54 Grammar & Vocabulary   Progress Check

CONTENTS

UNIT 5 — CHALLENGES

			Grammar	Functions and Skills	Pronunciation	Vocabulary
1	They haven't had any accidents yet	56	Present perfect with *just*, *already* and *yet*	Talking about what has and hasn't happened; Reading an article about a journey	/eə/ wh**ere** /eɪ/ w**ay**	Countries; Phrases with *go*, *learn* and *ride*
2	Have you ever wondered …?	58	Present perfect with *ever* and *never*; Present perfect and past simple	Talking about experiences; Reading an article about extreme sports; Writing about things you've wanted to do but haven't done	Word stress in compound nouns	Sport; Geographical features
3	I've wanted to win since I was 14	60	Present perfect with *for* and *since*	Talking about achievements; Describing events and things which are important to you; Interviewing	Syllable stress	Olympic Games; Personal information
4	Integrated Skills Describing personal experiences	62	Linking words: *so* and *because*	**Reading** Connecting ideas: website travelogue; **Listening** Checking details: conversation about itinerary; **Speaking** Planning a backpacking trip; **Writing** Email describing journey; **Learner Independence** Self assessment; Word creation: noun suffix *-ity*		Countries; Geographical features; Useful expressions

Inspiration Extra! 64 **Project** Extreme Sports File **Sketch** The Interview **Revision & Extension** **Your Choice!**

Culture 66 Your holiday, their home

UNIT 6 — THAT'S CLEVER!

			Grammar	Functions and Skills	Pronunciation	Vocabulary
1	He had won awards	68	Past perfect	Describing a sequence of past events; Reading an article about teenage inventors; Writing about what you did yesterday	Syllable stress	Disability
2	People didn't use to throw things away	70	*used to* + infinitive	Talking about past habits and states; Reading an article about recycled products; Writing about changes in your life	/eɪ/ w**a**ste /e/ w**e**st	Recycling; Household items; Materials
3	The first car was invented by him	72	Past simple passive	Describing past processes; Reading about Leonardo da Vinci's inventions; Doing a quiz; Writing about best/worst inventions	Syllable stress	Inventions; Phrases with *do* and *make*
4	Integrated Skills Describing a process	74	Linking word: *although*	**Reading** Connecting ideas: *Ancient Inventions* article; **Listening** Ordering pictures showing stages in a process; **Speaking** Matching sentences and pictures to describe a process; **Writing** Process description; **Learner Independence** Self assessment; Word creation: noun suffixes *-er*, *-or* and *-ist*		Inventions; Materials; Useful expressions

Inspiration Extra! 76 **Project** History of Our Town File **Song** Brown-eyed Girl **Revision & Extension** **Your Choice!**

Review Units 5–6 78 Grammar & Vocabulary Progress Check

CONTENTS

UNIT 7 — COMMUNICATION

		Grammar	Functions and Skills	Pronunciation	Vocabulary
1	He asked her not to go	80	ask/tell + object + infinitive	Reporting requests and commands Reading an article about animal language learners Describing parents' instructions	Linking	Animals Language Household tasks Phrasal verbs
2	He said it didn't bother him	82	Reported statements: say and tell	Reporting what someone said Reading an article about the invention of email Listening for differences between what was said and what actually happened Interviewing and reporting good news	/g/ dog /k/ dock	Email Communications media
3	We asked how he had got the idea	84	Reported questions	Reporting what someone asked Role play: interviewing an inventor Writing a report of an interview	Syllable stress	Mobile phones Emergency services Phrasal verbs with go
4	Integrated Skills Telling a story	86	Linking words: sequencing adverbs	Reading Details: *Amazing Rescue* newspaper story Listening Listening for details: radio news Speaking Comparing newspaper and radio news report of same story Writing News story about a rescue Learner Independence Using the Internet to practise language skills Word creation: noun suffix *-tion*		Sailing and the sea Useful expressions

Inspiration Extra! 88 Project News File   Sketch Hotel Reception   Revision & Extension   Your Choice!

Culture 90 Global English

UNIT 8 — NATURAL WORLD

		Grammar	Functions and Skills	Pronunciation	Vocabulary
1	They should have known	92	should(n't) have, ought to have	Criticising past actions Reading facts and an interview about water Describing past situations you regret	/dʒ/ jump /ʃ/ shark /tʃ/ punch	Water
2	What would you do?	94	Second conditional	Talking about imaginary or unlikely situations Giving advice Completing a questionnaire Listening to note down answers	Pronunciation of *gh*	Geographical features Weather Illnesses and ailments Survival kit
3	You'd like to stay there, wouldn't you?	96	Question tags	Asking for agreement and checking Doing a quiz Writing descriptions of people and places	Intonation in question tags	Homes and living spaces
4	Integrated Skills Describing a country	98	Revision	Reading Topics: *Australia* guidebook description Listening Specific information: description of Canada Speaking Exchanging information Writing Description of a country Learner Independence English resources outside school; Word creation: adjective suffix *-al*		Geographical features Animals Industry and agriculture Climate Useful expressions

Inspiration Extra! 100 Project Urban Survival File   Song I Will Survive   Revision & Extension   Your Choice!

Review Units 7–8 102 Grammar & Vocabulary   Progress Check

Communication Activities: Student A 106   **Communication Activities:** Student B 116

Grammar Summary 109   **Word List** 120   **Irregular Verbs** 127

1 TEEN LIFE

Learning Styles
WHAT KIND OF LANGUAGE LEARNER ARE YOU?

Which student are you more like: Paula or Paolo?

If you are more like Paula, read these statements. Are you more like Mario or Maria?

Paula
I'm learning English because I want to pass examinations.
I like grammar and I always learn the rules by heart.
I read a few pages of an English book every day, and I look up all the new words in my dictionary.
When I speak English, I try to use phrases from my coursebook.

Mario
When I listen to English, I always want to understand every word.
A mistake is when you break grammar rules.
A good learner of English never makes any mistakes.
When I speak English, I always try to remember the rules.

Paolo
Why am I learning English? So I can communicate with people.
I never worry much about grammar – it's boring.
I don't often look up words – I guess the meaning and I'm usually right!
When I speak in class, I try to say things in different ways.

Maria
We have English homework three times a week and I always bring it to school on time.
When I do an exercise, I choose my answers very carefully.
It's best when the whole class does the same thing – I don't like pair or group work.
Before I start an activity, I always want to know exactly what to do.

If you are more like Paolo, read these statements. Are you more like Alicia or Alex?

Alicia
I'm sometimes late with my homework – I'm not very organised!
I do exercises quickly – I don't spend a long time thinking about the answers.
I love it when we work in groups or play games.
I enjoy activities like projects because we can decide what to do.

Alex
When I listen, I want to understand what people mean – not every word they say.
A mistake is when people don't understand you.
I get things wrong in every English lesson – all learners do. It's nothing to worry about.
When I speak or write English, I say what I feel and forget about the rules!

UNIT 1

Now look at the Learning Styles below. Read about the learning style of the student you are most like. Then read about the other students' learning styles. Are you sometimes like them too?

LEARNING STYLES

CONSTRUCTION
You …
- enjoy grammar practice exercises.
- like working with the teacher.
- are good at homework and tests.
- enjoy writing more than discussion.
- don't like games or group work.

REFLECTION
You …
- always want to know why and find rules for things.
- like working hard on your own and getting things right.
- prefer listening, reading and writing to speaking.
- sometimes don't finish work and are unhappy if it isn't perfect.

ACTION
You …
- like listening and speaking more than reading and writing.
- enjoy fun activities and moving around the classroom.
- like doing lots of different things and working with other people.
- like games more than writing and grammar.

INTERACTION
You …
- really enjoy learning languages.
- love group and pair work and prefer speaking to writing.
- don't like exercises and rules.
- like discussing personal things and feelings.

The Revision and Extension section on page 17 has a *Your Choice!* section with activities for each learning style. It's good to know your learning style, but it's also good to try out other ways of learning too.

7

1 TEEN LIFE

1 How are you feeling?

Present tense review
Adverbial phrases of frequency
Talking about states and routines
Talking about what's happening now
Talking about future arrangements

Questionnaire Teenage Talk

Leo Evans is 16 and lives in a suburb of Manchester.

What do you usually do at weekends?
I go skateboarding, I play the guitar, and I listen to music with my mates. And we go to clubs every Saturday night.

How often do you go to the cinema?
Once or twice a month.

What are you reading at the moment?
A brilliant book called *Northern Lights* by Philip Pullman.

What are your favourite school subjects?
Drama, Spanish and computer studies.

What do you and your friends talk about?
Football and music.

Do you have a girlfriend?
No – all the girls like older boys, because they have cars and jobs and money. Anyway, I'm not looking for a girlfriend.

What are you wearing today?
A fleece, jeans and trainers.

How are you feeling?
I'm fed up with homework.

What are you looking forward to?
Half term – I'm spending a week with my cousins in New York. I can't wait!

What do you care about?
I think the environment is really important. We're destroying the planet.

What do you worry about?
There's a lot of crime round here because of drugs. Some people are too scared to go out at night.

What's your ambition?
I want to be an actor. And I'd like to travel round Latin America.

1 Opener

Look at the photo of Leo Evans. What does he look like? What's he wearing? What's he doing?

2 Reading

Read and listen to the questionnaire.

3 Comprehension

True or false? Correct the false sentences.

1 Leo lives in the city centre.
2 He goes to the cinema every Saturday night.
3 He's reading a boring book.
4 He's learning Spanish.
5 He doesn't want a girlfriend.
6 He's feeling happy.
7 He's looking forward to visiting New York.
8 He doesn't care about the environment.
9 He worries about crime.

4 Grammar

Complete.

Present simple
At weekends, I _____ to music.
He _____ in Manchester.
We _____ to clubs every Saturday night.
All the girls _____ older boys.
He _____ n't want a girlfriend.
_____ you have a girlfriend?

Present continuous
He _____ learning Spanish.
We _____ destroying the planet.
I _____ not looking for a girlfriend.
What _____ you reading at the moment?
I _____ spending a week in New York.

We use the present _____ to talk about states and routines.
We use the present _____ to talk about temporary events and what is happening now.
We can also use the present continuous to talk about future arrangements.

➡ Check the answers: Grammar Summary page 109

5 Grammar Practice

Complete the sentences with the present simple or continuous form of the verbs.

1 What _____ Leo usually _____ (do) after school?
2 He _____ (go) to the park with his friends and they _____ (play) football.
3 What _____ he _____ (do) at the moment?
4 He _____ (jump) on his skateboard.
5 Where _____ he _____ (spend) half term?
6 _____ you _____ (worry) about street crime?
7 I _____ (think) some city streets _____ (get) quite dangerous.
8 A lot of teenagers _____ (worry) about their weight.
9 Most British teenagers _____ (eat) chips at least twice a week!

6 Listening

Read this profile. There are eight mistakes in the text. Can you guess what they are? Then listen and see if you are right.

Tiffany Bell is 15 and lives in south London.
At weekends she meets her friends in town, and she goes to parties every Friday night. She goes to the cinema about once a week. She isn't reading anything at the moment. Her favourite school subjects are maths and art. She and her friends talk about clothes, TV and boys. Her boyfriend, Jake, is 18 and he's a student at sports college.

Today she's wearing a black top, a denim shirt and boots. She's feeling excited because she's 16 tomorrow and she's looking forward to her birthday cake.

She cares about politics, but she thinks most politicians are rubbish. She worries about flying because she gets very nervous. She wants to pass all her exams and go to Australia.

Now correct the mistakes in the text.

> She doesn't go to parties every Friday night.
> > She goes to parties every _____.

UNIT 1

7 Pronunciation

🎧 Listen and repeat.

college   cousin   drug
money   month   not   often
once   top   want   what
worry

Now write the words under /ɒ/ or /ʌ/ in the chart. Then listen again and check.

/ɒ/ job	/ʌ/ club

8 Speaking

Ask another student the questions in *Teenage Talk*. Note down the answers.

Adverbial phrases of frequency
How often?
every   day
                 night
once a   week
twice a   month
three times a   year

➡ Grammar Summary page 109

9 Writing

Write a profile of the student you interviewed in exercise 8. Use the profile of Tiffany to help you.

1 TEEN LIFE

2 I wanted to go home

Past simple review
Describing past events

1 Opener
Look at the photo of the girl. How is she feeling? Who is she talking to? What is she talking about?

2 Reading
🎧 Read and listen to Mel's online diary.

3 Comprehension
Answer the questions.
1. Who was Mel on holiday with?
2. Who did she miss?
3. Did Kate and Mel make the same friends on the first day?
4. Did Kate's new friends like Mel's accent?
5. What did Kate want Mel to do?
6. What did Mel want Kate's friends to do?
7. Why did Mel try to sound cheerful on the phone?
8. Who was also on the phone?

4 Grammar
Complete.

Past simple of *be*: was/were
This **was** our holiday.
We _____ really excited.
I _____ n't good enough.
_____ she also on the phone home?

Past simple: regular verbs
I want___ to go home.
She apologise___ for phoning.
I nearly cr___ when I heard my mother's voice.
It _____ n't bother me.
Why _____ I hate every minute of it?

Past simple: irregular verbs
It all **went** wrong from the start.
It _____ n't mean anything to me.
_____ she feel the same as me?

Regular and irregular verbs both form the _____ and _____ in the same way.

➡ Check the answers: Grammar Summary page 109

Diary of a teenager
Mel Dawson, 16

My first holiday without parents – just me and my best friend Kate. So why did I hate every minute of it?

I was 200 miles from home when Mum called. She apologised for phoning. But I wanted to talk to my mum. I was so pleased to hear her voice. I missed her and Dad, my brother Mike, and even Zoey, my little sister. I wanted to go home. We were on holiday in Brighton – it was a great place, trendy and cool. The beach life was fantastic and the parties lasted all night. But somehow it didn't mean anything to me – I was bored and depressed.

This was our holiday – just Kate and me. This was our week without parents. We wanted Brighton to be about friendship, about boys, about freedom, about being young and crazy. We were really excited. But it all went wrong from the start.

We both made new friends on the first day, but different friends. Kate's new friends didn't like my accent and I wasn't good enough for them. It didn't bother me. But it bothered Kate. She wanted me to speak better. I wanted her friends to leave me alone.

We didn't spend any time together. I was with my new friends and she was with hers. My friends laughed at my jokes and I wanted to have a good time. But in fact I felt really sad and lonely.

I was 200 miles from home, and I nearly cried when I heard my mother's voice. I tried to sound cheerful – I didn't want her to know I was miserable. Then I felt someone's eyes on me and turned round. It was Kate with her mobile to her ear. She didn't look very happy either. Did she feel the same as me? Was she also on the phone home?

8 Role Play

Kate did the same things as Mel yesterday, but at different times! Role play a phone conversation between Kate and her father.

Kate
- Say hello.
- Reply.
- Reply. Ask how everyone is at home.
- Thank him for calling and say goodbye.

Father
- Greet Kate and ask how she is.
- Ask what she did yesterday.
- Reply. Tell her to enjoy the rest of the holiday.

5 Grammar Practice

Complete with the past simple of the verbs.

1. Who _____ Mel _____ to talk to? (want)
2. Where _____ Kate and Mel _____ for their holiday? (go)
3. _____ Kate and Mel on holiday with their parents? (be)
4. How long _____ the parties _____? (last)
5. _____ Mel good enough for Kate's friends? (be)
6. _____ Kate and Mel _____ any time together? (spend)
7. What _____ Mel's friends _____ at? (laugh)
8. Why _____ Mel nearly _____? (cry)

Now find the past tense of the verbs in the diary and answer the questions with full sentences.

6 Listening

Listen to the phone conversation between Mel and her mother. Match Mel's activities yesterday with the times: morning (M), afternoon (A) or night (N).

fall asleep on the beach   go for a swim in the sea
go to a party   walk along the pier
dance for five hours   go on rides at the funfair
have a picnic   meet her friends in a club
visit a fortune teller

7 Speaking

Ask and answer questions about Mel's activities yesterday.

> What did Mel do yesterday morning?
> Did she fall asleep on the beach?

> No, she didn't. She ...

9 Pronunciation

Write the words under /θ/ or /ð/ in the chart.

anything   bother   brother   either   maths
month   mother   with   without

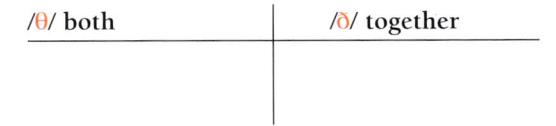

/θ/ both	/ð/ together

Now listen and check.

10 Vocabulary

Complete the chart with these adjectives. How many of the adjectives can you find in Mel's diary?

Feelings
angry   bored   cheerful   depressed   embarrassed
excited   happy   lonely   miserable   nervous
pleased   sad   scared   tired   worried

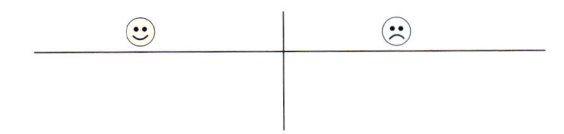

☺	☹

Now tell each other when you had ☺ or ☹ feelings.

A I felt excited when I watched the World Cup Final.
B I was angry when my brother borrowed my CDs without asking.

11 Writing

Imagine you went on holiday with a friend. Write your diary. Use Mel's diary to help you.

- Where did you go?
- Who were you with?
- Who did you meet?
- What did you do?
- How did you feel?

1 TEEN LIFE

3 Everyone was cheering

Past simple and past continuous
Describing what happened and what was happening

Tunnels Beach, Kauai Island, Hawaii
6.40 am October 31 2003

It was a beautiful morning. Bethany Hamilton was surfing with her best friend Alana. The girls got on well together and took part in surf competitions. Bethany hoped to become a professional surfer.

'I had no warning at all. The water was clear and calm. It was more like a swimming pool than the Pacific Ocean. I had my right hand on the board and my left hand in the cool water. We were waiting for the next big wave. I was thinking "I hope the surf gets better soon," when suddenly I saw the shark.

The attack happened so fast. The huge jaws of the four-metre shark covered the top of the board and my left arm. Then I watched in shock while the water around me turned bright red. I didn't scream. It's strange, but there was no pain at the time. But I knew I had to get back to the beach quickly.'

While Bethany was recovering in hospital she asked everyone the same question: 'When can I surf again?'

Kilauea Beach, Kauai Island, Hawaii
Late afternoon, November 23 2003

Less than four weeks after the shark bit off her left arm, Bethany was back on her surfboard.

'At first I couldn't stand up. My dad, who was in the water with me, was shouting "Bethany, try it one more time!" So I did.

When a wave came, I caught it, put my hand on the board to push up, and I was standing. Once I was on my feet everything was easy.

I was all wet, but I could still feel tears of happiness on my face. Everyone was cheering for me. It was a great moment!'

Bethany trained hard and entered surf competitions again. In 2005 she won her first national championship.

1 Opener

What is the girl in the photo holding?
What do you think happened to her?

2 Reading

Read and listen to the text.

3 Comprehension

Answer the questions.

1 Who was Bethany surfing with on October 31?
2 What did Bethany hope to become?
3 What was she thinking when the shark attacked?
4 What happened to the water after the attack?
5 When did Bethany start surfing again?
6 Who was shouting when Bethany tried to stand up?

4 Grammar

Complete.

Past simple and past continuous

Past simple
↓
―――――――――――― - - - - - - →
Past continuous

She _____ _____ (wait) for the next big wave **when** she _____ (see) the shark.
She _____ (ask) everyone 'When can I surf again?' **while** she _____ _____ (recover) in hospital.

We use the past _____ to describe an event or a short action in the past.
We use the past _____ to describe a longer activity, to give the background to an event.

➡ Check the answers: Grammar Summary page 109

5 Grammar Practice

Complete with the past simple or past continuous of the verbs.

Tourists in shark attack

Simon Donnell, 17, from Belfast, __1__ (escape) from a shark attack yesterday. Simon was on holiday in Florida with a group of friends. One day they all got together and __2__ (go) out in a small boat to see sharks.

'The sea was quite calm,' Simon said, 'and for the first two hours we __3__ (not see) any sharks at all. The boat __4__ (pull) bags of dead fish behind it to attract sharks but none __5__ (come). We __6__ (laugh) about our bad luck when suddenly everything __7__ (change). I __8__ (notice) that four or five small sharks __9__ (swim) around us. I __10__ (get) up and __11__ (go) over to the side of the boat. The boat __12__ (move) quite slowly and the water was clear. I __13__ (look) into the water when suddenly a huge white shark __14__ (appear). The shark __15__ (swim) fast and it __16__ (crash) into the boat. It was like *Jaws!* I __17__ (look) around. Most of my friends __18__ (scream) or __19__ (cry). But suddenly the shark __20__ (disappear) into the blue water.

It was a small boat and we were really lucky to get away from such a big shark.'

6 Listening

Listen to the radio broadcast and decide: true or false? Correct the false sentences.

1 Shane was helping his father in the garden.
2 He decided to swim in the lake.
3 While he was swimming, he heard a splash.
4 He saw a small crocodile which was swimming towards him.
5 When Shane shouted 'Help!', his father thought he was joking.
6 The crocodile took Shane's leg and pulled him under the water.
7 When Shane kicked the crocodile, it closed its jaws.
8 When he stood up, he saw the crocodile right behind him.
9 When Shane and the crocodile were face to face, he punched it on the mouth.
10 When he punched the crocodile, it turned and swam away.

7 Speaking

Student A Ask Student B questions 1–5.
Student B Close the book and answer the questions.

1 What was Shane doing in the garden?
2 Where did Shane go for a swim?
3 What did Shane hear while he was swimming?
4 What did Shane see when he turned?
5 What did Clive think when Shane shouted 'Help!'?

Now change roles. Ask and answer questions 6–10.

6 Where did the crocodile pull Shane?
7 What did the crocodile do when Shane kicked it?
8 What did Shane see after he stood up?
9 What did Shane do when he was face to face with the crocodile?
10 What did the crocodile do when Shane punched it?

8 Pronunciation

Listen and write the words in the correct column according to the pronunciation of the underlined letters.

change   cheer   competition   fish
national   ocean   professional   punch
push   shark   shout   splash   watch

/ʃ/ crash	/tʃ/ beach

9 Vocabulary

Match the phrasal verbs with their meanings. How many of the verbs can you find in this lesson?

1 get away   a be friends
2 get back   b reach
3 get on   c escape
4 get to   d stand up
5 get together   e return
6 get up   f meet

10 Writing

Write a short newspaper article describing what happened to Shane. Listen to the radio broadcast in exercise 6 again, and use the questions in exercise 7 to help you.

Teenager punches crocodile
Darwin, Australia

1 TEEN LIFE

4 Integrated Skills
Describing 'first times'

1 **Opener**

Martin Scorsese is a well-known film director. Do you know any of his films? He recently made a film about music. Look at the pictures and guess what kind of music.

Reading

2 Read and complete the text with phrases a–h.

a while he was performing
b and wrote down the name
c in a rock and roll show
d while she was doing the dishes
e when I was 16
f and we wanted to know more
g and found an old Leadbelly record
h from car radios

🎧 Now listen and check. Which words in the phrases helped you to complete the text?

3 Find the highlighted words in the text which mean:

1 feeling *n*
2 where something comes from *n*
3 very strong and clear *adj*
4 not common or normal *adj*
5 shop (American English) *n*
6 flats (American English) *n*
7 power, strength *n*
8 surprising, hard to believe *adj*

4 Can you remember the first time you heard a great song? Where were you? What were you doing? What was the song and who was the singer/band? How did you feel?

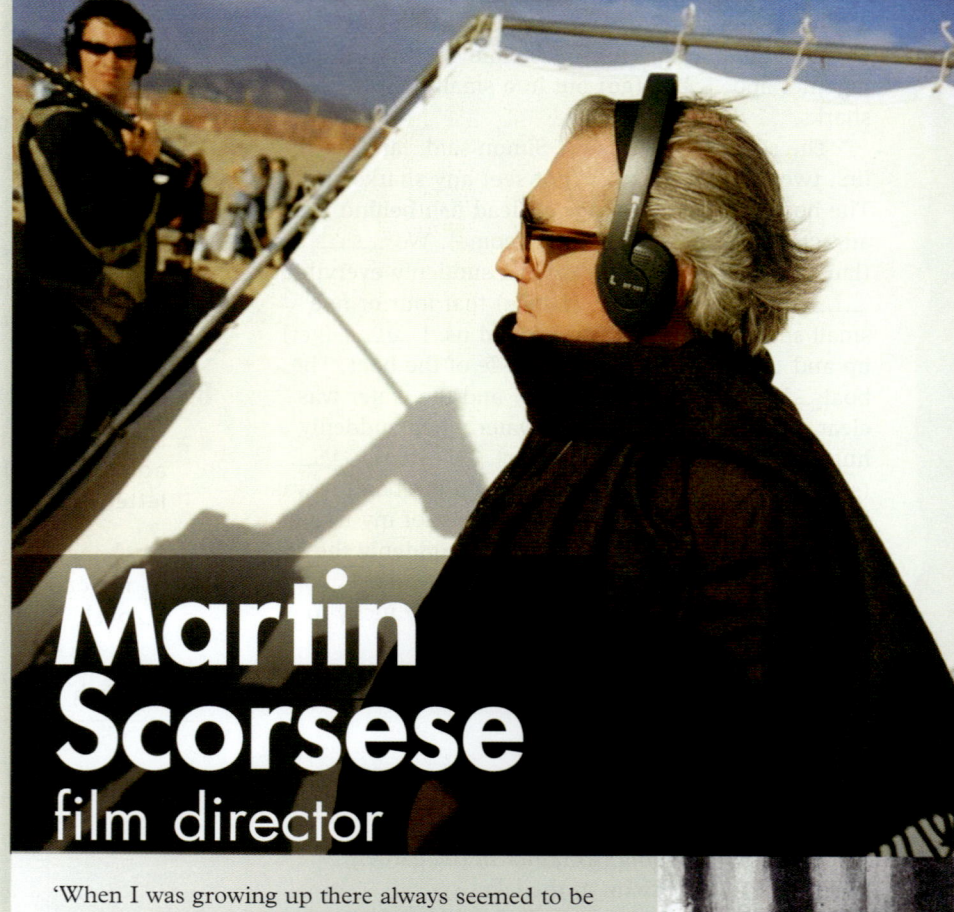

Martin Scorsese
film director

'When I was growing up there always seemed to be music in the air. It came in from the street, __1__, from restaurants and from the windows of apartments. At home my mother often sang – I have vivid memories of her singing __2__. My father played the mandolin, and my brother Frank played the guitar. And at that time there was an incredible range of music on the radio, everything from Italian folk songs to country and western.

One day, __3__, I heard something completely new. I'll never forget the first time I heard the sound of that guitar. The music was saying 'Listen to me!'. I ran to get a pencil and paper, __4__. The song was *See See Rider* and the name of the singer was Leadbelly. I ran up to the record store on Forty-ninth Street as fast as I could __5__. I listened to it again and again. When you listen to Leadbelly's music you feel inspired by its energy and truth, you really understand what it means to be human. That's the blues.

At around the same time, my friends and I went to see Bo Diddley. That was another great moment for me. He was playing at the Brooklyn Paramount __6__. He was a great performer and was always moving from side to side of the stage. But Bo Diddley also did something unusual __7__ – he explained the different drumbeats and which parts of Africa they came from. It gave us a sense of the history behind the music, the roots of the music. We all found this very exciting __8__.'

5 Listening

Listen and match the speakers with the photos.

Now listen again and complete texts 1–3.

1 I remember the first time I rode a motorbike. It was when I was 15. My friend Mike was __1__ and he had a new motorbike. One day he was cleaning his motorbike outside his house and he asked 'Do you want a go?' I said 'Yes, of course.' Mike started the engine and I put on the helmet. I felt excited and __2__ at the same time. 'Off you go,' Mike said and I started down the road. It was a __3__ feeling. I wasn't going fast, but I felt __4__. Mike ran after me. He was shouting something: 'Stop now!'. So I put on the brakes, the bike stopped suddenly, and I fell off! I wasn't hurt, but I was really __5__.

2 I'll never forget the first time I was close to a wild animal. It happened when I was __6__. I was on a camping holiday with my __7__ on Vancouver Island in Canada. It was a fine night and we were sleeping in the open around the fire. Suddenly I woke up in the middle of the night. The stars were really beautiful and I felt so __8__. But what woke me? Then I saw a dark shape. Something was sitting by the fire, only a metre away from us. It was a wolf! I was really __9__ – in fact I was terrified. Then the wolf stood up and slowly walked away. I couldn't believe it! And I couldn't go back to sleep. In the morning I was very __10__. But when I told my parents about the wolf, they didn't believe me!

3 The first time I played for the school ice hockey team was November 23rd – I can't forget the __11__! I was 15 and I was wearing a new pair of skates I got for my __12__. It was a home game and lots of people were watching. I felt quite __13__ at the start, but I soon relaxed. The crowd were cheering and screaming. And when we scored a goal the noise got even louder. It was a __14__ experience. I didn't score a goal, but that didn't matter. I was part of the hockey team now – that was the __15__ thing.

6 Speaking

Interview another student about the first time they did something and make notes. Use these questions to help you.

Tell me about an important 'first time' for you:
- What was it?
- How old were you?
- What were you and other people doing at the time?
- What happened?
- How did you feel?

Use your notes to tell a new partner about the event.

7 Writing

Write about an important 'first time' for you. Use the texts in this lesson and the questions in exercise 6 to help you.

Learner Independence

8 Keep a *Learning Diary* about your English language learning. Use these headings to help you.

Date: 13 September
What we did in class: Unit 1 Lesson 4
Activities I enjoyed: Talking about the first time I heard The Hives.
Difficulties I had: The past simple of some irregular verbs.
My plan: Learn the list of irregular verbs on page 127!
What I did outside class: I found the words to my favourite Hives song on the Internet. I looked up some of the difficult words in the dictionary.

9 Word creation: learn to create English words using prefixes and suffixes. Add the prefix *dis-* or *un-* to make the opposites of these words, and complete the sentences.

agree   appear   comfortable   friendly
happy   lucky   popular   usual

1 Mel didn't enjoy her holiday – she was *unhappy*.
2 It doesn't happen very often – it's very _____.
3 Mel _____ with Kate while they were on holiday.
4 I'm so _____ – I won the lottery but I lost my ticket.
5 No one wants to be his friend – why is he _____?
6 We didn't really enjoy the film because the cinema seats were _____.
7 Where's Tom? He _____ while I was on the phone.
8 I tried to talk to them but they were very _____.

10 Phrasebook

Listen and repeat these useful expressions. Then find them in this unit.

once or twice a month   I'm fed up with …
I can't wait!   It all went wrong.
It didn't bother me.   It was a great moment.
One day …   again and again
I'll never forget the first time I …
I couldn't believe it!

Which expression means:

a 'I didn't care.'?
b 'I was very surprised.'?
c 'I'm really looking forward to it.'?
d 'I'm tired of …'?

Unit 1 Communication Activity
Student **A** page 106
Student **B** page 116

1 TEEN LIFE
Inspiration *Extra!*

PROJECT Special Day File

Make a file about what happened on an exciting or unusual day.

1. Work in a group and make a list of people you know both in and outside your school. For example, think about members of sports teams, musicians, actors or teachers in your school; think about family and other people you know outside your school. Then choose one or two people to interview.

2. Make a list of questions to ask:

   Can you tell us about an exciting or unusual day in your life? When was it? How old were you? What happened? What did you do? What happened next? How did you feel? What do you remember most about that day? Other questions?

   Now interview the person or people you chose, and note down the answers.

3. Work together and make a Special Day File. Write out your questions and the answers. Read it carefully and correct any mistakes. Draw pictures or use photographs of the person or people and what they were doing. Show your Special Day File to the other groups.

GAME Word Maze

- Work in pairs to move from BEAUTIFUL to CALM.
- Move from line to line by finding pairs of opposites. For example, the opposite of BEAUTIFUL in the first line is *ugly*. Now find a word in the second line which is the opposite of one of the words in the first line.
- As you move through the Word Maze, write down all the pairs of opposites.
- The first two students to get to CALM are the winners.

BEAUTIFUL

trendy	funny	happy	ugly	hungry
boring	lonely	terrified	lucky	sad
tired	interesting	better	great	hot
exciting	worse	first	right	surprising
easy	wild	left	older	brilliant
important	favourite	scared	fast	difficult
hard	slow	unusual	tiny	bright
fantastic	huge	nervous	cool	different

CALM

SKETCH The Mirror

🎧 Read and listen.

MAN 1 Why are you looking at me like that?
MAN 2 I wasn't looking at you in any special way.
MAN 1 Oh yes, you were. I saw you.
       Both men touch their noses.
MAN 1 And stop copying me.
MAN 2 I wasn't copying you.
       Both men touch their noses.
MAN 1 Look! You did it again.
MAN 2 Did what?
MAN 1 Copied me. I touched my nose and you touched yours at the same time.
MAN 2 Did I? I didn't notice. I was thinking about something else.
MAN 1 Please stop copying me.
MAN 2 I can't help it. I'm a mirror, and I do what you do.
MAN 1 You're not a mirror – mirrors don't talk.
MAN 2 Well, I'm a talking mirror.
MAN 1 A talking mirror? No, you're not! You don't repeat what I say, do you?
MAN 2 Do you?
MAN 1 Sorry?
MAN 2 Sorry?
MAN 1 Look, I'm getting really angry now. Stop looking at me like that!
MAN 2 Stop looking at me like that!
MAN 1 Oh! Sorry.
MAN 2 Sorry.
MAN 1 That's better.
       Both men smile.
MAN 2 Better.
MAN 1 Bye.
       Man 1 turns to leave.
MAN 2 Bye. No, wait!
       Man 2 climbs through the frame and follows Man 1.

Now act out the sketch in pairs.

UNIT 1

REVISION for more practice

LESSON 1

Look at the profile of Tiffany Bell on page 9. Write a similar profile of Leo Evans using information from *Teenage Talk* on page 8.

Leo Evans is 16 and lives in a suburb of Manchester. At weekends he goes skateboarding, plays the guitar, and listens to music with his mates.

LESSON 2

Look at *Diary of a teenager* on page 10. Write questions beginning with *Who …?* and answer the questions. Use the past simple.

*Who hated every minute of her holiday?
Mel did.*

LESSON 3

Look at Bethany's story on page 12. Retell the story of the shark attack from Alana's point of view.

Beth and I were …

EXTENSION for language development

LESSON 1

Look at Tiffany's profile on page 9. Write a similar profile of yourself.

LESSON 2

Look at *Diary of a teenager* on page 10. Write the conversation between Mel and her mother about her holiday.

LESSON 3

Read Bethany, Simon and Shane's stories on pages 12–13 again. Imagine a shark attacked you when you were surfing and you escaped. A newspaper interviewed you about the attack. Write the newspaper article with the headline 'Teenage surfer escapes shark attack'.

YOUR CHOICE!

CONSTRUCTION Past simple or past continuous?

Complete with the correct form of the verbs.

In 1958 Martin Scorsese __1__ (listen) to the radio when he __2__ (hear) Leadbelly for the first time. At around the same time Scorsese and his friends went to see Bo Diddley, who __3__ (perform) in a show in Brooklyn. Scorsese __4__ (want) to play the guitar well, but he __5__ (be not) very good at it. In the 1960s he __6__ (discover) British bands like the Rolling Stones and Cream who __7__ (play) a new mixture of blues and rock. One of Scorsese's most important musical moments __8__ (come) when he __9__ (make) a film called *The Last Waltz* and __10__ (film) one of blues star Muddy Waters' greatest performances.

ACTION Alphabet sentences
- Work in groups of four.
- Student A says a letter of the alphabet.
- Student B says a verb beginning with that letter.
- Student C says the past simple of that verb.
- Student D says a sentence using the past simple verb.

REFLECTION Spelling rules

Complete.

Past simple
- Most regular verbs add _____ (example: _____).
- Verbs ending in *-e* add _____ (example: _____).
- When verbs end in a consonant + *y*, the *y* changes to _____ (example: _____).
  But we don't change the *y* after a vowel (example: _____).

Past continuous
- We form the tense with _____ / _____ + *-ing* (example: _____).
- Verbs ending in *-e* drop the *e* before *-ing* (example: _____).
  But we don't make a change when _____ comes after *-ee* (example: _____).

Doubling consonants
- For both tenses, most one-syllable words ending with a single vowel and a consonant (example: *stop*) double the consonant when adding _____ or _____ (example: _____, _____).
  But we don't double the consonants *w*, *x* or *y*.

INTERACTION
Doing and feeling
- Work in a small group.
- Ask each other about last weekend.
  *What were you doing at (time) on (day)?
  How did you feel? Why?*
  A What were you doing at 8am on Saturday?
  B I was having breakfast in the kitchen. I felt tired because I went to bed late.

culture
IDENTITY

identity /aɪˈdentəti/ noun
1 the fact of who you are or what your name is
2 the qualities that make someone or something what they are and different from other people

extract from Macmillan Essential Dictionary

We asked young people around the world what the word IDENTITY meant to them.

Anees Mansour, 18, Palestine
Our identity is the soul of our people, because that is all we have left. Everything else, our land, our dignity, our economic life, is gone. As a people we care about each other and we help each other with everything. We have big families and nobody lives alone. Nobody dies alone.

Sakiko, 19, Japan
My identity is in my art. I'm studying art at college now, but it has been my main interest since I was 13. I think art is one of the best ways to express myself.

Jakob, 19, Poland
My national identity is not as important to me as it was. I don't feel typically Polish – I live near the German border and my first name is German. I see myself more as a European than a Pole.

Dragan, 16, Austria
There is no one here in Austria I can identify with. My teachers don't inspire me and are only interested in school marks. I love my parents but I often don't agree with their ideas. When I'm older I want to move to America – that is already part of my identity.

1 Vocabulary

Read what young people say about identity. Match these words and phrases with their definitions.

1 inspire *v*   a to do with a country
2 criticise *v*   b with the usual qualities of a particular group of people or things
3 marks *n pl*   c numbers or letters which teachers give students for their school work
4 confusing *adj*   d make someone enthusiastic about something
5 typically *adv*   e say or show what you feel or think
6 soul *n*   f part of a person which thinks or feels
7 dignity *n*   g difficult to understand
8 national *adj*   h be a member or a possession of
9 express yourself *v*   i self-respect
10 belong to *v*   j say what you think is bad about someone or something

culture

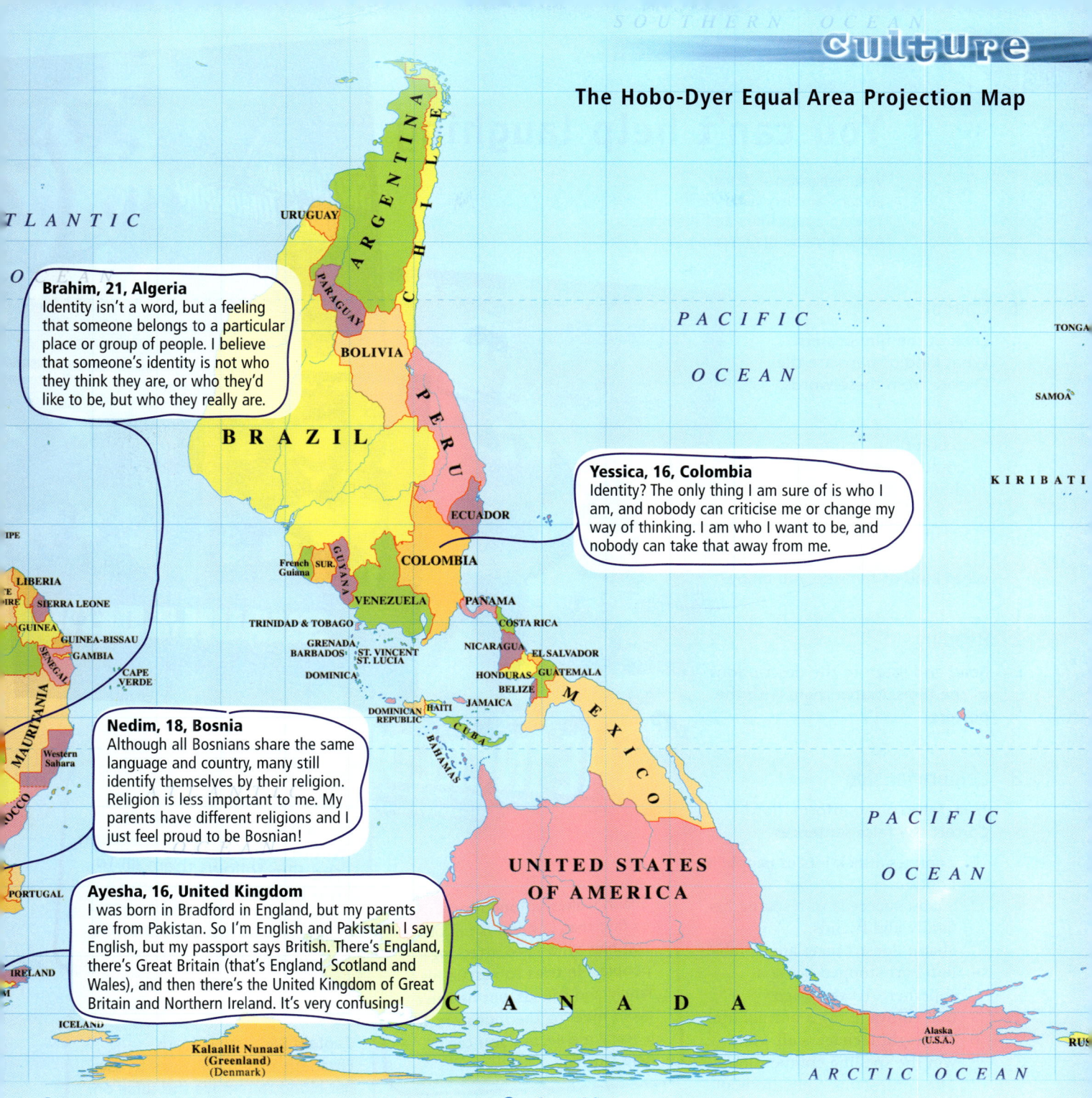

The Hobo-Dyer Equal Area Projection Map

Brahim, 21, Algeria
Identity isn't a word, but a feeling that someone belongs to a particular place or group of people. I believe that someone's identity is not who they think they are, or who they'd like to be, but who they really are.

Yessica, 16, Colombia
Identity? The only thing I am sure of is who I am, and nobody can criticise me or change my way of thinking. I am who I want to be, and nobody can take that away from me.

Nedim, 18, Bosnia
Although all Bosnians share the same language and country, many still identify themselves by their religion. Religion is less important to me. My parents have different religions and I just feel proud to be Bosnian!

Ayesha, 16, United Kingdom
I was born in Bradford in England, but my parents are from Pakistan. So I'm English and Pakistani. I say English, but my passport says British. There's England, there's Great Britain (that's England, Scotland and Wales), and then there's the United Kingdom of Great Britain and Northern Ireland. It's very confusing!

2 Comprehension

Answer the questions.

Who …

1 thinks nationality is more important than religion?
2 already feels partly American?
3 is an art student?
4 finds the different names for her country confusing?
5 feels part of a continent, not a country?
6 says that no one can take away her identity?
7 believes that identity is a feeling?
8 says she comes from a country where people look after each other?
9 says no one can make her change her mind?
10 doesn't identify himself by religion?

3 Speaking

Ask another student if he/she agrees with these statements and note down the answers.

1 There is no one in my town I can identify with.
2 I love my parents, but I often don't agree with their ideas.
3 No one can change the way I think.
4 My national identity is important to me.
5 I see myself as a citizen of the world, not of one country.

4 Writing

Do you agree with the statements in exercise 3? Write a paragraph comparing your views with those of the student you interviewed.

Hanna thinks there is no one in our town she can identify with, but I disagree.

19

2 ARTS

1 You can't help laughing

Verb/Preposition + gerund
so/nor + auxiliary verbs
Talking about likes and dislikes
Agreeing and disagreeing

1 Opener

Look at the film posters.
What kind of films are they?
Choose from these words.

Films
action film   animation
comedy   documentary
drama   horror film
musical   romantic film
science fiction film

What kind of films do you enjoy?

2 Reading

Read and listen to the descriptions of the films. Match them with the posters.

3 Comprehension

True, false, or no information?
Correct the false sentences.

1 Zombies attack lots of people in London.
2 Shaun succeeds in rescuing his family and friends.
3 Shaun doesn't meet any zombies.
4 Bob Parr stopped being a superhero 10 years ago.
5 Bob enjoys living a normal life.
6 The eight teenagers all want to win the spelling competition.
7 The contestants come from all over the USA.
8 Elizabeth Swann's life is in danger.
9 Enormous robots start attacking famous scientists.
10 Polly Perkins wants to stop Sky Captain destroying the planet.

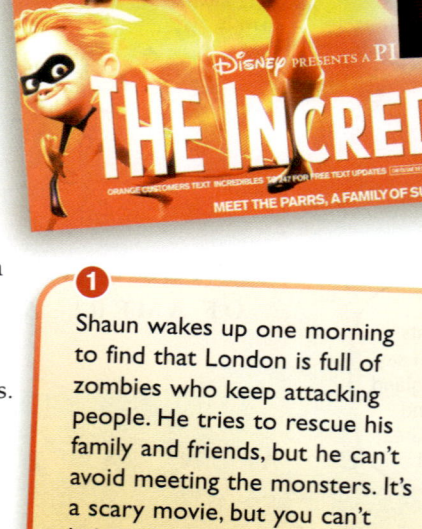

1
Shaun wakes up one morning to find that London is full of zombies who keep attacking people. He tries to rescue his family and friends, but he can't avoid meeting the monsters. It's a scary movie, but you can't help laughing.

2
Bob Parr gave up being a superhero 15 years ago, but he's fed up with living a normal life. When Bob receives an invitation to a secret meeting on a volcanic island, he and his family start fighting to save the world.

3
Eight teenage contestants dream of winning the US National Spelling competition. The film follows them all to the final in Washington DC. The kids are incredibly good at spelling, but only one of them can win.

4
Captain Barbossa kidnaps Elizabeth Swann. He plans to use her blood to remove the curse on his ship, the Black Pearl. Elizabeth risks losing her life – can her friend Will Turner and pirate Jack Sparrow succeed in rescuing her?

5
Famous scientists disappear and enormous robots start attacking cities, so newspaper reporter Polly Perkins and Joe Sullivan investigate. They fly to exotic places around the world – but can they stop Dr Totenkopf destroying the planet?

6 Speaking

Complete these sentences for yourself.

I love …   I'm not keen on …   I'm interested in …
I'm bored by …   I can't stand …   I'm scared of …
I don't mind …

Now read your completed sentences to another student. Do you agree or disagree?

A I love going to the cinema.
B So do I. OR Do you? I don't.

A I'm not keen on seeing horror films.
B Nor am I. OR Aren't you? I am.

so/nor + auxiliary verbs
I love …   So do I.
I'm scared of …   So am I.
I don't mind …   Nor do I.
I can't stand …   Nor can I.

➡ Grammar Summary page 110

4 Grammar

Complete.

Verb + gerund
You can't help laugh**ing**.
Zombies keep attack___ people.
He can't avoid meet___ the monsters.
They start fight___ to save the world.
She risks los___ her life.

Preposition + gerund
Bob gave **up** be**ing** a superhero.
He's fed up ___ liv___ a normal life.
They dream ___ win___ the competition.
They are incredibly good ___ spell___.
Can they succeed ___ rescu___ her?

➡ Check the answers: Grammar Summary page 110

5 Grammar Practice

Complete with the correct form of the verbs.

1 I feel like _____ a DVD. (buy)
2 Let's go _____. (shop)
3 I'm interested in _____ *Chicago*. (see)
4 I'm not keen on _____ musicals. (watch)
5 How about _____ *House of Horrors*? (get)
6 I don't like _____ scared! (be)
7 Let's stop _____ and get an action movie. (talk)
8 Steven Spielberg is famous for _____ action films. (make)

7 Vocabulary

Complete the chart with these adjectives.

Opinions
awful   boring   brilliant   disappointing
excellent   exciting   funny   interesting
scary   silly   terrible   terrific   thrilling

☺	☹

8 Pronunciation

🎧 Listen and check your answers to exercise 7. Repeat the words and mark the stress.

9 Listening

🎧 Listen to five people talking about the films in exercise 2. Which adjectives from exercise 7 do they use to describe each film?

10 Writing

Write a short review of a recent film. Use the descriptions in exercise 2 and these questions to help you.

- What kind of film is it?
- What's it about?
- Who's in it?
- What's your opinion of the film?

Now read out your review but don't say the film title. Can other students guess the film?

2 ARTS

2 Promise to work together

Verb (+ object) + infinitive
Talking about plans and abilities

1 Opener

Look at the magazine extract. What kind of show is it about? Are there shows like this on TV in your country?

2 Reading

Read and listen to *Star School*.

3 Comprehension

Match the questions with the answers. There are two wrong answers.

1 Who leaves Star School each week?
2 What two things does Robin expect the contestants to do?
3 What does the voice coach hope to do?
4 Who knows the secrets of some of the biggest names in the music business?
5 What does Adam ask the contestants to promise?
6 What does the songwriting coach say is important?

a Performing your own song.
b Robin did.
c To work together.
d Learning to fit the words to the music.
e To obey the rules of the school and to attend all their classes.
f The contestant with the lowest number of votes.
g To help the contestants to find their special voice.
h Jess does.

STAR SCHOOL

In this great reality TV show ten hopeful contestants spend nine weeks at the school. They learn to sing and each week they perform one of their own songs on TV. Viewers vote for the songs by phone and the contestant with the lowest number of votes leaves the show.

I'm **Robin**, the director of the school, and I'd like to welcome you and wish you every success. We expect you to obey the rules while you are here and to attend all your classes. The coaches here are great and we can help you to develop your talents.

Hi, I'm **Jess** and I'm your voice coach. Now I want you to listen carefully to me for a minute. Everyone can sing, but not everyone can sing like a star. I hope to help you to find your special voice. I expect you to practise hard and to help each other. In return I'll share some of the secrets of the biggest names in the music business.

I'm **Adam**, your dance coach. Think of me as your friend, your personal trainer and your choreographer. I can teach you to dance in a range of styles including ballet, jazz, breakdancing, ballroom and salsa. And if you like aerobics or yoga – I'm your man! But I want you to promise me one thing. Promise to work together because you can't learn to dance alone. Try out new dance steps and ideas and don't refuse to experiment.

My name's **Rachel** and I'm your songwriting coach. Songwriting is cool, but don't pretend to be a poet when you aren't one! The important thing is learning to fit the words to the music. Most contestants manage to do it, and performing your own song is a great feeling. Best of luck!

4 Grammar

Complete.

Verb + infinitive
I'd like **to welcome** you.
They learn _____ sing.
I hope _____ _____ you.
Promise _____ _____ together.
Don't refuse _____ _____ .
Don't pretend _____ _____ a poet.
Most contestants manage _____ _____ it.

Verb + object + infinitive
We expect **you to obey** the rules.
I want _____ _____ listen carefully.
I expect _____ _____ practise hard.
I can teach _____ _____ dance.
We can help _____ _____ develop your talents.

➡ Check the answers: Grammar Summary page 110

5 Grammar Practice

Complete with the infinitive of the verb. Include the correct object pronoun (*her, us, you*) where necessary.

Frank, one of the Star School contestants, writes his diary.

We had a great first day. Robin, the director, welcomed us and said he expected __1__ (obey) the rules. I like Jess, the voice coach, very much and I want __2__ (help) me with my singing. She said: 'I will help __3__ (find) your own special voice.' I also hope __4__ (learn) jazz dance with Adam. He wanted __5__ (promise) __6__ (work) together and try out new ideas. We all want __7__ (be) songwriters and Rachel is going to teach __8__ (write) songs. I hope I manage __9__ (do) it. I promise __10__ (try) hard.

6 Pronunciation

Write the words in the correct column.

attend   business   expect   hopeful   manage
obey   perform   practise   pretend   promise
refuse   return   secret   special   success   talent

■ .	. ■
business	attend

🎧 Now listen and check. Repeat the words.

7 Listening

🎧 Read the questionnaire and listen to the answers of two teenagers, Anna and Will.

TRUTH QUESTIONNAIRE
1 Do you promise to tell the truth?
2 What new skill do you want to learn?
3 What would you like to teach your friends to do?
4 Is there something you pretend to like but don't really like?
5 Is there anything you refuse to eat?
6 What do your parents ask you to do which you don't enjoy?
7 What can you just manage to do but would like to do better?
8 What do you hope to do when you leave school?

Listen again and decide: true or false? Correct the false answers.

Anna
1 Yes.
2 Ballroom dancing.
3 To speak to me sometimes.
4 Salad.
5 Peas.
6 To do the washing up.
7 PowerPoint.
8 To go to university.

Will
1 Yes.
2 To drive a bus.
3 Nothing.
4 I pretend to enjoy swimming.
5 Garlic.
6 They want me to write thank-you letters.
7 To speak Spanish.
8 To get a job.

Now compare Anna and Will's answers.

> Both Anna and Will promised to tell the truth.

8 Speaking

Do the *Truth Questionnaire* with two other students and note down their answers.

9 Writing

Write a paragraph comparing the students' answers to the *Truth Questionnaire*.

May wants to learn to do yoga, and Lucy wants to learn to swim.

2 ARTS

3 Books are left in public places

Present simple passive
Describing a system

Free books!

'FREE BOOK! Take me home and read me!' says the note on the cover of Jurassic Park. The paperback is lying on a café table. Is this a joke? No, it's an invitation. The book is registered at www.bookcrossing.com and you are invited to take it home and read it.

Ron Hornbaker, an American, came up with the idea of BookCrossing in 2001 and he set up the website, which is visited by thousands of members around the globe. 'Our goal is to make the whole world a library,' says Hornbaker.

How does BookCrossing work? Books are left in public places – on buses, on park benches, in cafés – and they are found by other people. Each book is labelled with a unique ID number, and people are asked to report back to the website when they find a book.

So why not try it? The next time you finish a good book, register it at the website with some enthusiastic comments and label it with its ID number. Then leave it in a public place for someone else to pick up and enjoy. Who knows? – your book may turn up on the other side of the world!

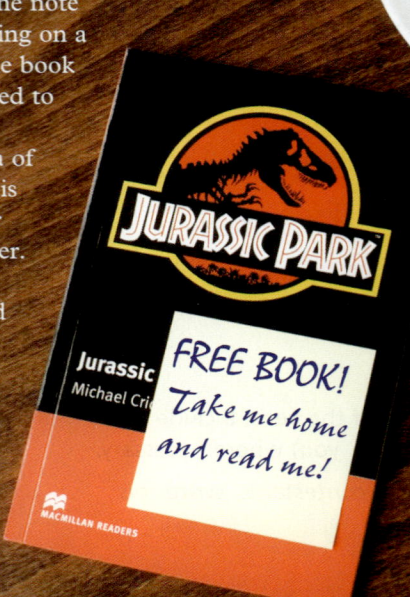

1 Opener

Think about the last book you read – where did you get it from?

Where else can you get books?

2 Reading

Read and listen to *Free books!*

3 Comprehension

Answer the questions.

1 What is the title of the paperback?
2 What are you invited to do?
3 Whose idea was BookCrossing?
4 Who is the website visited by?
5 Where are books left?
6 What are finders of books asked to do?
7 'So why not try it?' Try what?

In what other public places could you leave a book?

4 Grammar

Complete.

Present simple passive
The book _____ registered at www.bookcrossing.com.
You _____ invited to pick it up.
Each book _____ labelled.
The books _____ found **by** other people.

We form the present simple passive with the present tense of _____ + past participle.

➔ Check the answers: Grammar Summary page 110
Irregular Verbs page 127

5 Grammar Practice

Complete with the verbs in the present simple passive.

Books __1__ (make) of paper, and most of the world's paper __2__ (produce) from pine trees. These trees __3__ (grow) by countries such as Canada, the USA, Sweden, Finland and Japan.

A book __4__ (publish) somewhere in the world every thirty seconds. Most books __5__ (sell) by town bookshops, but now increasing numbers __6__ (buy) online through 'virtual' bookshops like Amazon.

In the UK, about 60% of the population __7__ (register) with a library. Nearly half the books which __8__ (take) out of libraries __9__ (borrow) by children. More books __10__ (read) by girls than boys, and most reading __11__ (do) in bed.

It __12__ (say) that a good book is the best of friends. So find a new friend today!

24

6 Speaking

Ask and answer the quiz questions using the present simple passive.

A Where are the most newspapers sold?
B I think it's …

World Records Quiz

1 where/the most newspapers/sell?
  A Germany B Japan C the UK

2 where/the most films/make?
  A China B India C the USA

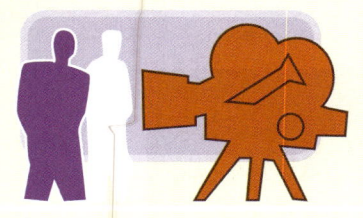

3 where/the most cars/sell?
  A the USA B Germany C Japan

4 where/the most coffee/produce?
  A Brazil B Kenya C Mexico

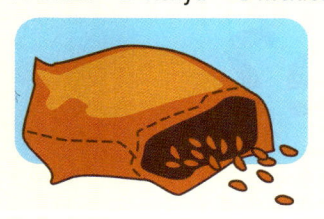

5 where/the most coffee/drink?
  A Italy B Poland C Scandinavia

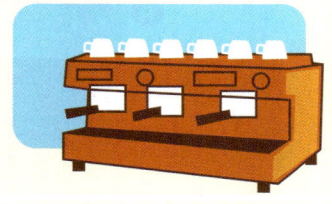

6 where/the most tea/produce?
  A Australia B China C India

7 where/the most tea/drink?
  A Canada B Russia C India

8 where/the most bananas/grow?
  A Colombia B India C Mexico

9 where/the most rice/grow?
  A China B Japan C Vietnam

Now listen and check.

7 Vocabulary

Match the phrasal verbs with their meanings. How many of the verbs can you find in *Free books!*?

1	come up with	a	appear, be found
2	give up	b	become an adult
3	grow up	c	find in the dictionary
4	look up	d	lift, collect
5	pick up	e	rise to your feet
6	set up	f	stop
7	stand up	g	start, create
8	turn up	h	think of

8 Pronunciation

Listen and repeat.

Linking: consonant sound + vowel
It's_an_invitation.
Take_it home and read_it.
Books_are left_in public places.
Each book_is labelled with_a unique_ID number.
Leave_it_in_a public place for someone_else to pick_up_and_enjoy.

9 Speaking

Ask and answer the questions.

1 What book would you like someone else to read?
2 Who is it written by?
3 What's on the cover of the book?
4 What's it about?
5 Which is your favourite character? Why?
6 Why did you enjoy the book?

10 Writing

Write a short review of a good book, using the questions in exercise 9 to help you. Put your review inside the book or on the class noticeboard. Then start BookCrossing – exchange books with other students in your class.

25

2 ARTS

4 Integrated Skills
Describing a picture

What's your favourite picture?

1 I don't really have a favourite picture, but there's a painting which means a lot to me. I saw a film about it last year – Scarlett Johansson, who's one of my favourite film stars, was the girl with the **pearl** earring. The young girl in the painting is beautiful, and I like the way the light shines on her face. I also like the colours of her clothes. I **wonder** what she's thinking, because she looks a little sad. But the painting makes me feel very calm.

2 My favourite picture? I have a different one every day – it depends on how I'm feeling. But this picture of Ruby is one of my favourites. She has an **expression** on her face which always **cheers me up** when I feel depressed. I like the fact that she's a woman doing a man's job, and she's wearing men's clothes – except for the hat! The picture shows that she's a strong person, but also that she's a woman who has feelings.

3 This definitely isn't my favourite picture, but it's a painting which means **a great deal** to me. You can't expect to enjoy every picture you see and this one really isn't a lot of fun. It shows someone who is suffering pain – you can almost hear the scream. The expression on the person's face speaks straight to my heart. It **reminds me** of a time when I felt bad and thought all the world was against me. We all have painful times like that in our lives. The picture isn't painted in a **realistic** way, but it gives a truthful **account** of what life can be like – perhaps that's why it is stolen so often!

The Scream by Edvard Munch © The National Museum of Art, Architecture and Design

1 Opener

Look at the three pictures. Which one do you like most and why? Is there one you don't like? Why?

Reading

2 Read and match the pictures with the texts. Then listen and check.

Do you agree with the opinions?

26

3 Find the highlighted words in the texts which mean:
1 look *n*
2 true to life *adj*
3 ask myself *v*
4 makes me remember *v*
5 small round white shining jewel *n*
6 description *n*
7 makes me feel better *v*
8 a lot *n*

4 What do the words in *italics* refer to?

Text 1
1 … I saw a film about *it* last year.
Text 2
2 I have a different *one* every day.
Text 3
3 *It* reminds me of a time when I felt bad …
4 We all have painful times like *that* in our lives.
5 … *it* is stolen so often!

5 Linking words: *which* and *who*

We use the relative pronouns *which* for things and *who* for people. Find three examples of each in the texts in exercise 2. Which words do they refer to?

6 Listening

Listen and choose the correct answer.

> **Do you have a favourite picture, or one which means a lot to you?**
> Yes, there are several pictures which I like a lot, but there's one in particular.
>
> **What kind of picture is it?**
> It's a painting/poster on my bedroom/kitchen wall.
>
> **Can you describe it?**
> It's a picture of a sunset in the Greek islands. There aren't any people or boats/cars in it, just the sea, the sky and the islands. I don't know who painted it but there's a date on it – 57/75. So I think it's from 1957/1975.
>
> **Why is it important to you?**
> It reminds me of holidays in Greece. I love travelling around the islands.
>
> **How does it make you feel?**
> Happy and relaxed. The colours are fantastic – the sea is black/blue and grey, some of the islands are green and blue, but the mountains in the background are pink/red. And the sky is yellow and blue.

7 Speaking

Ask another student about their favourite picture or a picture which means a lot to them. It could be a photo, an album cover, a painting or a poster. Use the questions in exercise 6 to help you.

8 Writing

Write a short description of your favourite picture or a picture which means a lot to you.

Learner Independence

9 Classroom English: match the questions with the answers.
1 How is *island* pronounced?
2 Can you teach us to read phonetic script?
3 Excuse me. How is /sək'ses/ spelt?
4 Do you want us to finish the writing for homework?
5 What's this called in English?
6 What's a good way to practise speaking?

a Earring.
b S-U-double C-E-double S.
c Yes, please.
d Of course. Let's have a look at the pronunciation guide at the back of the book.
e Phone a friend in English every evening.
f /'aɪlənd/

10 Word creation: add the suffix *-ful* or *-less* to these words to make adjectives, and complete the sentences.

care (x2)   colour (x2)   hope (x2)
pain (x2)   success   truth

1 The team win all their matches. They're very _____ .
2 He was very _____ and dropped the picture.
3 My foot hurts a lot – it's _____ .
4 You can trust her – she's always _____ .
5 His clothes are usually very _____ .
6 There are ten _____ contestants at Star School.
7 Please be _____ with the new TV.
8 It doesn't hurt at all – it's _____ .
9 I feel depressed – everything seems _____ .
10 Water is _____ .

11 Phrasebook

Listen and repeat these useful expressions. Then find them in this unit.

> You can't help laughing.   The important thing is …
> Best of luck!   Do you promise to tell the truth?
> Why not try it?   Who knows?
> It depends.   I like the fact that …
> It means a great deal to me.   It reminds me of …

Now write a five-line dialogue using three of the expressions.

Unit 2 Communication Activity
Student **A** page 106
Student **B** page 116

2 ARTS
Inspiration Extra!

PROJECT Two-Minute Talks

Give two-minute talks about books, films, or plays.

1 Work in a group and make a list of books, films or plays you have read or seen recently. Then choose two to prepare two-minute talks about.

2 Make notes:

> What is it about?
> Where and when does it happen?
> Who are the main characters?
> How does it begin? How does it end?
> What is your opinion of it?

3 Work together and prepare the talks. Use this structure:

Opening – Say what you are going to talk about (book, film or play) but don't say the title.
Description – Describe the book, film or play.
Opinion – Say what you think of it.
Ending – Summarise what you have said.

Take turns to practise giving the talks. Check carefully that the talks are not longer or shorter than two minutes. Choose two speakers to give the talks. Each speaker practises giving the talk to the rest of the group. Then give your talks to the other groups, who guess what the title is.

POEMS

Write another verse for each poem.

YES/NO POEM
Peace
Yes to listening and understanding.
No to shouting and arguing.
Yes to meeting and talking.
No to fighting and killing.
It's peace, peace, peace.

Yes to _____.
No to _____.
Yes to _____.
No to _____.
It's _____. (x3)

HELLO/GOODBYE POEM
Fun
Hello to smiles and laughter.
Goodbye to feeling sad.
Hello to holidays and happiness.
Goodbye to empty days and loneliness.
It's fun, fun, fun.

Hello to _____.
Goodbye to _____.
Hello to _____.
Goodbye to _____.
It's _____. (x3)

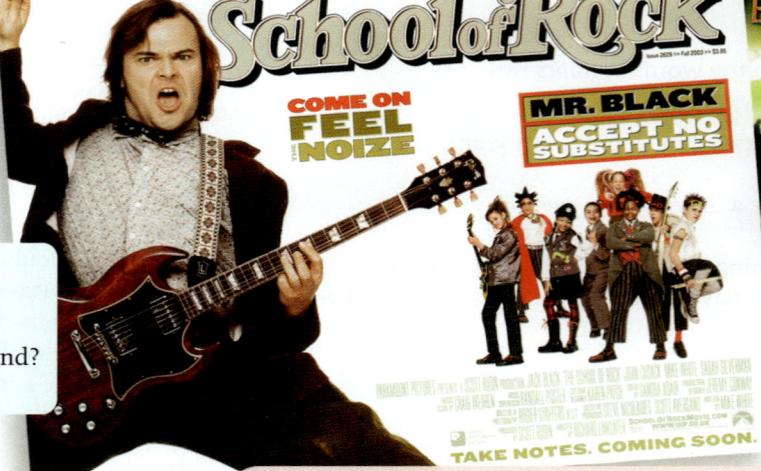

Give your poems to your teacher and listen. Can you guess who wrote each poem?

SONG

Read and try to guess the missing words.

You've Got A Friend
Carole King

When you're down and troubled
And you need some loving care
And nothing, nothing is going right
Close your __1__ and think of me
And soon I will be there
To brighten up even your darkest __2__

Chorus
You just call out my __3__
And you know wherever I am
I'll come running to see you again
Winter, __4__, summer or fall
All you have to do is call
And I'll be there
You've got a friend

If the __5__ above you
Grows dark and full of clouds
And that old north __6__ begins to blow
Keep your head together
And call my name out loud
Soon you'll hear me knocking at your __7__

Chorus

Ain't it good to know that you've got a friend
When __8__ can be so cold?
They'll hurt you, and desert you
And take your soul if you let them
Oh, but don't you let them

Chorus

🎧 Now listen and check.

UNIT 2

REVISION for more practice

LESSON 1

Look at exercise 1 on page 20. Copy out the kinds of film and write a list of at least three films for each kind.

Animation
Shrek ...

LESSON 2

Look at exercise 4 on page 23. Write sentences about Star School using six verbs from the box.

Jess helps the contestants to find their special voice.

LESSON 3

Look at the World Records Quiz on page 25. Write the answers to the quiz questions.

1 The most newspapers are sold in Japan.

EXTENSION for language development

LESSON 1

Read the review you wrote in exercise 10 on page 21 again. Now write another review of the same film giving the opposite opinion.

LESSON 2

Look at the questions in exercise 7 on page 23 again and write a paragraph answering them for yourself.

LESSON 3

Complete with the verbs in the present simple passive.

Do you know how paper is __1__ (make)? Trees __2__ (cut) down and __3__ (send) to a paper factory. There the wood __4__ (chop) into tiny pieces and these __5__ (mix) with water to make pulp. Then the water __6__ (remove) and the pulp __7__ (dry) between heated rollers. During this process, the pulp __8__ (turn) into paper.

YOUR CHOICE!

CONSTRUCTION Present simple active or passive?

Complete with the correct form of the verbs.
When you __1__ (buy) a notebook computer, you are buying something which __2__ (design) in one country and __3__ (build) in another country with parts which __4__ (come) from all over the world. Workers in Malaysia __5__ (build) notebooks with hard drives which __6__ (make) in Singapore, microprocessors which __7__ (make) in Costa Rica and batteries which __8__ (come) from Mexico. The notebook __9__ (fly) to the USA, it __10__ (put) in a bag which __11__ (make) in China, and then it __12__ (sell) on the Internet.

REFLECTION Infinitive or gerund?

Complete.
Verbs which take only one form
- *ask*, *decide* and *promise* all take the _____ :
  I promised _____ (phone) her.
- *dislike*, *enjoy* and *keep* all take the _____ :
  I kept _____ (phone) her.

Verbs which take either form with same meaning
- Some verbs take either the _____ or the _____ with no change in meaning. For example, *start* and *continue*:
  Suddenly it started to rain. Suddenly it started _____ .

ACTION Star game

- Play in two teams.
- Each team thinks of popular books, songs, and films. For books or songs, think of who they are written by or sung by. For films, think of who the film is directed by.
- The teams ask each other questions. When a team answers correctly, they ask the next question.
  A Who are the Harry Potter books written by?
  B Who is *Gangs of New York* directed by?

INTERACTION Childhood memories

- Work in a small group.
- Think about your favourite activities and people when you were a child. Make a list of activities and people. For example:
  Favourite activities: *I enjoyed eating ... , drinking ... , playing ... , watching ... , sitting in ... , hiding in ... , listening to ...*
  Favourite people: *friend, relative, teacher, neighbour ...*
- Take turns to ask and answer questions about your favourite childhood activities and people. For example:
  A What did you enjoy eating?
  B Who was your favourite friend?

29

REVIEW UNITS 1-2

Grammar

1 Read and complete. For each number 1–10, choose word or phrase A, B or C.

TEENAGERS AND MONEY

Two-thirds of British teenagers know exactly how much an Apple iPod Mini costs. But when they __1__ for the price of a bottle of milk, three-quarters have no idea. So teenagers are good at __2__ the price of things they want to buy, but they are __3__ at knowing the price of everyday things. The survey was of over 300 British teenagers and you can't help __4__ at some of the results:

- 77% of teens do not know the price of a bottle of milk and 34% seem __5__ that it costs over £1.
- However, 66% know exactly how much the successful Apple iPod Mini __6__ .
- And how much __7__ to bring up a child until they're 21? Just under two-thirds think the cost was £50,000 or less. In fact, the true cost is a painful £140,000 and only one in five teenagers __8__ that.
- Over half of teens are more worried about __9__ good than having money.
- Some think that the British Prime Minister is a very rich man. A third of teenagers believe that he gets over £1 million a year (he actually gets £178,000, which isn't bad!).
- And what about __10__ no money? 12% of teenagers think that the expression 'being in the red' (which means you've borrowed money, or spent money you don't have) means being embarrassed. How embarrassing for a few red-faced teenagers!

	A	B	C
1	ask	are asked	are asking
2	know	to know	knowing
3	hopeless	hoping	hopeful
4	laugh	laughing	to laugh
5	think	thinking	to think
6	costs	is costing	was costing
7	costs	is it costing	does it cost
8	know	knows	is knowing
9	look	looking	to look
10	having	have	to have

2 Complete with the present simple or present continuous of the verbs.

1 'What ____ you usually ____ on Saturday nights?' (do) 'I ____ to the cinema.' (go)
2 'How ____ you ____ at the moment?' (feel)
3 Leo ____n't ____ French, he ____ Spanish. (learn)
4 'What ____ you ____ about?' 'I ____n't ____ about anything.' (care)
5 'How often ____ you ____ to parties?' (go) 'About once a month. But I ____ to two parties next weekend!' (go)
6 Leo ____ jeans and trainers because he's on his skateboard. (wear)
7 Tiffany ____ forward to the holidays. (look) But the exams are first and she always ____ nervous about them. (get)
8 Why ____n't Leo ____ a girlfriend? (have) He ____n't ____ for one at the moment. (look)

3 Complete with the past simple of these verbs.

apologise   cry   go   hear   laugh
like   make   want   try

1 The holiday ____ wrong from the start.
2 Mel ____n't ____ to stay in Brighton.
3 Mel and Kate both ____ new friends.
4 Kate's new friends ____n't ____ Mel's accent.
5 Mel's new friends ____ at her jokes.
6 Mel's mum ____ for phoning her.
7 Mel nearly ____ when she ____ her mother.
8 Mel ____ to sound cheerful on the phone.

4 Write sentences using the past simple or past continuous.

Bethany (surf) with Alana because they (get) on well together.
Bethany was surfing with Alana because they got on well together.

1 The girls (wait) for a big wave when the shark (attack).
2 Bethany (think) about the surf when she (see) the shark.
3 Bethany (not scream) or (feel) pain at the time.
4 What question she (ask) everyone while she (recover) in hospital?
5 She (feel) very happy when she (surf) again for the first time.

5 Complete with the gerund of these verbs.

borrow   go   have   laugh   listen   make   watch

1 Sometimes when a film is really bad, it's funny and you can't help ____ .
2 Walt Disney was famous for ____ animated films.
3 I'm fed up with ____ to people talking in the cinema.
4 When I feel like ____ to the cinema, there's nothing on I want to see!
5 How about ____ a DVD and ____ it at home?
6 She dreams of ____ her own cinema at home.

30

UNITS 1-2 REVIEW

6 Complete with the infinitive of these verbs.

become   dance   go
help   listen   sing

1 Star School teaches contestants _____ and dance.
2 The director expects them _____ to all their classes.
3 The school helps them _____ better singers.
4 Jess wants the contestants _____ carefully to her.
5 She also expects the contestants _____ each other.
6 Adam can teach them _____ in lots of different styles.

7 Gerund or infinitive: match the beginnings with the endings.

1 Tiffany's parents want her
2 But Tiffany feels like
3 She promises
4 Her parents want to avoid
5 So they allow her
6 She's dreaming of

a to phone her parents every night.
b having an argument with her.
c to go on holiday with them.
d having lots of parties when her parents are away.
e to do what she wants.
f staying at home and being with her friends.

8 Complete with the present simple active or passive of the verbs.

Books of the past, present and future
You want to buy a book? Simple! Or is it? You __1__ (buy) books in bookshops. But today many books also __2__ (sell) in supermarkets and other shops. A lot of people __3__ (buy) books over the Internet and the books __4__ (send) to them by post. In fact you don't have to read paper books any more. Lots of books __5__ (record) and people __6__ (listen) to them on cassette or CD. And there are e-books which __7__ (download) onto MP3 players and __8__ (listen) to by people on the bus or train, or on their way to school.

Vocabulary

9 Complete with these words.

avoid   bench   bothers   brakes   calm   denim
helmet   library   scream   warning

1 Blue jeans are made of _____.
2 If something worries you, it _____ you.
3 'Be careful!' is a _____.
4 People _____ when they are hurt.
5 When water is _____, it doesn't move very much.
6 You wear a _____ on your head when you're on a motorbike.
7 You use _____ to stop a car or bike.
8 You _____ something by staying away from it.
9 You can borrow books from a _____.
10 A _____ is a long seat, usually made of wood.

10 Match these words with their definitions.

accent   chop   coach   enthusiastic   freedom
incredible   obey   paperback   robot   terrified

1 being able to do what you want
2 the way you pronounce words
3 very very frightened
4 surprising or difficult to believe
5 machine which does things people can do
6 do what someone tells you to do
7 someone who trains people
8 cut into small pieces
9 book which hasn't got a hard cover
10 very interested, keen or excited

11 Match the verbs in list A with the words and phrases in list B.

A	B
1 break	an invitation
2 go	the truth
3 pass	a website
4 perform	rules
5 receive	examinations
6 tell	a song
7 visit	boots
8 wear	wrong

12 Find the odd word.

1 awful   brilliant   disappointing   terrible
2 bored   excited   interested   keen
3 hopeful   nervous   scared   terrified
4 blues   hip-hop   documentary   folk
5 aerobics   ballet   ballroom   salsa
6 make   produce   grow   destroy

PROGRESS CHECK

Now you can ...

1 Talk about states and routines
2 Talk about what's happening now
3 Talk about future arrangements
4 Describe past events
5 Describe what happened and what was happening
6 Talk about likes and dislikes
7 Agree and disagree
8 Talk about plans and abilities
9 Describe a system

Look back at Units 1 and 2 and write an example for 1–9.

1 *She goes to parties every Friday night.*

How good are you? Tick a box.

★★★ Fine ☐   ★★ OK ☐   ★ Not sure ☐

Not sure about something? Look back through the lesson again.

31

3 OPINIONS

1 It can't be her

must and *can't*
could, *may* and *might*
Verbs of perception
Making logical deductions and discussing possibility
Describing sensations (1)

Personality Profiles

Profile	Colin	Stella	Ed	Rose	Tessa	You	Winner
Fish							
Meat							
Hip-hop							
Heavy metal							
Phoning							
Texting							
Cinema							
DVD							
Skiing							
Swimming							

1 Opener

Look at the photo. What TV game shows are there in your country? What do the contestants do to win?

2 Listening

Read and listen to the beginning of *Personality Profiles*.

HOST Good evening and welcome. I'm your host and here are Colin, Stella, Ed, Rose and Tessa, who are tonight's contestants. So let's play *Personality Profiles*! I'm sure you all know the rules by now. Our viewers have voted for a winning profile by phone. I'm going to ask you five questions. If all five of your answers match the winning profile then you're tonight's winner. OK? And the first question is: which do you prefer, fish or meat?

Now listen to the rest of the show and complete the chart for the contestants.

3 Comprehension

Complete the chart for yourself.

Now listen to the profile of the winner. After each answer, stop and discuss the possible winner(s).

A It can't be … because he/she prefers …
B It could/may/might be … or … because they prefer …
C It must be either … or … or … because they prefer …

Who is the winner? Do any of the class match the winner's profile?

32

4 Grammar

Complete.

> **must** and **can't**
> It _____ be Colin because he prefers meat.
> It _____ be you because your answers match the profile.
>
> We use _____ to show that we are sure that something is true.
> We use _____ to show that we are sure that something is untrue.
>
> **could, may** and **might**
> We use **could**, **may** and **might** to show we think something is possibly true.
>
> ➡ Check the answers: Grammar Summary page 110

5 Grammar Practice

Complete with *must* or *can't*.

1 'Where's she going?' 'It _____ be somewhere important because she's wearing her best clothes.'
2 He had two pizzas for lunch, so he _____ be hungry now.
3 'Can you see Ruth on the bus?' 'There _____ be many people with red hair and a green coat!'
4 Her new album is so popular – everyone loves it. It _____ be number one next week.
5 Lost your keys? You _____ be serious! They _____ be somewhere in your room.
6 'Oh, no! He failed his exams.' 'But that _____ be true – there _____ be some kind of mistake.'

6 Speaking

Look at photos 1–6 and discuss what they show. Choose from these words.

> balloon carpet coconut comb fork hair
> knife lemon lobster melon prawn roots
> salt sand spaghetti spider string sugar

> It looks like a comb because it's got teeth.
>> It could/may/might be …
>>> It must/can't be … because …

7 Vocabulary

Match these words and phrases with their definitions.

> chilli sauce DVD helicopter ice motor boat
> spaghetti tuna steak vacuum cleaner

1 It sounds like a motorbike but it goes on water.
2 It looks like lots of very small white snakes but it tastes great.
3 It sounds like a plane but it doesn't have wings.
4 It looks like meat but it's fish.
5 It looks like tomato sauce but it tastes hot.
6 It sounds like a plane but it cleans the floor.
7 It looks like a CD but it shows films.
8 It looks like snow but it feels hard.

8 Pronunciation

Five of these words contain silent letters. Which ones and which are the letters?

> album answer comb contestant knife
> melon spaghetti tomato tonight

🎧 Now listen and check.

9 Writing

Look at exercise 7 again and write five definitions beginning *It looks/sounds/tastes like …* Give the definitions to two other students and ask them to guess the words.

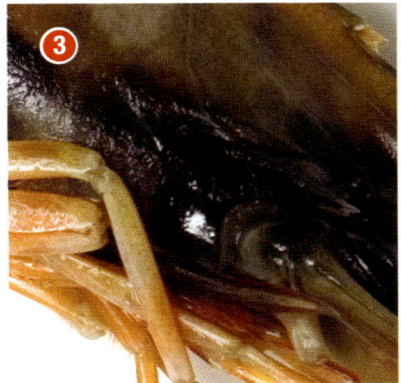

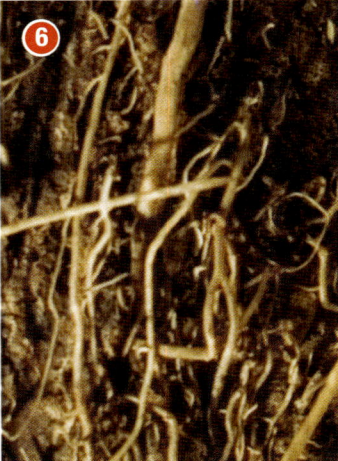

3 OPINIONS

2 You can't take a lion to the cinema

must and *mustn't/can't*
have to and *don't have to*
Reflexive pronouns
Expressing obligation and prohibition

1 Opener

Look at the cartoons. They show people breaking two strange laws. What do you think the laws are?

PARTNERS IN CRIME

Two British students plan to spend their summer vacation crossing the USA. But they have to avoid the police because they aim to break as many American laws as possible.

Americans don't have to worry, because Richard Smith and Luke Bateman only want to break silly laws. Smith, who came up with the idea, said 'There are thousands of stupid laws in the United States, but we are limiting ourselves to breaking about forty-five'. The pair intend to start their law-breaking holiday in Los Angeles – riding a bike underwater in a swimming pool. They also want to go whale-hunting in Salt Lake City, Utah (1,500 km from the ocean), and cross the road on their hands in Hartford, Connecticut.

Smith enjoys himself more on holiday when he has a purpose. 'I am not really one of those people who likes going away and sitting by a pool.'

The students had to plan their 28,000 km journey across the continent carefully. It will take about two months – as long as they don't get themselves arrested on the way!

Other laws that Smith and Bateman hope to break include:
- You mustn't fall asleep in a cheese factory in South Dakota – you must stay awake.
- You aren't allowed to play golf in the streets of Albany, New York.
- You can't take a lion to the cinema in Baltimore.
- It's illegal to say 'Oh boy!' in Jonesboro, Georgia.
- It's forbidden to give lighted cigars to pets in Zion, Illinois.
- You mustn't drive round the town square in Oxford, Mississippi more than 100 times.

2 Reading

Read and listen to *Partners in Crime*. Which phrases describe the cartoons?

3 Comprehension

Match the questions with the answers. There are two wrong answers.

1 Why do the students have to avoid the police?
2 How many laws do they hope to break?
3 What's the strange law in Los Angeles?
4 What mustn't you do in Salt Lake City?
5 What can't you do in Hartford, Connecticut?
6 Does Smith enjoy himself sitting by a pool?

a You mustn't ride a bike in a swimming pool.
b Not really.
c They don't want to get themselves arrested.
d Crossing the USA.
e Go whale-hunting.
f About 45.
g They don't have to worry.
h Cross the road on your hands.

4 Grammar

Complete.

must and mustn't/can't
You _____ stay awake in a cheese factory.
You _____ fall asleep.
You _____ take a lion to the cinema.

have to and don't have to
They _____ _____ avoid the police.
Americans _____ _____ _____ worry.

You must/You _____ to = It's obligatory.
You mustn't/You _____ = It's not allowed.
You can = It's allowed.
You don't _____ to = It's not necessary.

The past tense of both *must* and *have to* is *had to*.
The students _____ _____ plan their journey carefully.

➡ Check the answers: Grammar Summary page 111

34

5 Grammar Practice

Here are some more strange US laws. Rewrite them using the correct form of the verb in brackets.

1 You aren't allowed to whistle underwater in Vermont. (can)
2 You can't sing in the bath in Pennsylvania. (must)
3 It's against the law to keep a donkey in the bath in Georgia. (can)
4 You must wear shoes when driving in Alabama. (have to)
5 It's forbidden to eat ice cream on Sundays in Oregon. (can)
6 In Elko, Nevada, everyone walking in the street must wear a mask. (have to)
7 In North Dakota it's illegal to lie down and fall asleep with your shoes on. (can)
8 In Oklahoma City it's forbidden to walk backwards while you're eating a hamburger. (must)
9 All cats must wear three bells in Cresskill, New Jersey. (have to)
10 You aren't allowed to sleep outside on top of a refrigerator in Pennsylvania. (must)

6 Speaking

When can you do these things in your country? How old do you have to be? Discuss and complete the first column of the chart.

You can drive a car when you're …
You can't drive a car until you're …
You have to be … to drive a car.

	Age in my country	Age in the UK
You can drive a car.		
You can get married.		
You can join the army.		
You can vote in an election.		
You can live by yourself.		
You can buy a pet.		
You can leave school.		
You can buy a lottery ticket.		
You can fly a plane.		
You can get a part-time job.		

Do you agree with these laws?

7 Listening

Listen to two British people talking about the laws and complete the chart for the UK.

What are the differences between your country and the UK?

8 Grammar Practice

Look at the box and find three reflexive pronouns in *Partners in Crime*. Then complete these sentences.

1 We all enjoyed _____ at the party.
2 She's looking forward to living by _____.
3 He fell off his bike, but he didn't hurt _____.
4 Please everyone, help _____ to more food.
5 I sometimes talk to _____ when I'm thinking.
6 Have fun, Richard, and take care of _____.

Reflexive pronouns
myself   ourselves
yourself   yourselves
himself/herself/itself   themselves

➡ Grammar Summary page 111

9 Pronunciation

Write the words in the correct column.

allowed arrest asleep avoid backwards
cigar donkey factory himself include
intend journey limit ocean partner
police purpose ticket

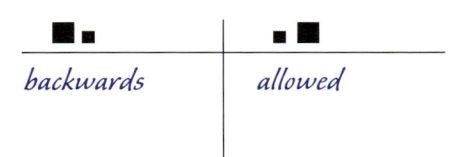

■ ▪	▪ ■
backwards	*allowed*

Now listen and check. Repeat the words.

10 Writing

Write ten more laws for your country. You can write 'silly' laws!

You must/have to …
You mustn't/can't …
You can …
You don't have to …

You mustn't eat eggs on Mondays.

Now compare your laws with other students.

3 OPINIONS

3 You should calm down!

should/ought to and shouldn't
had better
Adjective + infinitive
Giving advice

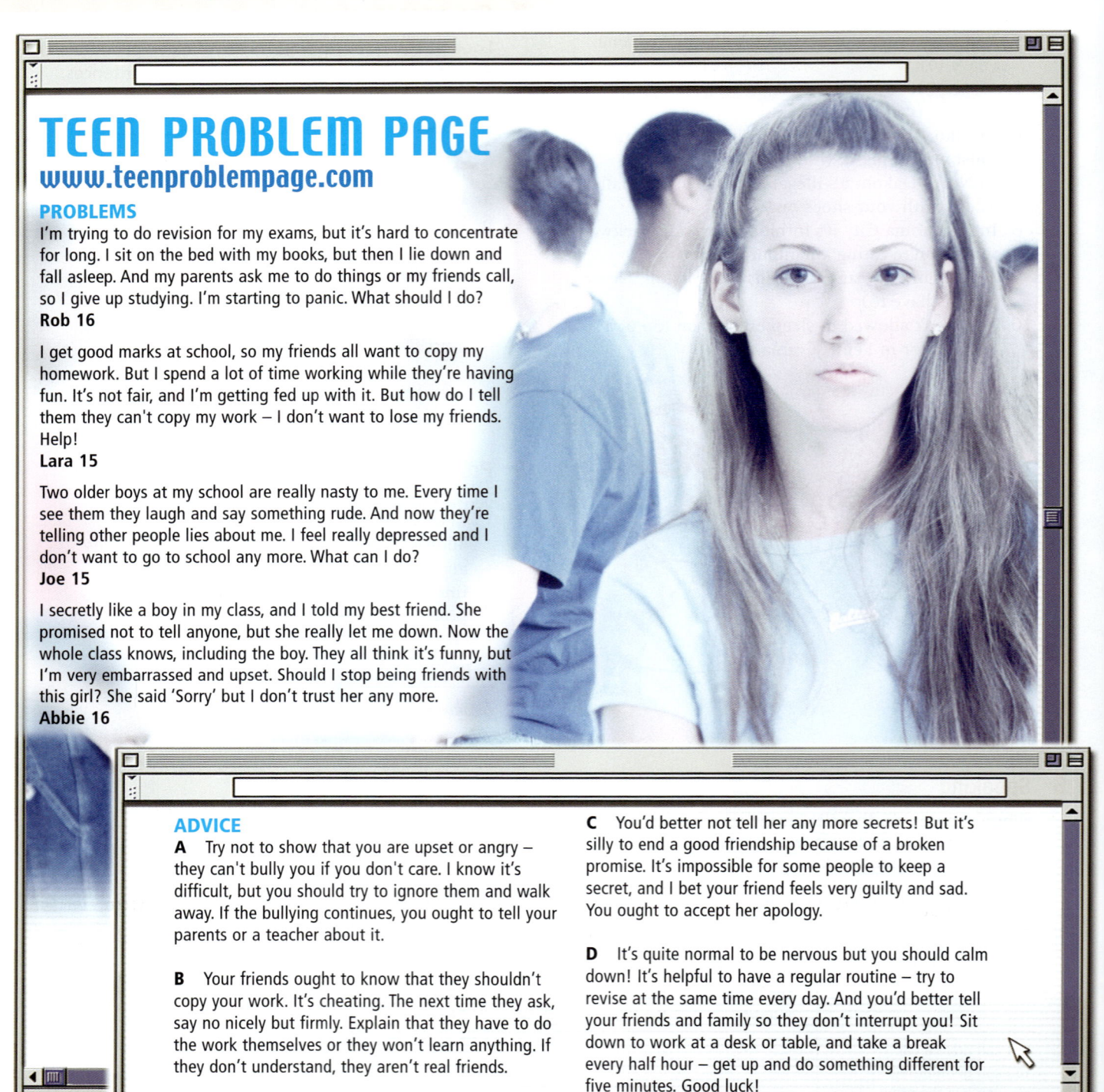

TEEN PROBLEM PAGE
www.teenproblempage.com

PROBLEMS

I'm trying to do revision for my exams, but it's hard to concentrate for long. I sit on the bed with my books, but then I lie down and fall asleep. And my parents ask me to do things or my friends call, so I give up studying. I'm starting to panic. What should I do?
Rob 16

I get good marks at school, so my friends all want to copy my homework. But I spend a lot of time working while they're having fun. It's not fair, and I'm getting fed up with it. But how do I tell them they can't copy my work – I don't want to lose my friends. Help!
Lara 15

Two older boys at my school are really nasty to me. Every time I see them they laugh and say something rude. And now they're telling other people lies about me. I feel really depressed and I don't want to go to school any more. What can I do?
Joe 15

I secretly like a boy in my class, and I told my best friend. She promised not to tell anyone, but she really let me down. Now the whole class knows, including the boy. They all think it's funny, but I'm very embarrassed and upset. Should I stop being friends with this girl? She said 'Sorry' but I don't trust her any more.
Abbie 16

ADVICE

A Try not to show that you are upset or angry – they can't bully you if you don't care. I know it's difficult, but you should try to ignore them and walk away. If the bullying continues, you ought to tell your parents or a teacher about it.

B Your friends ought to know that they shouldn't copy your work. It's cheating. The next time they ask, say no nicely but firmly. Explain that they have to do the work themselves or they won't learn anything. If they don't understand, they aren't real friends.

C You'd better not tell her any more secrets! But it's silly to end a good friendship because of a broken promise. It's impossible for some people to keep a secret, and I bet your friend feels very guilty and sad. You ought to accept her apology.

D It's quite normal to be nervous but you should calm down! It's helpful to have a regular routine – try to revise at the same time every day. And you'd better tell your friends and family so they don't interrupt you! Sit down to work at a desk or table, and take a break every half hour – get up and do something different for five minutes. Good luck!

1 Opener

Which of these words do you expect to find in the messages on the *Teen Problem Page*?

bullying cheating comedy concentrate embarrassed
exams factory marks revision secret shark

2 Reading

🎧 Read the messages and match the problems with the advice. Then listen and check.

3 Comprehension

Answer the questions.

Who …
1 wants to stop going to school?
2 should have a regular routine?
3 ought to say no to her friends?
4 should try to ignore the bullies?
5 had better accept an apology?
6 shouldn't study on his/her bed?
7 spends a lot of time doing homework?
8 told her friend a secret?

Do you agree with all the advice?

4 Grammar

Complete.

should/ought to and shouldn't
You _____ try to ignore them.
They _____ copy your work.
What _____ I do?

We can use *ought to* instead of *should*.
You _____ _____ accept her apology.

had better
You'd _____ tell your friends and family.
You'd _____ _____ tell her any more secrets!

We can use *had better* when something is important **now**.

➡ Check the answers: Grammar Summary page 111

5 Grammar Practice

Rewrite the sentences using the correct form of the verb or phrase in brackets.

1 It's important to do your homework. (should)
2 He was rude to me and he should apologise. (ought)
3 The music is very loud – we ought to turn it down. (had better)
4 It's wrong to borrow my things without asking. (should)
5 They shouldn't be late for school today. (had better)
6 You should go to bed earlier. (ought)

6 Pronunciation

🎧 Listen and repeat.

/æ/ sad	/e/ said
and	end
bad	bed
had	head
sand	send
sat	set

Now listen and write the words you hear.

7 Speaking

Tell another student your opinion. Use adjectives from the box below and these phrases.

keep a secret   feel nervous about exams   tell lies
listen to the teacher   learn English
concentrate in a noisy place   talk to friends
break a promise   talk to my parents
make a revision timetable   laugh at people
wear uncomfortable shoes

> I think it's difficult to keep a secret.
>> So do I.

Adjective + infinitive
We can use *to* + infinitive after these adjectives.

difficult   easy   good   hard   helpful   important
(im)possible   normal   rude   silly   wrong

➡ Grammar Summary page 111

8 Vocabulary

Match the phrasal verbs with their meanings. How many of the verbs can you find in this lesson?

1 calm down   a disappoint
2 let down   b go more slowly
3 lie down   c reduce the noise, heat etc
4 sit down   d put on paper
5 slow down   e lie flat
6 turn down   f stop panicking, relax
7 write down   g opposite of *stand up*

9 Speaking

What should you do in these situations? Tell each other what you think.

1 A friend of yours steals a DVD from the supermarket.
2 A friend of yours says 'Do you like my new jacket?' You think it's awful.
3 You find a 50-euro note in the street. There's no one else around.
4 Your aunt gives you a sweatshirt for your birthday. You don't like the colour.
5 Your friend Maria doesn't know that her boyfriend is going out with another girl.

10 Writing

Write a note describing a problem, and ask for advice.

Now exchange notes with another student. Write a reply giving your partner some helpful advice.

3 OPINIONS

4 Integrated Skills
Discussing facts and opinions

1 Opener

What is the population of the world? 2.5 billion, 4.5 billion or 6.5 billion?

Reading

2 *World Poverty* contains facts, but *The Aid Debate* contain both facts and opinions. Which are facts and which are opinions? How can you tell? Make a list of the verbs which tell you that you are reading an opinion and not a fact.

3 Find the highlighted words and phrases in the texts which mean:

1. guns, for example *n*
2. responsibility for something bad *n*
3. opposite of clean *adj*
4. make better *v*
5. probably going to happen *adj*
6. buying and selling between countries *n*
7. help for people or countries *n*
8. illnesses *n*
9. poor countries *n*
10. when people don't have enough money for basic things *n*
11. basic things that everyone should be allowed to have or do *n*
12. each year *adj*

4 Are you surprised by any of the facts in the texts? Why? Do you agree with any of the opinions? Why?

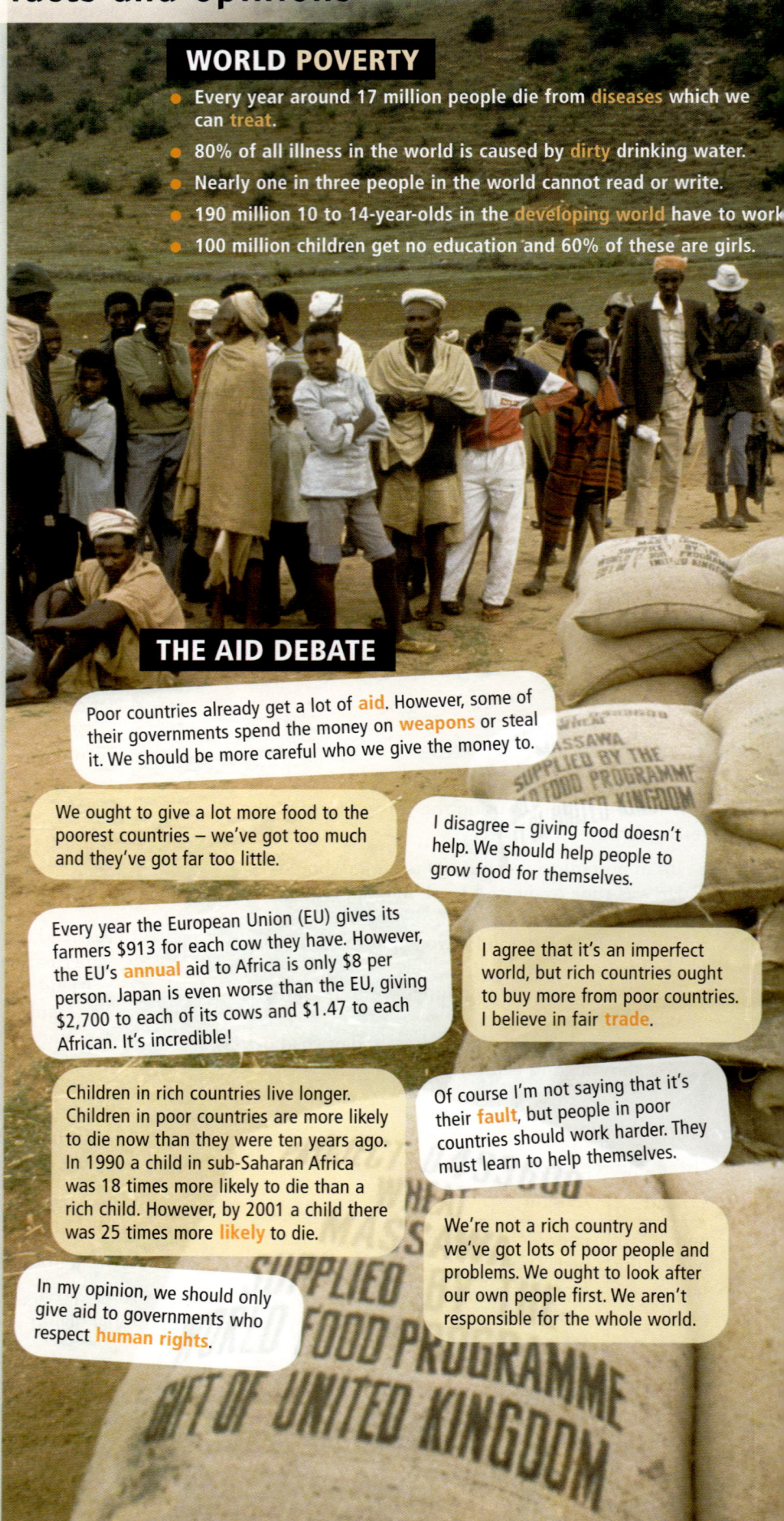

WORLD POVERTY

- Every year around 17 million people die from diseases which we can treat.
- 80% of all illness in the world is caused by dirty drinking water.
- Nearly one in three people in the world cannot read or write.
- 190 million 10 to 14-year-olds in the developing world have to work
- 100 million children get no education and 60% of these are girls.

THE AID DEBATE

Poor countries already get a lot of aid. However, some of their governments spend the money on weapons or steal it. We should be more careful who we give the money to.

We ought to give a lot more food to the poorest countries – we've got too much and they've got far too little.

I disagree – giving food doesn't help. We should help people to grow food for themselves.

Every year the European Union (EU) gives its farmers $913 for each cow they have. However, the EU's annual aid to Africa is only $8 per person. Japan is even worse than the EU, giving $2,700 to each of its cows and $1.47 to each African. It's incredible!

I agree that it's an imperfect world, but rich countries ought to buy more from poor countries. I believe in fair trade.

Children in rich countries live longer. Children in poor countries are more likely to die now than they were ten years ago. In 1990 a child in sub-Saharan Africa was 18 times more likely to die than a rich child. However, by 2001 a child there was 25 times more likely to die.

Of course I'm not saying that it's their fault, but people in poor countries should work harder. They must learn to help themselves.

In my opinion, we should only give aid to governments who respect human rights.

We're not a rich country and we've got lots of poor people and problems. We ought to look after our own people first. We aren't responsible for the whole world.

38

5 Linking words: *however* and *and*

Find examples of *however* in *The Aid Debate*. Then complete this text with *however* and *and*.

It is true that more aid is now given to the poorer countries __1__ more is promised in the future. __2__, what is needed is both more aid __3__ fairer trade. Many people believe that individuals cannot make a difference. __4__, we can help by choosing to buy things from the poorer countries when we go shopping.

6 Listening

Listen and complete the text.

HOW YOU CAN SAVE ENERGY

How can you make a difference to the world? Easy! Take control of your environment.

1. Switch off the lights when you leave a _____.
2. When you make hot drinks, just boil the water you need. In a _____ you can save enough energy to light your house for a _____.
3. Run the washing machine at 40°C not 60°C and use a _____ less energy.
4. Turn down the heating in your house by 1°C – it will cost _____ less!
5. Turn your TV, radio or DVD off at the wall. When you leave them on standby, it uses 10 to _____ % more electricity.
6. Walk, cycle or, if you must, take the _____ to school. Don't let your parents drive you – be impolite and say no!
7. Buy local food, not fruit or vegetables from the other side of the _____.
8. Think before you fly. A New York–Paris flight gives out _____ tonnes of CO_2 (a greenhouse gas) per passenger.

7 Speaking

Either: Make questions from the statements 1–8 in exercise 6 and interview two other students about how they save energy. Note down the answers.

> Do you switch off the lights when you …?

Or: Look at the texts in exercise 2 again. With another student, role play a discussion for and against more aid for the poorest countries. Express opinions and give facts to support them.

Expressing opinions
We should/ought to/must …
I believe in …
I'm not saying …, but …
I think that …
In my opinion, …
I agree/disagree.

8 Writing

Either write a paragraph giving the results of the interviews in exercise 7, or a dialogue based on the role play about aid.

Learner Independence

9
Learning contracts: there are human rights and there are also classroom rights.

1. The student's right to learn
2. The teacher's right to teach
3. Everybody's right to safety, dignity and respect

It is a good idea for the class and teacher to discuss these rights and the responsibilities which go with them. Together you can make an agreed list of rules.

Students
We should respect each other's opinions.
We must be punctual.

Teacher
I should discuss each week's learning plan with you. I must mark your homework within three days.

10
Word creation: add the prefixes *il-*, *im-* or *in-* to make the opposites of these adjectives, and complete the sentences.

| correct | credible | legal | logical |
| perfect | polite | possible | visible |

1. It's against the law. It's _____.
2. I can't believe it. It's _____.
3. They can't be seen. They're _____.
4. I can't do it all. It's _____.
5. It's not right, it's wrong. It's _____.
6. It doesn't agree with the facts. It's _____.
7. When you are rude you are _____.
8. It's not how it should be. It's _____.

11 Phrasebook

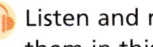

Listen and repeat these useful expressions. Then find them in this unit.

> You can't be serious!   That can't be true.
> There must be some kind of mistake.
> I'm not one of those people who …   Have fun.
> Take care of yourself.   What should I do?
> It's not fair.   Help!   It's incredible!

Which expression(s):

a show that you don't believe what is said to you?
b is a request for advice?
c is a strong request for advice?
d could you say to someone who is going out for the evening?

Unit 3 Communication Activity
Student **A** page 107
Student **B** page 117

3 OPINIONS
Inspiration *Extra!*

PROJECT *Debate*

Hold short class debates.

1 Work in a group and make a list of topics. Then choose one for a debate and write a topic statement with *should*, for example:

> People should always tell the truth.
> Students should stay at school until they are 18.
> Everyone should vote in a national election.

2 Divide the group into two sides: *For* and *Against*. The *For* side agrees with the topic statement and the *Against* side disagrees. Each side makes notes to support their point of view.

3 Each side chooses two speakers, who can each speak for one minute. Practise speaking from your notes.

4 Hold your debate for the rest of the class. Write the topic statement on the board. Speakers take turns to argue for and against, starting with a *For* speaker.

Finally the class votes for or against. Did anyone change their mind?

PUZZLE

Look at the chart below. The five people all have different jobs:

> artist   nurse   politician   reporter   scientist

They all have different pets:

> cat   dog   goldfish   rabbit   snake

They all like different activities:

> dancing   riding   skiing   surfing   swimming

Work in pairs. Discuss the clues and complete the chart.

> He must be a reporter.
> He can't have a snake.
> She can't like swimming.

Name	Job	Pet	Activity
Alice			
Ben			
Claudia			
Dave			
Elena			

Clues
Elena likes skiing.
Ben works in a hospital.
Claudia doesn't like horses or watersports.
The woman with a snake likes riding.
One of the men is a reporter.
The scientist has a rabbit and likes dancing.
Alice isn't a politician.
The nurse has a dog and likes swimming
Dave doesn't have a goldfish.

SKETCH *Sign Language*

🎧 Read and listen.

OFFICER Excuse me, sir. What are you doing?
MAN I'm taking photographs.
OFFICER Yes, I know. But you can't do that.
MAN Yes, I can. I'm very good at taking photos.
OFFICER No, sir, I mean you aren't *allowed* to do that.
MAN It's not against the law to take pictures.
OFFICER Not usually, sir, but you can't take pictures *here*.
MAN Why not?
OFFICER Look at the sign – it says: Police No Entry.
MAN Oh, that's OK. I'm not a police officer.
OFFICER Exactly. That's why you shouldn't be here.
MAN No, that's why *you* shouldn't be here.
OFFICER I beg your pardon?
MAN You're a police officer, so you shouldn't be here.
OFFICER Are you trying to be funny?
MAN Certainly not! The sign says that police mustn't come in here.
OFFICER No, it doesn't!
MAN You don't have to shout.
OFFICER Sir, that is a *police* sign. It says *no one* can come in here.
MAN No one?
OFFICER That's right.
MAN Then you're breaking the law. You'd better leave before I take a photo of you!

40

UNIT 3

REVISION for more practice

LESSON 1

What are these things? Write sentences with *must/can't* using the words in brackets.

A is round and red. (orange/tomato)
B has 1250 pages. (dictionary/newspaper)
C is a large animal. (elephant/mouse)
D has two wheels. (car/motorbike)
E can fly. (helicopter/train)

A must be a tomato.
It can't be an orange.

LESSON 2

Look at the six laws at the end of the text on page 34. Rewrite all of them using *mustn't*, *can't* and *have to*. For example, in the first law, replace *mustn't* with *can't*.

You can't fall asleep in a cheese factory in South Dakota.

LESSON 3

Look at the *Teen Problem Page* advice on page 36. Rewrite some of the advice using *should(n't)* and *ought to*.

A You shouldn't show that you are upset or angry. You ought to try to ignore them.

EXTENSION for language development

LESSON 1

Match the sounds in the yellow box with the words in the blue box and write sentences.

baa   cluck   ding dong   hiss   miaow
moo   pop   quack   splash   tick tock

balloon   bell   cat   chicken   clock
cow   duck   sheep   snake   water

baa   It sounds like a sheep.

LESSON 2

Write sentences about things you must and mustn't/can't do:

on a plane   in a church   in a museum   in a shop

You can't carry a knife on a plane.

LESSON 3

Read this message from *Teen Problem Page* and write some helpful advice.

I'm at a new school because we've moved to another town. I had lots of friends at my old school but now I feel very lonely. What can I do to make new friends?

I think you should ...

YOUR CHOICE!

CONSTRUCTION must, mustn't or don't have to?

Complete with *must*, *mustn't* or *don't have (to)*.
Travelling in other countries is exciting, but if you really want to enjoy your trip, you __1__ make some plans in advance. To enter most countries, you __2__ have a passport. Maybe you __3__ to get a visa, but you __4__ check before you leave. And you __5__ take enough money. You __6__ to spend a lot, but you __7__ find yourself without enough money for food and a place to stay. You __8__ to organise everything in advance, but you should book somewhere to stay on the first night. And you __9__ take the right clothes for the climate. But remember, if you're flying, you __10__ take more luggage than the airline allows.

ACTION What is it? game

- Work in a small group.
- Take turns to choose an imaginary object. Don't say what it is! Pick up your object and use it. You can mime and make noises, but don't say anything.
- The rest of the group try to guess what your object is.
    A It looks like a box.
    B It can't be a computer.
    C It must be a TV!

REFLECTION Modal auxiliary verbs: must and can

Match the examples a–e with language functions 1–5.
1 *must* is used to express obligation.
2 *can* is used to express permission.
3 *can* and *can't* are used to talk about ability.
4 *must* and *can't* are used to make deductions.
5 *mustn't* and *can't* are used to express prohibition.

a He can swim but he can't dive.
b You must listen to me.
c You must be joking – it can't be true!
d We can't talk during the exam.
e You can borrow my bike.

INTERACTION Your ideal holiday

- Work in a small group.
- Plan your ideal fortnight's holiday. Discuss where you should go, how to get there, where to stay, and what you want to do on your holiday. Think about when you should go and what you should take with you.
    A I think we should go to the UK so we can practise speaking English.
    B But the weather isn't great there – I think we ought to go to Australia!

41

culture

Great Novels

Reading

1 Read the biographies 1–3 of three famous British writers and match them with the novels and texts a–c below.

1 He was born in Edinburgh in 1859 and was one of ten children. He studied medicine and in 1880 he went to the Arctic as a ship's doctor for six months. In 1882 he moved to London, working as a doctor and writing. In 1887 he wrote his first story about the famous detective, Sherlock Holmes.

2 Born in 1775, she was one of eight children. She was well-educated and learnt French, Italian and music. Four of her six books were published during her lifetime, and the other two after she died. Unlike most of her heroines, she never married. She died in 1817, but remains one of the most popular English novelists.

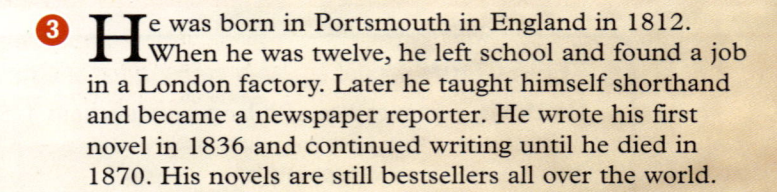

3 He was born in Portsmouth in England in 1812. When he was twelve, he left school and found a job in a London factory. Later he taught himself shorthand and became a newspaper reporter. He wrote his first novel in 1836 and continued writing until he died in 1870. His novels are still bestsellers all over the world.

The Sign of Four
Sir Arthur Conan Doyle

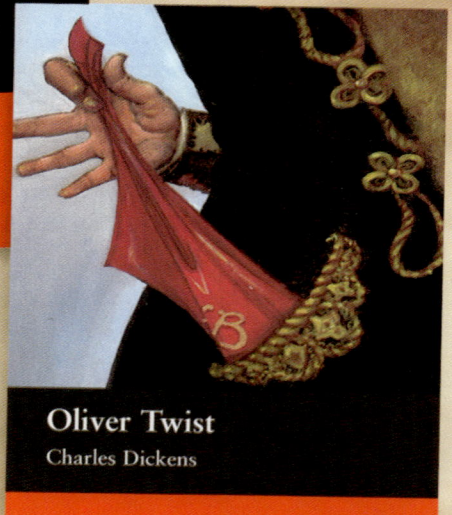

Sense and Sensibility
Jane Austen

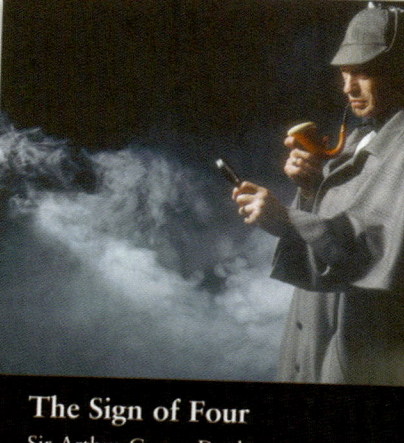

Oliver Twist
Charles Dickens

a 'I'm afraid,' said Miss Morstan. 'What should I do, Mr Holmes?'
Holmes jumped up excitedly. 'We shall go tonight to the Lyceum Theatre – the three of us – you and I and Doctor Watson. We'll meet your unknown friend. And we'll try to solve the mystery.'

b A poor young boy, brought up without parents, runs away to London. There he finds friends – and makes enemies.
The author paints a dramatic picture of life on the streets of nineteenth-century London, and Fagin is one of the most memorable villains in English literature.

c After the death of her husband, Mrs Dashwood and her daughters, Elinor, Marianne and Margaret, must leave their family home and move to a small cottage in Devon.
There Marianne falls in love with the handsome John Willoughby and Elinor misses Edward Ferrars, the man she had to leave behind.

culture

2 Read these extracts. Which novel on page 42 is each extract from?

❶

One morning, Marianne looked out of the sitting-room window and saw that the rain-clouds had disappeared. The sky was now blue and the sun was shining.

'Look, the sun is shining at last,' she said. 'Let us all go out for a walk!'

Elinor was drawing and Mrs Dashwood was reading, and they did not want to go out. Only Margaret wanted to go walking with her sister. Soon the two girls were walking up the nearest hill.

'What exciting weather!' Marianne cried as the wind blew in their faces. 'I could walk here for a long time without getting tired!'

The girls walked on, laughing and talking. Suddenly, the rain-clouds returned and the sky became dark. Soon rain began to fall heavily.

There were no trees or buildings nearby. There was nowhere for the sisters to shelter from the rain. They turned back at once to go home. They ran as fast as they could, down the hill and back towards the cottage. Soon, they were both very wet.

❷

There were stalls and shops selling books on one side of the square. At one of the stalls, an old gentleman was looking at the books. He picked one up and began to read.

The Dodger stopped. 'He'll do,' he said quietly.

'Right,' Charley whispered.

The two boys walked across the square. Oliver followed. The old gentleman went on reading. He had grey hair and wore gold glasses. He wore a long, dark green coat and white trousers.

The Dodger moved nearer. The next moment, the old gentleman's silk handkerchief was in the Dodger's hand. The Dodger and Charley ran and hid in the doorway of a house.

The old gentleman touched his pocket. He turned round quickly. He saw Oliver standing behind him.

'That boy's got my handkerchief!' the old gentleman cried.

Oliver turned and ran.

'Stop thief! Stop thief!'

In a few moments, a hundred people were shouting. A hundred people were running after Oliver.

❸

There were many people outside the theatre. Everyone was meeting friends and going in to see the play. We waited. Suddenly a small dark man appeared.

'Are you Miss Morstan and her friends?' he asked.

'Yes,' she said.

'You must promise me that these men are not policemen,' said the stranger.

'They are not policemen,' replied Miss Morstan.

'Then come with me,' said the man.

We passed through so many streets that I was very soon lost. I had no idea where we were going. I was feeling nervous and Miss Morstan's face looked white. Sherlock Holmes was calm.

At last we stopped. We were outside a house in a dark quiet street. It had only one light in the kitchen window. There were no lights in any of the other houses in the street.

3 Listening

Listen to three extracts which continue the story from the novels. Match the extracts with pictures A–C below. Which novel is each extract from?

4 Speaking

Which of the three novels would you most like to read? Tell each other why.

OR

Close your book. Tell another student what you remember about one of the novels.

A

B

C

43

4 MIND OVER MATTER

1 They hear him singing

Verbs of perception + present participle
can/could + verbs of perception
Describing sensations (2)

1 Opener

Look at the photo. What do you know about Elvis Presley?

2 Reading

Read and listen to *Elvis lives and speaks!*

Elvis
lives and speaks!

Elvis Presley died on August 16, 1977, at the age of 42, but today he is more alive than ever. Many believe that he often returns from the 'Other Side'. This may be true. People see Elvis walking out of a café, they watch him driving by in a flashy car, or they hear him singing. But he doesn't stay long enough for them to be absolutely sure – they say it could be him or it might be him, but not that it is him.

But Dorothy Sherry was different. She not only saw Presley, but she talked to him and travelled with him! In 1978 Dorothy visited Dr Hans Holzer, a psychic investigator, at his office in Manhattan, New York, with an incredible story.

It was in early January 1978 at around eleven at night. Dorothy was sitting alone at home when she suddenly noticed Elvis Presley standing in front of her.

'I was fully awake at the time,' Dorothy explained, 'and I saw him smiling at me. I didn't dare say anything. He held out his hand, saying 'Come with me, now.' I took his hand and we went through a sort of tunnel with bright lights at the end. I could hear birds singing and we were soon in a beautiful field full of flowers.'

Elvis and Dorothy talked for four hours that first night. Then he kissed her on the cheek and took her back through the tunnel to her home. After the first time Elvis returned frequently. He took Dorothy on trips to Las Vegas to see the hotel where he performed, and to Graceland, the house where he lived. At Graceland Dorothy hurt her knee on a low table in the garden and the next morning she had a bruise on her knee!

'Is Elvis real?' Dr Holzer asked. 'Can you actually feel him?'

'Oh, yes,' Dorothy replied. 'I can feel his shirt, his face and I can feel him holding my hand. His fingers feel rough at the ends because he bites his nails. I saw him biting his nails several times.'

3 Comprehension

Choose the best answer.

1. When people see Elvis walking out of a café, he
   A says hello to them.   B gets into a car.   C disappears quickly.
2. People think it
   A can't be Elvis.   B might be Elvis.   C must be Elvis.
3. Dorothy Sherry saw Presley
   A in her house.   B in Dr Holzer's office.   C on stage.
4. Dorothy suddenly noticed Elvis Presley
   A standing in front of her.   B sitting beside her.   C holding her hand.
5. After she went through the tunnel, Dorothy heard
   A people singing.   B Elvis singing.   C birds singing.
6. Dorothy says Elvis came to see her
   A once.   B three times.   C lots of times.
7. Dorothy knows that she went to Graceland with Elvis because
   A Elvis took her there.   B she had a bruise the next day.
   C she has a photo.

Do you believe that people can come back from the dead?

4 Grammar

Complete.

> **Verbs of perception + present participle**
> People see Elvis walk**ing** out of a café.
> They hear him sing_____.
> I saw him bit_____ his nails.
>
> We can also use this construction with *watch*, *notice*, *listen to*, *smell* and *feel*.

> **can/could + verbs of perception**
> I can _____ him holding my hand.
> I could _____ birds singing.
>
> We can also use *can/could* before *see*, *smell* and *taste*.

➡ Check the answers: Grammar Summary page 111

5 Grammar Practice

Complete with the present participle of these verbs.

> cook   dance   leave   play
> sing   sit   touch   walk

1 She listened to Elvis _____ *Blue Suede Shoes*.
2 Sh – can you hear someone _____ up the stairs?
3 Let's watch the contestants _____ the salsa.
4 I could see people _____ tennis from my window.
5 Mmm – I can smell supper _____.
6 When we saw the bus _____ we knew we were late.
7 She felt a snake _____ her foot and screamed.
8 He noticed a new student _____ at the back and asked her name.

6 Listening

Listen and say what you can hear.

A I can hear a door banging.
B I can hear someone cheering.

> door bang   car come   cheer
> clap   cry   phone ring   laugh
> run   scream   motorbike leave

7 Speaking

Look at the picture and say what you can see.

A I can see a girl flying a kite.
B I can see a boy juggling.

8 Listening

Listen and complete.

It was last Saturday afternoon and I was at home. I heard a car __1__ down the street outside, two car doors __2__ and then two people __3__. I went to the window and saw a tall man and a woman __4__ down the street. The woman was holding a small black bag. Soon I couldn't see them any more. Then I heard a woman __5__ again and again, and then __6__ 'Help! Help!'. I ran out of the house and at that moment I heard a motorbike __7__. The motorbike went past me very fast, but I could see the tall man on it with the bag. I heard the woman __8__ and I went up to her.

What happened next? Listen to the end of the story and see if you are right.

9 Pronunciation

Listen and repeat.

/eə/ **hair**	/ɪə/ **hear**
air	ear
chair	cheer
dare	dear
pair	pier
wear	we're

Now listen and write the words you hear.

10 Writing

Close your eyes. Imagine you are at home. It's Saturday morning and you are still in bed. What can you hear? What can you smell?

Now write five sentences beginning *I could hear/smell …*

I could hear my parents talking.

4 MIND OVER MATTER

2 I'll keep my fingers crossed!

Future review: *will/won't*, *shall* and *going to*
Making predictions, promises and offers
Talking about plans and intentions

How superstitious are you?

Are you down-to-earth, or on another planet? Find out here!

1 **A friend says 'Shall I read out your horoscope?' Do you …**
   A say yes, listen carefully and follow all the advice?
   B say yes, but only believe it if it says something good?
   C ask your friend to read out the sports results instead?

2 **You know that tomorrow is Friday the 13th. What are you going to do?**
   A Stay at home all day.
   B Go out, but be very careful.
   C Take no notice – it makes no difference anyway.

3 **You see a painter up a ladder on your way to school. Will you …**
   A walk round the ladder to avoid bad luck?
   B walk under the ladder to prove it's not unlucky?
   C walk round the ladder because it's safer?

4 **You accidentally break a mirror. What do you say?**
   A 'Oh dear, I'll have seven years' bad luck!'
   B 'I won't be unlucky, touch wood.'
   C 'Never mind – I'll buy another one.'

5 **A friend is worried about an important exam tomorrow. What do you say?**
   A 'Don't worry – I'll lend you my lucky charm.'
   B 'Good luck – I'll keep my fingers crossed!'
   C 'Shall I help you to revise this evening?'

6 **You're in an old building and are told that it's haunted. What do you say?**
   A 'I can hear footsteps coming this way – we're going to see the ghost!'
   B 'I hope we won't see any ghosts.'
   C 'I don't believe in ghosts – it's all nonsense!'

Now turn to page 119 to find out your score.

1 Opener

Here are the top UK superstitions and the percentage of people who believe in them.

- ☺ Touching wood **86%**
- ☺ Crossing fingers **64%**
- ☹ Walking under a ladder **49%**
- ☹ Breaking a mirror **34%**
- ☹ Worried about number 13 **25%**
- ☺ Carrying a lucky charm **24%**

Do you have these superstitions in your country?

2 Reading

Read and answer the questionnaire
How superstitious are you?

3 Speaking

Compare your score with other students.
Do you agree with your score?

4 Grammar

Complete.

> **will/won't and going to**
> We use *will/won't* to say what we predict or hope for the future.
> **I'll** have seven years' bad luck.
> I hope we _____ see any ghosts.
>
> We also use *will/won't* for offers, promises and decisions made at the time of speaking.
> I _____ lend you my lucky charm.
> I _____ keep my fingers crossed!
> Never mind – I _____ buy another mirror.
>
> We use *going to* to talk about plans and intentions.
> I _____ _____ to stay at home all day.
> Are _____ _____ to go out?
>
> We also use *going to* to predict the future from present evidence.
> I can hear footsteps – we _____ _____ to see the ghost!
>
> ➡ Check the answers: Grammar Summary page 112

5 Grammar Practice

Complete with *'ll/won't* or *(be) going to*.

WOMAN   I must hurry or I __1__ miss the train.
MAN   I __2__ drive into town. I __3__ give you a lift to the station.
WOMAN   Oh, thank you. Wait a second – I __4__ get my jacket.
MAN   And you'd better take an umbrella. Look at the sky.
WOMAN   Yes, it __5__ start raining soon.
MAN   I'm sure you __6__ be late. We __7__ be there in five minutes.
WOMAN   You're driving too fast – you __8__ have an accident! Look out!
MAN   Sorry, I __9__ slow down.

6 Listening

🎧 You are going to hear a short story. Read and listen to the beginning.

> A doctor is driving home along a quiet country road. It's late at night and it's raining hard. Suddenly he sees a girl walking along the road. She looks like a student.

What do you think the doctor will do?

Now listen to the rest of the story. Continue to make predictions, and find out if you predicted correctly.

Do you think this is a true story? Why/Why not?

7 Speaking

Make promises in response to statements 1–5.
Use *I will/won't …* with these phrases.

> phone once a week   drive carefully
> forget anything   be away for long   look at the map

1 Remember your passport.
2 Have a safe journey.
3 Don't get lost!
4 Please keep in touch.
5 Come back soon.

Now make offers in response to statements 6–10.
Use *Shall I …?* and *I'll …* with these phrases.

> close the window   turn down the heating
> carry it for you   lend you one   turn off the lights

6 I want to go to sleep.
7 I don't have a pen.
8 It's quite cold in here.
9 I'm feeling rather hot.
10 My suitcase is very heavy.

> **Making offers**
> **Shall I** read out your horoscope?
> **I'll** read out your horoscope.
>
> ➡ Grammar Summary page 112

8 Pronunciation

🎧 Listen and repeat the sentences. Mark the stressed words.

1 Never mind – I'll buy another one.
2 Don't worry – I'll lend you my lucky charm.
3 Good luck – I'll keep my fingers crossed!
4 Shall I help you to revise this evening?
5 We're going to see the ghost!
6 I don't believe in ghosts.

9 Vocabulary

Match the phrasal verbs with their meanings. How many of the verbs can you find in this lesson?

1 find out   a be careful
2 go out   b read aloud
3 look out   c discover
4 read out   d opposite of *stay in*
5 take out   e experiment with
6 try out   f remove

10 Writing

Write a paragraph about next week. Say what you *know* is going to happen because you have decided to do it, or because it is planned. You can also say what you *think* or *hope* will happen.

4 MIND OVER MATTER

3 If you fly in a small plane ...

First conditional
Talking about future possibility

I've always been afraid of flying – I'm afraid of heights! However, when I was 18 my parents gave me an unusual present. 'If you fly in a small plane first, you'll feel better about going up in a big one,' my father said. So on my birthday I met Carol, my instructor, on the runway at our local airfield. The plane was a Cessna 152, registration G-KBCX. Carol was full of confidence as she showed me the plane's controls and instruments. Then Carol spoke on the radio to Matt in the control tower and we took off, climbing to 500 metres. We turned back towards the airfield and that was when I got my first surprise.

CAROL Here, you take over now. If you keep your hands steady, everything will be fine.

Carol took her hands off the controls and suddenly I was flying the plane! I couldn't believe it! But a moment later I got another, much worse, surprise. 'Aaah!' Carol cried out. Her face went white and she held her head in her hands.

CAROL It's my head – I feel awful. Gary, it's up to you now. You'll have to land the plane yourself. It's our only chance.
GARY But ...
CAROL See the button on top of your controls – that's the radio. If you press that button, you'll talk to Matt. He'll help you.

Carol closed her eyes. So I pressed the radio button.

GARY Help!!! Help!!!
MATT This is the control tower. Who are you and what's your problem?
GARY It's G-KBCX calling. Carol is unconscious!! I'm Gary and I don't know how to fly! Get me out of here! Please ...
MATT OK Gary, take it easy. I can see you above me now. If you listen carefully, I'll tell you what to do. All right? First, let's practise a little. Push the controls forward, and the plane's nose will drop.
GARY Oh no!
MATT That's too much. If you pull the controls back towards you gently, the nose will come up again. Good – now can you see the black knob in front of you? That's the throttle and it controls the engine. If you pull the throttle towards you, the plane will start to go down. Try it. Great. But make sure you keep the nose up.
GARY But how am I going to land?
MATT If you do exactly what I say, everything will be fine.

1 Opener

Look at the picture. Who is the woman and what has happened to her?

What's the boy doing? How do you think he is feeling?

2 Reading

Read and listen.

What do you think will happen next? What will happen if Gary makes a mistake? Listen to the rest of Gary's amazing story.

3 Comprehension

Answer the questions.

1 What was Gary scared of?
2 What was Gary's first surprise?
3 Why did Gary have to land the plane himself?
4 What happened when Gary pulled the controls towards him?
5 What happened when Gary pulled the throttle towards him?
6 Who went to hospital, and who never wanted to fly again?

Would you like to learn to fly? Why or why not?

4 Grammar

Complete.

> **First conditional**
> *If* + present simple, future simple
> If you **fly** in a small plane, you**'ll feel** better about going up in a big one.
> _____ you press that button, you _____ talk to Matt.
> If you _____ carefully, I _____ _____ you what to do.

➡ Check the answers: Grammar Summary page 112

5 Grammar Practice

Murphy's Law says that 'If something can go wrong, it will.' Match the beginnings and endings of these sentences, which are all examples of Murphy's Law at school.

1 If a subject is interesting to the teacher,
2 If you want a book from the library,
3 If you are allowed a calculator in an exam,
4 If you are early,
5 If you are late,
6 If you do homework on a computer,
7 If you copy someone else's homework,
8 If you lend friends your notes,

a it will be out.
b the school bus will be late.
c they will lose them.
d it will crash before you save your work.
e the battery will be flat.
f the teacher will find out.
g it will bore the students.
h the school bus will be on time.

6 Speaking

Complete the sentences in the cartoons using these phrases.

> have to pay for them   help me with my maths
> let you go to the party   miss the train
> tidy your room   turn it off

7 Pronunciation

Count the syllables and mark the stress.

> airfield   ambulance   confidence
> control   however   instructor
> instrument   registration   unconscious

■

airfield 2

🎧 Now listen and check. Repeat the words.

8 Speaking

Interview two other students. Ask them the questions in the *What if …?* questionnaire and note down the answers.

> **Questionnaire** *What if …?*
> 1 What will you do tonight if you don't have any homework?
> 2 What will you do at the weekend if the weather's bad?
> 3 What will you reply if a friend invites you to the cinema after school?
> 4 What will you say if your family asks you to cook supper tonight?
> 5 What will you do if you can't sleep tonight?
> 6 What will you do if you forget your bag when you go home today?
> 7 What will you do if you find someone's purse in the street on the way home?
> 8 What will you say if a classmate wants to copy your work after class?

9 Writing

Use your notes from the *What if …?* questionnaire to write sentences comparing the two students.

If they don't have any homework tonight, Anna will watch TV and Stefan will go out with his friends.

If we don't hurry, we …
If you drop any, you …
If you aren't home by midnight, we …
I'll let you borrow my new top if you …
You'll find your Walkman if you …
If you don't turn the music down, I …

4 MIND OVER MATTER

4 Integrated Skills
Telling a story

1 Opener

Rebecca is a novel by Daphne du Maurier. In the book, Maxim de Winter marries again after the death of his first wife, Rebecca. Maxim never talks about Rebecca, but other people talk about her …

What problems do you think Maxim's new wife will have when they return to his home?

2 Reading

Read the first part of the story and answer the questions.

A shy young girl of 21 was working for an American woman in Monte Carlo when she met Maxim de Winter, a rich and handsome Englishman. People said that Maxim couldn't get over the death of his beautiful wife, Rebecca, who drowned in a boating accident. But Maxim asked the young girl to marry him. After a honeymoon in Italy, Maxim took his new wife back to his beautiful home, Manderley, on the south-west coast of England.

But when she arrived at Manderley, the second Mrs de Winter didn't feel at all confident in her new role. She found herself in charge of a huge house with lots of servants, including the unfriendly housekeeper, Mrs Danvers. She soon realised that Mrs Danvers adored Rebecca. In fact, Rebecca seemed to haunt the house, and the second Mrs de Winter felt Rebecca's presence everywhere. But Maxim never talked about her.

One afternoon, Maxim and his wife went for a walk on the beach with the dog. When she followed the dog to an empty cottage, Maxim called her back. He was quite cross, and explained impatiently that the cottage held bad memories. Later, she discovered that Rebecca often stayed there.

1 Where did Maxim de Winter meet his second wife?
2 Who was Rebecca?
3 What did people say happened to Rebecca?
4 Where did Maxim de Winter live?
5 Why didn't the second Mrs de Winter feel confident?
6 What was Mrs Danvers like?
7 Why didn't Maxim want his wife to go to the cottage?
8 Who often stayed in the cottage?

Speaking

3 Look at the pictures and tell each other what happened in the second part of the story. Then listen and check.

The second Mrs de Winter wanted to be the perfect wife at Manderley's annual fancy dress ball.

1
What are you going to wear for the ball?
I don't know.
Why don't you copy one of the paintings in Manderley? I like the picture of the girl in white, with a hat in her hand.

2
I'll have to wear a wig.

50

Tell me about your costume.

It's a secret! You won't know it's me – you'll have the surprise of your life.'

Go and change immediately! It doesn't matter what you wear.

4 Before you listen to the third part of the story, discuss the possible answers to these questions about it.

1. Why was Maxim so angry about Mrs de Winter's dress?
2. Why did Mrs Danvers suggest the white dress?
3. What did Mrs de Winter say to Mrs Danvers the next day?
4. What did Mrs Danvers reply?
5. What did a diver find in the sea that night?
6. What did Maxim confess to his wife?
7. Did anyone else know what really happened to Rebecca?
8. Did Maxim ever love Rebecca?

Listening

5 Listen to the third part of the story and check your answers to exercise 4.

6 Read these phrases from the last part of the story. How does it end?

inquest into Rebecca's death … verdict was suicide … Rebecca's diary … a doctor in London … the day she died … the next day … went to London … asked the doctor about Rebecca … very ill … only six months to live … never have a child … afterwards … dinner in a restaurant … Rebecca wanted me to kill her … laughing when she died … wife didn't reply … all over now … looked very worried … suddenly … must drive back to Manderley … something's wrong … early hours of the morning … reached the top of the hill … sky above their heads was black … sky above Manderley was red

Now listen to the last part of the story and check.

7 Writing

Write the last part of the story using the phrases in exercise 6.

There was an inquest into Rebecca's death, and the verdict was suicide.

Learner Independence

8 When you come across a new word, try to guess what it means.

- What could the word mean in the context?
- What part of speech is it?
- Has it got a prefix or suffix?
- Is it like another English word you know?
- Is it like a word in your language?

Look at the text in exercise 2 again. Could you guess the meanings of the new words?

9 Word creation: complete the two charts with words from Unit 4.

Noun	Adjective	Verb	Noun
anger		calculate	
care		instruct	
confidence		investigate	
friend		paint	
luck		predict	
presence		revise	
superstition		teach	

10 Phrasebook

Listen and repeat these useful expressions. Then find them in this unit.

Take no notice. It makes no difference.
Touch wood. Never mind.
I'll keep my fingers crossed!
It's all nonsense! Look out!
It's up to you. It's our only chance.
Get me out of here! Take it easy.
It's a secret!

Which expression means:

a 'It doesn't matter.'?
b 'Relax.'?
c 'Be careful!'?
d 'It doesn't change anything.'?

Unit 4 Communication Activity
Student **A** page 107
Student **B** page 117

4 MIND OVER MATTER
Inspiration *Extra!*

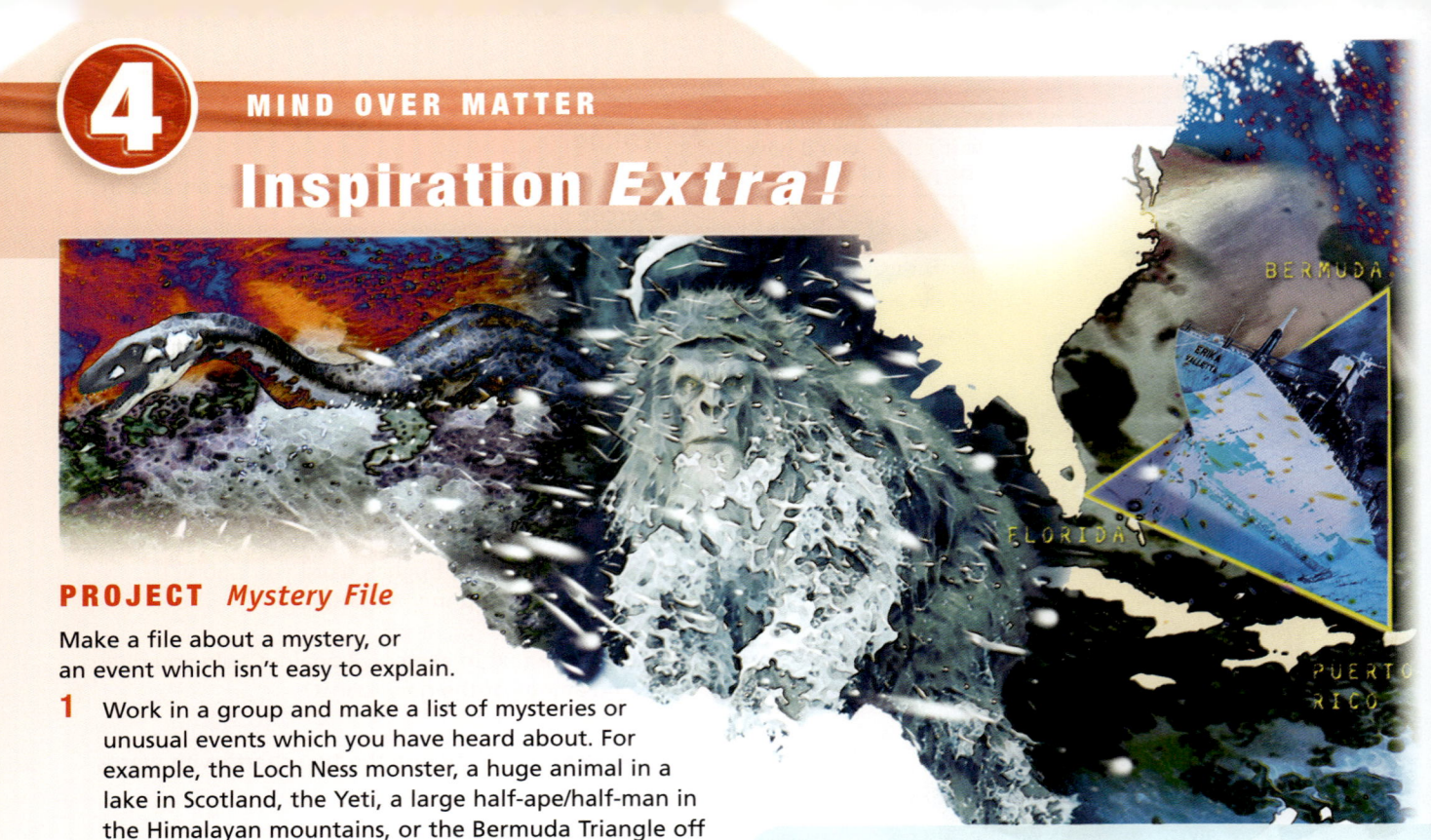

PROJECT Mystery File

Make a file about a mystery, or an event which isn't easy to explain.

1. Work in a group and make a list of mysteries or unusual events which you have heard about. For example, the Loch Ness monster, a huge animal in a lake in Scotland, the Yeti, a large half-ape/half-man in the Himalayan mountains, or the Bermuda Triangle off the coast of the USA where planes and ships disappear. Then choose one or two to write about.

2. Find out information about the mysteries or events using the Internet or a library:

   > When and where does or did it happen?
   > What happens/happened? How do we know about it?
   > What explanations are there for it?
   > What is your opinion?

3. Work together and make a Mystery File. Read it carefully and correct any mistakes. Draw pictures or use photographs from magazines or newspapers. Show your Mystery File to the other groups.

GAME Where Am I?

- Imagine you're somewhere outside the classroom. You could be in a town, in the country, by water … . Think about these questions and make notes.

   > What time of day is it?
   > What's the weather like? Do you feel hot, warm, cold, wet?
   > What can you see around you?
   > Are there any people or animals? What are they doing?
   > What sounds can you hear?
   > What can you smell?
   > How do you feel – happy, relaxed, …?

- Now describe your experience to other students. Can they guess where you are?

   It's the afternoon, it's a beautiful day, and I feel quite warm. I can see hundreds of people all around me, and we're all watching animals running. I can hear people cheering and clapping and I can smell the grass. I feel excited!

SONG

Read and complete with these words. One word is used twice.

> celebration   hand   history   make
> share   tomorrow   true   world

Celebrate The Future

The Future's coming
You got to catch it if you can
The magic's unfolding
When you can hold it in your __1__
We can touch tomorrow today
To __2__ some memories that never fade away
Put your hands on the future
There are dreams together around the __3__
With the voice from every country
Face from every land
We'll celebrate the future hand in hand
We'll celebrate the future hand in hand
The magic of __4__
Lives inside of you
Join the __5__
It's a fairy tale come __6__
Harmony
It's harmony
All of us together making __7__
Put your hands on the future
__8__ our dreams together around the __9__
With the voice from every country
Face from every land
We'll celebrate the future hand in hand
We'll celebrate the future hand in hand
We'll celebrate the future hand in hand

🎧 Now listen and check.

52

UNIT 4

REVISION for more practice

LESSON 1

Write five sentences beginning *I could see/hear someone/something ...* and use these verbs.

bang   cry   fall   laugh   run   wave

I could hear someone crying.

LESSON 2

Write ten predictions for another student about the next 24 hours.

Greg will help cook supper this evening.

Tomorrow, give your predictions to the student. How many of your predictions were correct?

LESSON 3

Complete these superstitions from different countries.

1 If you _____ (drop) your comb, you _____ (get) bad luck.
2 You _____ (be) well all year if you _____ (eat) an apple at Christmas.
3 If you _____ (start) a trip on a Friday, things _____ (go) wrong.
4 You _____ (be) unlucky if you _____ (point) at the moon.
5 If there _____ (be) a cat on a ship, it _____ (bring) good luck.

EXTENSION for language development

LESSON 1

Think about your journey to school today and all the sounds you heard. Write a paragraph describing the journey.

While I was waiting at the bus stop, I heard the birds singing.

LESSON 2

Look at exercises 4–7 on page 47 and write:

1 Three predictions with *will*.
2 One offer with *shall*.
3 One promise with *will*.
4 One future plan with *going to*.
5 One prediction from present evidence with *going to*.

Today will be your lucky day.

LESSON 3

Complete these sentences.

1 If there's nothing good on TV tonight, I …
2 If I can't understand today's homework, I …
3 If I lose my house key, I …
4 If my parents tell me to go to bed early, I …
5 If I'm really lucky and win the lottery, I …

YOUR CHOICE!

CONSTRUCTION Words beginning with *in-*

In this unit find words beginning with *in-* which mean:
1 teacher *n*
2 equipment which measures something, eg speed *n*
3 someone who tries to find out all the facts *n*
4 makes you want to know more about it *adj*
5 ask someone to do something with you *v*

What other words beginning with *in-* do you know? Check in the Word List.

REFLECTION *will/won't*, *shall* or *going to*?

Complete the rules.
We use _____ to talk about future plans and intentions.
I _____ go shopping after school.
We use _____ or _____ to make offers.
I _____ get it for you.   _____ I phone the doctor?
We use _____ to say what we hope or predict.
She _____ get better soon.
We use _____ for promises.
I _____ be home before midnight.
We use _____ to predict the future when we can see that something is likely to happen.
It _____ rain – look at those clouds.

ACTION Speed dictation

- Work in teams of three, A, B and C.
- Student A goes to the other side of the classroom and chooses a paragraph from this unit.
- Student B crosses the room and Student A reads out the first sentence of the paragraph. Student B repeats the sentence and then returns.
- Student B says the sentence to Student C, who writes it down. Then Student B goes across to Student A for the next sentence. At the end compare Student C's paragraph with the book.

INTERACTION Celebrity memories

- Work in a small group.
- Look at *Elvis lives and speaks!* in Lesson 1 again. Imagine that you met a famous person who is dead! Imagine what happened, what you did and what you said.
- Ask and answer questions about the celebrities.
  Who did you meet and where? What was he/she wearing? What did he/she say?

REVIEW UNITS 3-4

Grammar

1 Read and complete. For each number 1–12, choose word or phrase A, B or C.

Mystery in the sky

Many people see strange things in the sky and think they __1__ be UFOs (Unidentified Flying Objects). It's certainly difficult __2__ what happened to a young Australian pilot in 1978.

At 6.19pm on 21 October, 20-year-old Frederick Valentich took off in a Cessna 182 from Melbourne. He __3__ to fly over the sea to King Island, between Australia and the island of Tasmania.

AUSTRALIA
Bass Straight
King Island
TASMANIA

At 7.06pm, Valentich contacted Steve Robey at Air Traffic Control in Melbourne, because he __4__ see a large aircraft __5__ over him. Robey was very surprised – he knew there __6__ be any other aircraft in the area. But the small Cessna wasn't alone. Valentich watched the UFO flying above __7__. The object was long and very fast with a green light. It __8__ like metal, but it wasn't a plane. Then it disappeared from the sky.

At 7.11pm, when Valentich was still 30 minutes from land, he reported engine problems. 'I'm going __9__ to reach King Island,' he told Robey. Suddenly he shouted 'I __10__ see that strange thing above me again, and it's not an aircraft!' Robey __11__ a strange noise over the radio, and then there was silence.

The Cessna 182 never reached King Island; the plane and pilot completely disappeared. We __12__ probably never know what happened to Frederick Valentich.

	A	B	C
1	can	could	mustn't
2	to explain	explain	explained
3	must	have	had
4	can	could	did
5	to fly	flying	flew
6	ought	should	shouldn't
7	him	his	himself
8	saw	watched	looked
9	try	to try	trying
10	can	could	might
11	listened	heard	sounded
12	will	won't	can't

2 Write responses using *must* and *can't*.

It's next to Spain. *Germany or Portugal?*
It can't be Germany — it must be Portugal.

1 He comes from South America. *Brazilian or Italian?*
2 It lives in Antarctica. *A parrot or a penguin?*
3 They're made of glass. *Curtains or windows?*
4 She works in a hospital. *A pilot or a doctor?*
5 It's white and very cold. *Snow or rain?*
6 They're long and yellow. *Cucumbers or bananas?*
7 They perform on stage. *Actors or reporters?*
8 It has wings. *A plane or a helicopter?*

3 Complete the sentences with *must* or *mustn't*.

SCHOOL RULES
1 You _____ be polite at all times.
2 You _____ shout or make unnecessary noise.
3 You _____ run in the school building.
4 You _____ arrive on time for lessons.
5 You _____ listen to the teacher.
6 You _____ copy other students' work.
7 You _____ use mobile phones in class.
8 You _____ wear clean, tidy clothes.

4 Rewrite the sentences replacing the words in italics with the correct form of *have to*.

1 *Must we* go to school every day?
2 *You don't need to* work all weekend.
3 *It's necessary for you to* hand in homework on time.
4 *He must* do some revision before the test.
5 *It was necessary for us to* answer 20 questions.
6 *They didn't need to* look up any words.

5 Choose the correct object or reflexive pronoun.

1 I'm teaching me/myself yoga from a book.
2 You have to believe in you/yourself.
3 He gave her/herself a glass of orange juice.
4 Look – we can see us/ourselves on TV!
5 We're going out with them/themselves tonight.
6 Well done! You must be proud of you/yourselves!
7 It's so noisy I can't hear me/myself think!
8 It's hard to understand him/himself.

6 Complete with *'d better (not)* where possible. Otherwise write *should(n't)*.

1 You _____ always wash your hands before meals.
2 His ankle is broken – we _____ call an ambulance.
3 You _____ go out in this awful weather.
4 Everyone _____ eat lots of vegetables.
5 If you want to pass the exam, you _____ do some work!
6 I don't think people _____ break promises.

7 Write sentences using *It's* + adjective + infinitive.

good/see you again
It's good to see you again.

1 hard/remember dates
2 impossible/walk round the world
3 rude/stare at people
4 important/tell the truth
5 easy/forget phone numbers
6 nice/meet you

54

UNITS 3-4 REVIEW

8 Complete with the present participle of these verbs.

burn   eat   play   run   sing   wait

1 I can hear someone _____ the piano.
2 Is there a fire? Can you smell something _____?
3 Did you notice anyone _____ at the bus stop?
4 She felt the rain _____ down her neck.
5 Please don't watch me _____ lunch – I'm embarrassed!
6 I like listening to the birds _____.

9 Complete the phone conversation with *'ll/won't* or *(be) going to*.

JACK   Hi, Tim, what are you doing?
TIM   I __1__ wash my father's car.
JACK   Oh, there's no point – it __2__ rain. Come to the cinema with me instead.
TIM   But I haven't got any money.
JACK   No problem, I __3__ pay for you.
TIM   OK, I __4__ wash the car tomorrow. I'm sure Dad __5__ mind. Just a minute – I __6__ tell him. Dad, I __7__ see a movie with Jack.
FATHER   So you __8__ (not) wash my car today.
TIM   I promise I __9__ wash it tomorrow. I __10__ let you down. Jack, I __11__ meet you at the cinema in 15 minutes. Er, Dad, could you …?
FATHER   I don't believe it – you __12__ ask me to give you a lift to the cinema!

10 Write sentences using the correct form of the verb: present simple or *will*.

1 I (cook) supper tonight if you (like).
2 If we (not hurry), we (miss) the plane.
3 My sister (be) a doctor if she (pass) her exams.
4 If the team (score) another goal, they (win) the game.
5 We (not get) lost if we (look) at the map.
6 If it (rain) tomorrow, we (not have) a barbecue.
7 You (sleep better) if you (open) the window.
8 If I (not finish) my project, I (be) in trouble!

Vocabulary

11 Complete with these words.

annual   army   boil   button   concentrate
election   electricity   horoscope   ladder   wig

1 There's going to be an _____ for a new prime minister.
2 The music is very loud – it's hard for me to _____ on my work.
3 Our school has its _____ Sports Day in June.
4 It takes longer to _____ an egg in the mountains than at sea level.
5 We should switch off the lights to save _____.
6 He wanted to be a soldier, so he joined the _____.
7 She has short dark hair, but today she's wearing a blonde _____.
8 A fire-fighter climbed up a _____ to the roof of the house.
9 Tell me your star sign and I'll read out your _____.
10 You press this _____ to start the washing machine.

12 Match these words with their definitions.

adore   apology   forbidden   frequently   handsome
honeymoon   ignore   lie   nasty   purpose

1 not allowed
2 opposite of *nice*
3 love very much
4 good-looking
5 holiday after a wedding
6 often
7 aim or goal
8 something that isn't true
9 take no notice of
10 statement saying sorry

13 Match the words in list A with the words and phrases in list B.

A	B
1 break	asleep
2 do	a bike
3 fall	a button
4 feel	the law
5 press	depressed
6 ride	lies
7 spend	revision
8 tell	money

14 Find the odd word.

1 embarrassed   guilty   noisy   upset
2 helicopter   refrigerator   vacuum cleaner   washing machine
3 bruise   cheek   nail   neck
4 feel   like   smell   taste
5 lobster   prawn   snake   tuna
6 bang   clap   notice   whistle

PROGRESS CHECK

Now you can …

1 Make logical deductions
2 Discuss possibility
3 Describe sensations
4 Express obligation and prohibition
5 Give advice
6 Make predictions, promises and offers
7 Talk about plans and intentions
8 Talk about future possibility

Look back at Units 3 and 4 and write an example for 1–8.

1 My alarm clock is ringing – it must be 7.30.

How good are you? Tick a box.

★★★ Fine ☐   ★★ OK ☐   ★ Not sure ☐

Not sure about something? Ask your teacher.

5 CHALLENGES

1 They haven't had any accidents yet

Present perfect with *just, already, yet*
Talking about what has and hasn't happened

1 Opener

Look at the photo. Do you recognise either of the people? Where do you think they are?

2 Reading

Read and listen to the newspaper report, and look at the route of the journey.

Route of the journey

14 April – Belgium
15 April – Germany
16 April – Czech Republic
19 April – Slovakia
21 April – Ukraine
27 April – Russia
1 May – Kazakhstan
16 May – Russia
19 May – Mongolia
2 June – Russia
1 July – USA (Alaska)
8 July – Canada
17 July – USA
29 July – New York City

LONG WAY ROUND

Actors Ewan McGregor and Charley Boorman have just arrived in Kazakhstan on a 20,000-mile motorcycle trip. The pair are on their way round the world – they've already travelled across Europe, but they haven't completed a quarter of their journey yet. McGregor (famous for films such as *Moulin Rouge* and *Star Wars*) and Boorman are spending more than three months travelling on motorbikes from London through Europe, Asia, Canada and the USA. It's a long and challenging journey – fortunately they haven't had any accidents yet.

3 Comprehension

Match the questions with the answers. There are two wrong answers.

1. Where have McGregor and Boorman just arrived?
2. How many countries have they already been to?
3. How many miles have they travelled?
4. How long have they been on the road?
5. Have they crossed Asia yet?
6. How long will the whole journey take?

a No, not yet.
b About 15 weeks.
c Yes, they have.
d Over two weeks.
e Six.
f In Asia.
g Over 5,000.
h Under 5,000.

4 Grammar

Complete.

> **Present perfect with *just, already, yet***
> They have _____ arrived in Kazakhstan.
> They have _____ travelled across Europe.
> They haven't completed a quarter of their journey _____.
> Have they crossed Asia _____?
>
> We can use the present perfect with _____ to talk about *very* recent events.
> We use the present perfect with _____ to emphasise that something has happened.
> We can use the present perfect with _____ to show that we expect something to happen.
>
> ➡ Check the answers: Grammar Summary page 112

5 Grammar Practice

Write questions about McGregor and Boorman's trip using the present perfect and *yet*.

Have they been to Germany yet?

1. they/go to Germany?
2. they/reach Alaska?
3. they/go to Russia?
4. they/cross Mongolia?
5. they/travel through Ukraine?
6. they/arrive in Canada?

Now look at the route of the journey and answer the questions using *just, already* or *yet*. It's 1st May.

Yes, they've already been to Germany.

Make more true statements about McGregor and Boorman's journey so far.

A They've just left Russia.
B They've already been to Belgium.
A They haven't reached the USA yet.

6 Listening

Look at *10 things to do before you're 20* and listen to 16-year-old Tiffany. Tick the things she's already done.

10 things to do before you're 20
- Go to a gig
- Learn first aid
- Perform in a play
- Ride a horse
- Write a poem
- Go camping with friends
- Organise a birthday party
- Go skiing
- Fly a kite
- Hold a baby

7 Speaking

Check your answers to exercise 6.

Has Tiffany been to a gig yet?
Yes, she's already been to lots of gigs.
Has she learnt first aid yet?
No, she hasn't done that yet.

Now ask another student questions about *10 things to do before you're 20* and note down the answers.

8 Writing

Write sentences about the student you interviewed in exercise 7.

Robert hasn't been to a gig yet, but he's already learnt first aid.

9 Vocabulary

Complete with *go, learn* or *ride*.

1. _____ a bicycle
2. _____ camping
3. _____ on holiday
4. _____ a horse
5. _____ an instrument
6. _____ a language
7. _____ first aid
8. _____ motorbike
9. _____ skiing
10. _____ to a gig

10 Pronunciation

🎧 Listen and repeat.

/eə/ where	/ɪə/ way
pair	pay
their	they
stare	stay
bear	bay
dare	day
hair	hey

Now listen and write the words you hear.

11 Writing

Write a list of ten things you'd like to do in the future. Then exchange lists with another student. Write sentences about the things on your partner's list that you've already done and haven't done yet.

Meet a famous person
Travel round the world
Appear on television

I've already met a famous person — I've just met Ewan McGregor!

5 CHALLENGES

2 Have you ever wondered …?

Present perfect with *ever* and *never*
Present perfect and past simple
Talking about experiences

1 Opener
Look at the photos of extreme sports. Which one would you like to try and why?

2 Reading
Read and match the extreme sports with the photos. Then listen and check.

3 Comprehension
Answer the questions.

Which sport(s) …
1 gives you a new view of a city?
2 is like going on a roller coaster?
3 is more enjoyable than water-skiing?
4 makes you look at things differently?
5 do you do on water?
6 makes you laugh so much that you can't stop?
7 needs no equipment?
8 came from France?
9 uses the wind?

In which sport do you …
10 do nothing?
11 start very high up?
12 steer with lines?

Zorbing
Zorbing – or sphereing – started in New Zealand in the mid-1990s. What's it like? It's like bungee jumping, it's like floating, it's like going on a roller coaster, and it's unlike anything you've ever done before! Imagine being inside a giant bouncy beach ball rolling down a steep hill at up to 50 km an hour. Two people are strapped into the two-metre sphere and pushed over the top of a hill.

'I didn't have a clue what was going on,' says someone who has tried it. 'I saw colours whizzing by – blue sky, green grass, blue sky, green grass – and I could hear myself laughing uncontrollably.'

Have you ever wondered what it's like inside a washing machine? Well, try Hydro-Sphereing, where one person rolls down the hill in a sphere containing 30 litres of water!

Free running
This new sport – free running through the city, climbing walls, crossing roofs and jumping from building to building – started in Paris. It has become well known in Britain through a BBC advertising film called *Rush Hour*.

Free-runner Paul Clifford says 'I've never tried anything like it before. It's not about exercise – it's about finding new ways to do things and new ways of looking at life.'

Kite surfing
Kite surfing started in France in the 1980s and has recently become very popular worldwide. You use a small surfboard and a large kite on 30-metre lines. The kite pulls you through the water and you can steer with the lines. You can just speed through the water, or you can do jumps as high as a house.

Kirsty Jones, Women's UK Kite Surfing Champion, took up the sport in 2001. 'I've never enjoyed myself so much,' says Kirsty. 'It's much more fun than water-skiing behind a boat.'

Paraskiing
Have you ever wanted to ski off a mountain and fly? If you like skiing and paragliding, then this is the sport for you, because it combines skiing and flying!

The way to do it is to ski straight down the hill with the parachute wing behind you. Then let the parachute come up in the air behind you and whoosh! Suddenly you're flying.

4 Grammar

Complete.

> **Present perfect with *ever* and *never***
> Have you _____ wondered what it's like?
> Have you _____ wanted to ski off a mountain?
> I've _____ tried anything like it.
> I've _____ enjoyed myself so much.
>
> We use *ever* and *never* with the present perfect to talk about the time up to now. We mainly use _____ in questions and _____ in statements.
>
> **Present perfect and past simple**
> Kite surfing **started** in France **in the 1980s** and **has recently become** very popular worldwide.
>
> We can use the _____ _____ to talk about an indefinite time in the past.
> We use the _____ _____ to talk about a specific time in the past.

➡ Check the answers: Grammar Summary pages 112–13

5 Grammar Practice

Put the verbs in the present perfect and complete with *ever* or *never*.

1. She _____ _____ _____ (see) anything like it.
2. _____ you _____ _____ (think) about going on holiday on your own?
3. I _____ always _____ (want) to, but I _____ _____ (have) enough money.
4. Why _____ n't you _____ _____ (learn) to swim?
5. Because I _____ _____ _____ (live) near the sea, and I hate swimming pools.
6. _____ your parents _____ _____ (leave) you at home when they _____ _____ (go) away on holiday?

6 Grammar Practice

Complete with the present perfect or past simple of the verbs.

1. _____ you ever _____ (try) snowboarding?
2. Yes, I _____ (have) a go last winter. It _____ (be) great fun.
3. _____ your parents ever _____ (let) you drive their car?
4. No, because we haven't got one! My dad _____ (have) a motorbike for a while but he _____ n't _____ (let) me ride it.
5. _____ you ever _____ (do) something that you regretted?
6. You mean something I _____ (feel) bad about afterwards? Yes, once I _____ (steal) some chocolate from a shop. It _____ (be) a long time ago, but I _____ never _____ (forget) it.

7 Speaking

Ask each other questions using *Have you ever wanted to …?* and these phrases.

> change your name   move to another town
> live in another country   visit …   meet …
> learn to …

A Have you ever wanted to change your name?
B No, I haven't.
A Why not?
B Because I'm happy with it!

8 Pronunciation

🎧 Listen and repeat the compound nouns. Mark the main stress.

> bungee jumping   ice hockey   kite surfing
> paragliding   roller coaster   water-skiing

9 Speaking

Ask other students questions and complete the chart.

Activity	Name	When/What it was like?
Go on a roller coaster		
Try bungee jumping		
Go water-skiing		
Play ice hockey		
Go sailing		
Do aerobics		
Win a race		
Ride a motorbike		

A Have you ever been on a roller coaster?
B Yes, I have.
A When did you do it and what was it like?
B I did it on holiday last year. I was really scared on the ride, but I felt great afterwards.

Compare your chart with three other students. How many of the activities have you tried? Write a paragraph saying what you have tried, when and what it was like.

10 Vocabulary

Make a word map for sport. Use words from this lesson, and add other words you know.

paraskiing — AIR — SPORT — WATER — *water-skiing*
LAND — *ice hockey*

11 Writing

Write a paragraph about five things you've always wanted to do but have never done. Say why you've never done them.

5 CHALLENGES

3 I've wanted to win since I was 14

Present perfect with *for* and *since*
Talking about achievements
Describing events and things which are important to you

KELLY – IN HER OWN WORDS

At the Athens Olympic Games in 2004 Kelly Holmes (aged 34) became the oldest woman to win either the 800 metres or the 1500 metres – and she won both of them! So what is it like to win two Olympic gold medals?

> Fantastic! People ask me why I've suddenly won two gold medals. It's because this year I haven't had any injuries. I've been a full-time runner for 12 years, but I've had injuries in seven of those years.

> I've wanted to win a gold medal since I was 14 and now I've done it. But I won't let success go to my head. What I've done hasn't changed me. It just means I've achieved my dreams. Really I'm no different from how I was before.

> I've dreamt of winning a gold medal for 20 years and now I've got not one, but two. Since I came back from the Olympics the support from the public has been overwhelming.

> A few days after I got back from Athens there was a parade through Tonbridge, my home town. I said to my mum 'It'll be really embarrassing if no one comes.' I was a bit worried about it, but there were 80,000 people! I'll never forget that day.

> My family have supported me since I started running and I'm really grateful to all of them. And of course my first coach Dave Arnold helped me through the ups and downs of my career for over 14 years.

> I met Tom Cruise before a TV chatshow, and he gave me a big hug and said he watched me at the Olympics. I thought 'I don't believe this – Tom Cruise knows who I am!'

1 Opener

Look at the photo of Kelly Holmes. How is she feeling? What has she done?

2 Reading

Read and listen to the text.

3 Comprehension

Answer the questions.

1. What races did Kelly Holmes win at the 2004 Olympics?
2. What has she had in seven of her 12 years as a full-time runner?
3. Has success changed Kelly?
4. How long has she dreamt of winning a gold medal?
5. What kind of support has she had from the public?
6. How many people came to the parade in Kelly's home town?
7. How long did Dave Arnold help Kelly?
8. When did Tom Cruise give her a hug?

4 Grammar

Complete.

> **Present perfect with *for* and *since***
> I've been a full-time runner _____ 12 years.
> I've wanted to win a gold medal _____ I was 14.
>
> We can use the present perfect with *for* and *since* to talk about the unfinished past.
> We use _____ to say *how long* something has lasted.
> We use _____ to say *when* something started.
>
> Check the answers: Grammar Summary pages 112–13

5 Grammar Practice

Complete these phrases with *for* or *since*.

1 _____ a couple of minutes   2 _____ I got up   3 _____ last Wednesday
4 _____ four days   5 _____ a week   6 _____ Christmas
7 _____ last summer   8 _____ two months   9 _____ a while
10 _____ June 13   11 _____ ages   12 _____ 2005   13 _____ I was born
14 _____ the lesson began   15 _____ three years

6 Grammar Practice

Put the verbs in the present perfect and complete with *for* or *since*.

1 People _____ (ask) Kelly lots of questions _____ the Athens Olympics.
2 She _____ (be) a full-time runner _____ 1992.
3 She _____ (dream) of winning a gold medal _____ 20 years and now her dream _____ (come) true.
4 She _____ (have) fantastic public support _____ the Olympics.
5 Her family _____ (support) her _____ she started running.
6 Her coaches _____ (help) her _____ 20 years.

7 Speaking

Make questions and interview another student. Note down the answers.

How long/you/be/at this school?

> How long have you been at this school?
>
> For three years./Since September 2005.

When/you/get/to school today?

> When did you get to school today?
>
> At eight o'clock.

1 How long/we/have/this coursebook?
2 When/you/start/learning English?
3 Who/you/know/the longest in this class?
   When/you/first/meet/them?
4 Which friend/you/have/the longest?
   How long/you/be/friends?
5 What's your favourite band?
   When/you/first/hear/them?
6 What's your favourite sport? How long/you/play/it?
7 How long/you/live/in this town?
8 How long/you/live/in the same house or flat?
9 What colour are your favourite shoes? When/you/get/them?
10 Has your family got any pets? How long/you/have/them?

Now tell another student about the most interesting answers.

8 Grammar Practice

Complete with the correct preposition: *about, at, in, to.*

1 be _____ the Olympic Games
2 let something go _____ your head
3 worry _____ something
4 be grateful _____ someone
5 be _____ a class
6 be _____ school
7 live _____ a house

9 Pronunciation

Write the words in the correct column.

> achieve   answer   career
> different   grateful   medal
> parade   public   success
> support

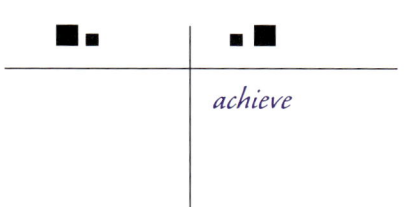

■ .	. ■
	achieve

Now listen and check. Repeat the words.

10 Writing

Look at questions 3–10 in exercise 7 again. Write a paragraph about yourself answering some of the questions.

5 CHALLENGES

4 Integrated Skills
Describing personal experiences

1 Opener

Look at the photos. Where do you think they were taken? Use these words to describe what you can see.

> boat   buildings   clouds
> grass   island   lake
> llamas   mountains   ruins
> stones   tourists   walls

Students Julie and Simon are backpacking round South America. Julie is recording a diary of their journey on the Internet.

We've just arrived in Puno on the western shore of Lake Titicaca, which is on the border between Peru and Bolivia. It's the largest freshwater lake in South America and one of the highest in the world – __1__. Puno is nothing special, but we're very glad to be here after a long and uncomfortable overnight bus ride from Cuzco.

We've been busy since we arrived in Peru a week ago! First we took a bus from Lima to Cuzco (24 hours!). Somewhere on the journey I lost my watch, but it wasn't **valuable**, so it didn't really matter. Cuzco is a beautiful old town surrounded by the Andes mountains – __2__. We spent a night in a **hostel**, and the next morning we started on the Inca trail to the city of Machu Picchu. The trail is often very **steep** __3__, so lots of people suffer from **altitude** sickness. I've been lucky because I haven't felt ill, but Simon has had a bad headache for a couple of days.

The trek along the Inca **trail** took four days and it was **exhausting**. But it was well worth it. On the last day, we got up at 4am to get to Machu Picchu in time for sunrise. When we got there, the city was **invisible** because it was covered in cloud. But suddenly the cloud lifted, and there was Machu Picchu __4__. It was magic! Apparently half a million people now visit Machu Picchu every year, and its popularity isn't surprising.

We spent several hours **wandering** round the site – what an incredible place! Then back to Cuzco by bus and train __5__. We've had some interesting food in Peru. I've already tried llama, __6__. A local speciality in Cuzco is roast guinea pig, but I couldn't face it!

Tomorrow we're going on a boat trip to visit some of the islands on Lake Titicaca. The weather has been great – let's hope it stays that way.

Reading

2 Read and complete the text with phrases a–f.

a and rises to over 4,000 metres in some places
b which tastes a bit like beef
c on the edge of the mountain
d it was the capital of the Inca empire
e for a hot shower and a rest before dinner
f it's 3,809 metres above sea level

🎧 Now listen and check. Which words in the phrases helped you to complete the text?

62

3 Find the highlighted words in the text which mean:
1. cheap hotel *n*
2. height *n*
3. walking in a relaxed way *v*
4. path through the countryside *n*
5. rising quickly *adj*
6. very tiring *adj*
7. worth a lot of money *adj*
8. something you can't see *adj*

4 Linking words: *so* and *because*

Find examples of *so* and *because* in the text. Then complete these rules.

We use _____ to talk about reason or cause.
We use _____ to talk about consequence or result.

Now complete these sentences with *so* or *because*.
1. They were tired _____ the bus journey was uncomfortable.
2. Cuzco is surrounded by mountains, _____ it gets very cold at night.
3. We got up early _____ we wanted to see the sunrise.
4. Thousands of people visit Machu Picchu _____ it's very beautiful.
5. I haven't got much money, _____ I can't go on holiday this year.

5 Listening

🎧 Listen to Julie and Simon talking to an American backpacker in Cuzco. Number the countries in the order they're visiting them.

> Argentina   Brazil   Chile   Colombia
> Ecuador   Peru   Uruguay   Venezuela

Speaking

6 Look at your answers to exercise 5. Tell each other which countries Julie and Simon have already visited, and which countries they haven't visited yet.
A They've already visited Venezuela.
B They haven't been to … yet.

7 Plan a backpacking trip with another student. Choose a country or group of countries, and decide which places you want to visit. Plan your itinerary.

8 Writing

Imagine you are on the road! Write an email to your friends about your backpacking trip. Use the text in exercise 2 to help you, and include this information.
- Where are you now?
- Where is it exactly, and what's it like?
- How did you get there?
- Where have you already been?
- What have you done?
- Where are you going next?

9 Learner Independence

Self assessment: look back over this unit, think about what you've learnt and make a list.

Grammar   *I've learnt how to use 'already' and 'yet' with the present perfect.*
Vocabulary   *I've learnt new words for sports.*
Information   *I've found out more about Machu Picchu.*

If there are any areas where you have problems, look back at the lesson again and refer to the Grammar Summary.

I haven't learnt how to use 'for' and 'since' yet.

10 Word creation: make nouns ending in *-ity* from these adjectives and complete the sentences.

> active   electric   national   popular
> possible   real   responsible   special

1. Seafood is a _____ in this restaurant.
2. Reading is my favourite leisure _____.
3. There's a _____ of rainstorms later today.
4. The _____ of backpacking holidays has grown recently.
5. Where are you from? What's your _____?
6. Parents have a _____ to look after their children.
7. If we turn off the lights, we'll save _____.
8. Snowboarding looks difficult, but in _____ it's quite easy.

11 Phrasebook

🎧 Listen and repeat these useful expressions. Then find them in this unit.

> I didn't have a clue.
> Have you ever wondered what it's like?
> I've never tried anything like it.
> I've never enjoyed myself so much.
> I'm really grateful.   It's nothing special.
> It was well worth it.   It was magic!
> What an incredible place!   I couldn't face it.
> Let's hope it stays that way.

Now write a five-line dialogue using three or more of the expressions.

> **Unit 5** Communication Activity
> Student **A** page 107
> Student **B** page 117

UNIT **5**

63

5 CHALLENGES

Inspiration *Extra!*

PROJECT *Extreme Sports File*

Make a file about Extreme Sports.

1. Work in a group, look at the photos above and the sports in Lesson 2 again, and make a list of extreme sports. For example, skydiving, bungee jumping, snowboarding, scuba diving, and rock climbing. Then choose one or two sports to write about.

2. Find out information about the sports using the Internet or a library:

   > When and where do people do it?
   > What exactly do they do?
   > What equipment do they need?
   > Why do they do it?
   > Is it popular?   Is it dangerous?   *Your opinion.*

3. Work together and make an Extreme Sports File. Read it carefully and correct any mistakes. Draw pictures or use photographs from magazines or the Internet. Show your Extreme Sports File to the other groups.

GAME *Help!*

- Work in small groups.
- One group member is a tourist on holiday in a country where he/she doesn't speak the language. The other members are people who live in that country.
- The tourist has a problem and needs help. But because the tourist doesn't speak the language he/she has to mime the problem. The other group members try to guess what the problem is.
- The group member who guesses what the problem is becomes the tourist and the game is played again.

> Your plane goes at ten o'clock, but you've lost your watch and don't know what the time is.

> There's a crocodile in your room and it's eaten your bag.

SKETCH *The Interview*

🎧 Read and listen.

WOMAN Are you ready?
MAN Yes, sorry. Right. Um. Now. Which job have you applied for?
WOMAN Deep-sea diver.
MAN And what experience have you got of diving?
WOMAN Well, none, really, but I …
MAN I'm sorry. Let me ask you again. Have you ever been underwater?
WOMAN Oh yes, lots of times.
MAN I see. So you have dived.
WOMAN No, I haven't. Not in the sea, that is.
MAN Then where have you dived?
WOMAN Do I have to answer that?
MAN Come on. Answer the question! Where have you dived if you haven't dived in the sea?
WOMAN You've already asked me that.
MAN I know I have! And what's the answer?
WOMAN In the bath at home.
MAN That's not deep-sea diving!
WOMAN I know. But you see – there's a problem. I can't swim.
MAN So why have you applied for a job as a deep-sea diver?
WOMAN Why? Because it's very well paid and there's lots of foreign travel.
MAN Well paid! Travel! Stop wasting my time and get out! You've failed to get the job! The interview is over.
WOMAN No, I'm sorry, but you're the one who has failed. We were looking for a good interviewer and you were terrible. Goodbye. Next!

Now act out the sketch in pairs.

64

UNIT 5

REVISION *for more practice*

LESSON 1

Look at *10 things to do before you're 20* on page 57. Use your answers to exercise 6 to write eight sentences about Tiffany.

She's already been to lots of gigs. She hasn't learnt first aid yet.

LESSON 2

Look at exercise 7 on page 59. Write six sentences about the student you arrived.

Helena has never wanted to change her name because she likes it.

LESSON 3

Look at exercise 5 on page 61. Write sentences using five of these phrases.

She's only been here for a couple of minutes.
I haven't felt well since I got up.

EXTENSION *for language development*

LESSON 1

Look at *Long Way Round* on page 56. Imagine it is 17 July. Write eight questions about McGregor and Boorman's trip using verbs from the text in the present perfect and *yet*. Answer the questions using *just*, *yet* or *already*.

Have they been to the Czech Republic yet?
Yes, they've already been there.

LESSON 2

Look at the chart you completed in exercise 9 on page 59 and write a paragraph about the students you interviewed.

Kris and Stephanie haven't been water-skiing, but Nadia has. She went water-skiing when she was on holiday in Spain last summer.

LESSON 3

Look at the notes you made in the interview in exercise 7 on page 61. Write a paragraph about the student you interviewed.

YOUR CHOICE!

CONSTRUCTION Present perfect or past simple?

Complete with the present perfect or past simple of the verbs.

Zorbing is a new sport and not a lot of people __1__ (try) it yet. Dwane van der Sluis and Andrew Akers __2__ (invent) zorbing in New Zealand in the 1990s. The inventors __3__ (want) to design a ball so that people could 'walk' on water but it __4__ (not work) very well. Then they __5__ (try) rolling it down a hill with great success. Zorbing centres now __6__ (open) around the world and soon everyone will know someone who __7__ (try) the sport. 'Once you __8__ (have) a go, you want to do it again and again,' a teenage zorber said.

REFLECTION Present perfect

Choose the correct rule.
We use *for* to refer to
  A a period of time   B a point in time.
We use *since* to refer to
  A a period of time   B a point in time.
We use the present perfect with *just* to talk about things that
  A happened a long time ago.   B happened very recently.
We use the present perfect with *already* to talk about things that
  A have happened.   B haven't happened.
We use the present perfect with *yet* to talk about things that
  A we expect to happen.   B have happened recently.
We usually use *ever* in
  A questions.   B negative statements.
We use *never* in
  A affirmative statements.   B negative statements.

ACTION
Make yourself look good!

- Work in groups of four. Use these verbs:
  go, kiss, meet, see, talk, win.
- Student A makes a sentence using one of the verbs in the present perfect.
  I've been to India.
- Student B repeats the sentence and adds to it.
  I've been to India and China.
- Student C repeats Student B's sentence and adds to it.
  I've been to India, China and Egypt.
- Student D repeats Student C's sentence and adds to it.
  I've been to India, China, Egypt and Antarctica.

INTERACTION
The present I've always wanted

- Work in a small group.
- We are given presents on our birthdays and at other times of the year. Imagine it's one of those days and you can choose the present.
- What present have you always wanted but never got? It could be a thing, or an event, or a skill you'd like to have, or something you'd like for someone else.
- Take turns to tell each other about the present you've always wanted and why it has been such an important wish.

65

culture
Your holiday, their home

PACKAGE TOURISM

What a great place …

… and we don't need to go out for anything. We've got everything we want here.

Anyway when we do go out it can be difficult …

… because all these people want to show us places or sell us things.

They must think we're millionaires. But we're not. I worked hard for this holiday.

… so you don't get all the 'locals' bothering you.

It's OK by the pool, and part of the beach is private …

I don't really like seeing all the poor people around the resort – especially the children. Some of them look really hungry. They make me feel a bit guilty – but what can I do?

THE TOURISTS ARE COMING
Benjamin Zephaniah

Tell them to be careful
If they're not give them an earful
The tourists are coming
The tourists are coming.

They may want to party nightly
But tell them they must be tidy
The tourists are coming
The tourists are coming.

They must respect what we've planted
They should not take us for granted
The tourists are coming
The tourists are coming.

They should practise what they preach
When they're lying on our beach
The tourists are coming to play.

Because our land is sunny
They come here with their money
The tourists are coming
The tourists are coming.

culture

Who do these tourists think they are? It's our beach, but we can't go on it.

When I try to sell them things they always bargain for the lowest price. The tourists have got much more money than me – they can afford to pay a good price.

My son works at the resort as a waiter – it's a job and he helps us with money. But he works very long hours and when no tourists come there is no work.

All the showers and the swimming pools take a lot of water …

… and our village has only got one tap.

What I hate is the way they dress – when they leave the beach they still wear their bikinis and swimming things. It really offends me.

Well, they don't care about our culture and way of life at all. They're only here for the beaches and the sun. And lots to eat and drink.

But they don't eat our food. The hotels don't buy from our farmers. Instead they import nearly all the food from Europe – it's crazy.

1 Vocabulary

Read the texts and match these words with their definitions.

1 private *adj* a tell people what to do
2 resort *n*   b opposite of *public*
3 bargain *v*   c something you turn on to get water
4 afford *v*   d place where people go for a holiday
5 tap *n*   e try to reduce the price
6 offend *v*   f show you think something is important
7 respect *v*   g be able to pay for something
8 preach *v*   h make someone angry

2 Comprehension

1 The tourists give reasons for not leaving the hotel. Can you name three?
2 The 'locals' give reasons for not liking tourists. Can you name five?
3 In *The Tourists Are Coming* the poet tells the tourists to do four things. What are they?

3 Listening

Listen and choose the correct answer.

Are tourists destroying the famous places they visit? Let's look at some well-known tourist sites around the world and see what's happening.

Machu Picchu
This Inca site in Peru receives **50,000/500,000** visitors a year. There are so many tourists that you can only walk along the Inca Trail to the site if you are in a **group/on** your own.

Angkor Wat
More and tourists come to Cambodia to visit the Angkor Archaeological Park. One way of **reducing/increasing** numbers is to have two prices for entry: Cambodians go free but foreigners pay **£12/£20** for a day ticket.

Pompeii
The Roman town is one of the best-known sites in the world but it is also one of the ones which is in most danger. In 1981 **86,300/863,000** visitors came to see what life was like in Roman times, but now the numbers have increased to **two/ten** million people a year.

Taj Mahal
The Taj Mahal is the most popular tourist site in India – in 2003 it had **300,000/3,000,000** visitors – and now you are never alone there. One plan is to close the Taj Mahal completely and only let visitors look at it from a distance.

4 Writing

Write two paragraphs giving your views on tourism. Think about:

- Ways in which package tourism could become more responsible: money, jobs, the environment, respect.
- Problems which more responsible tourism could face: numbers of people, accommodation, travelling to and from remote places.

67

6 THAT'S CLEVER!

1 He had won awards

Past perfect
Describing a sequence of past events

1 Opener
Look at your hands. How many things can you do with them?

2 Reading
Read and listen to *Teenage Inventors*.

TEENAGE INVENTORS

From bicycle helmets to road materials

Canadian teenager Gina Gallant has always been an inventor. She became interested in science because her father had taken her to science fairs from the age of four. Soon after she started school, she made a kind of paper out of broccoli for her science project! By the age of 12, she had invented a safer bicycle helmet for kids. She did this after her little brother had a cycling accident – luckily he was OK because he had put his helmet on properly. And by the age of 16, Gina had designed a new kind of road material which used recycled plastic bottles. What will she invent next?

The waterbike

Californian Krysta Morlan was 16 when she invented the waterbike. She thought of the idea when she was doing exercises in the swimming pool. She had spent a lot of time in hospital and needed to do exercises to recover her strength. 'I loved cycling, but I hadn't ridden a bicycle for a long time.' she explained. 'The idea of the waterbike was to have fun and still get the advantage of a workout in the pool.' Anyone can have fun on Krysta's invention, whether they are disabled or not.

The glove that translates

18-year-old Ryan Patterson found the inspiration for his invention in a fast food restaurant. 'There was a group of deaf people who needed help to order their food,' Ryan remembers. Although deaf people can use sign language to communicate, many people don't understand it. Ryan had been fascinated by electronics as a child and had won awards for designing robots by the time he was 16. Now he used his skills to invent a Sign Language Translator – a glove which translates sign language into letters. All the deaf person does is put on the glove, make a sign, and the letter appears on a computer screen.

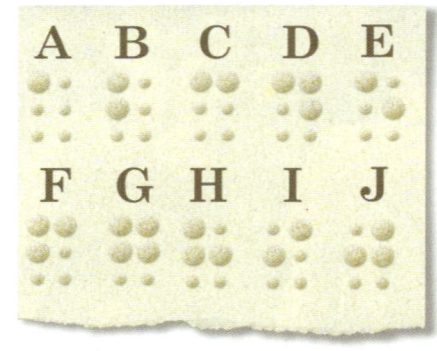

Braille

In 1824, when he was 15, Louis Braille invented a way for blind people to read. Louis himself had been blind since the age of three. When he was 10 he went to a school for the blind in Paris. Two years later, an old soldier called Charles Barbier visited the school. Barbier told Louis about something he had learnt in the war called 'night-writing'. It was a way for soldiers to communicate in the dark so that the enemy did not hear them speak. However, 'night-writing' was hard to learn because it used 12 raised dots on a page. For three years Louis simplified the system that Barbier had told him about. Louis's system uses only six dots and blind people 'read' by moving their fingers over the dots.

68

3 Comprehension

Answer the questions. Whose invention(s) …

1 uses recycled plastic bottles?
2 are to do with language?
3 is the oldest?
4 are to do with cycling?
5 uses computers?
6 helps people who cannot see?
7 helps people who cannot hear?
8 is fun whether you are disabled or not?
9 are to do with hands?

4 Grammar

Complete.

> **Past perfect**
>
> Past perfect   Past simple
>   ↓   ↓   NOW
>
> She **had spent** a lot of time in hospital.
> By the age of 12, she _____ _____ a safer bicycle helmet.
> He was OK because he _____ _____ his helmet on properly.
> Ryan _____ _____ awards by the time he was 16.
> Louis Braille _____ _____ blind since the age of three.
>
> We form the past perfect with _____ + past participle.
> Contractions: _____/you'd/he'd/she'd/we'd/they'd
> We use the _____ _____ to describe the earlier of two past events.
>
> ➡ Check the answers: Grammar Summary page 113

5 Grammar Practice

Complete with the past simple or past perfect of the verbs.

1 Gina _____ (visit) science fairs with her father from the age of four and _____ (know) a lot about science.
2 Gina _____ (invent) the bicycle helmet after her brother _____ (be) in an accident.
3 Ryan _____ (think) of the Sign Language Translator after he _____ (see) deaf people in a restaurant.
4 Krysta _____ (invent) the waterbike because she _____ (not ride) a bike for a long time.
5 Charles Barbier _____ (visit) the school for the blind after Louis _____ (be) there for two years.
6 Louis _____ (develop) Braille from the communication system that Barbier _____ (tell) him about three years before.

6 Pronunciation

Mark the stress. Which words are stressed on the first syllable?

> advantage   bicycle   communicate   disabled
> electronics   enemy   inspiration   invention   operation
> recover   recycled   remember   simplify   translator

🎧 Now listen and check. Repeat the words.

7 Speaking

Why did these things happen? Use the phrases in the box to complete the sentences in the past perfect.

1 The players were delighted because …
2 I didn't do my homework because …
3 She was upset because he …
4 He didn't call her back because …
5 She couldn't get into the house because …
6 They were really happy because …
7 I was hungry because …
8 The man climbed the tree because …

> forget her number   leave my books at school
> lose the key   not eat anything all day
> win the match   not remember her birthday
> the dog bite him   pass the exam

8 Speaking

Ask each other questions about last year.

Last year, did you …

- talk to someone who you'd never talked to before?
- discover a singer who you'd never heard before?
- like a kind of food which you'd never tried before?
- visit a place which you'd never been to before?
- get a present which you'd always wanted?
- do something which you'd never wanted to try before?
- do something which you'd always wanted to do?

9 Writing

Make a list of things you did yesterday after you had come home from school. Think about:

> have something to eat   have a shower   watch TV
> play football   do my homework   phone a friend
> listen to music   go shopping   read a magazine
> clean my teeth   go to bed

Then write sentences, using *after* and the past perfect and past simple.

After I'd come home from school, I phoned Alexis.
After I'd phoned Alexis, I went for a walk.

6 THAT'S CLEVER!

2 People didn't use to throw things away

used to + infinitive
Talking about past habits and states

Don't throw it away!

People didn't use to throw things away. We used to mend our clothes and we used to wear shoes until they wore out. When we bought things, we used to carry shopping baskets, so we didn't need countless plastic bags. And we didn't use to buy so much in the first place.

But now we consume more and so we produce more rubbish. The UK is one of the worst recyclers in Europe but the Recycle Now campaign aims to change that. Its series of TV commercials shows the recycling of metal cans, glass bottles and paper into interesting new everyday items. One ad shows a town with cars, trains, buildings and even planes made of metal cans.

Top UK designer Oliver Heath is a strong supporter of the campaign – in 2005 he designed the first home constructed entirely from recycled materials, including yoghurt pots and glass bottles. And he is excited by the imaginative recycling of waste. 'There's an awful lot of exciting design stuff out there. I like all the new uses for ordinary products – plastic bottles turned into fleeces, glass bottles into bricks, rubber car tyres into pencil cases and carpets, plastic cups into pencils.' You can also buy pens made from recycled computer printers, rulers made from juice cartons, jewellery made from plastic bags, and bags made from bottle tops or CDs.

So don't throw things away! All the items you recycle are valuable resources and can be made into something useful, even stylish and fun. As Recycle Now says: 'The possibilities are endless!'

1 Opener

Look at photos 1–6. They are all recycled items. What are they? And what do you think they are made from?

2 Reading

Read and listen to *Don't throw it away!* Check your answers to exercise 1.

3 Comprehension

Answer the questions.

1 Why did we use to buy fewer clothes?
2 Why did we use to buy fewer shoes?
3 Why didn't we need plastic shopping bags?
4 Why do we produce more rubbish now?
5 What does the Recycle Now campaign aim to do?
6 Which kinds of rubbish are recycled in its TV ads?
7 What recycled materials did Oliver Heath use in the home he designed?

Now say what the items in photos 1–6 used to be.

4 Grammar

Complete.

> **used to + infinitive**
> I _____ _____ be a car tyre.
> We _____ _____ mend our clothes.
> We _____n't _____ to buy so much.
> Why _____ we _____ to buy fewer shoes?
>
> We can use *used to* when we talk about past habits and states.
>
> ➡ Check the answers: Grammar Summary page 113

5 Grammar Practice

Complete with *used to* or *didn't use to*.

1 ✗ People _____ spend so much time shopping.
2 ✓ We _____ produce less rubbish.
3 ✗ We _____ consume so much.
4 ? _____ you _____ make your own clothes?
5 ✗ I _____ recycle bottles and paper.
6 ? _____ you _____ throw them away?

6 Speaking

Look at the picture of a sitting room 200 years ago and say what's wrong. Use *They used to …/They didn't use to …* and these phrases.

> clean with a brush   have electric light
> have vacuum cleaners   light candles
> make phone calls   paint pictures   play cards
> take photos   watch TV   write letters

Now talk about other differences in life 200 years ago.

7 Vocabulary

Ask and answer questions about what these things are made of.

> boots   a computer   a desk   envelopes   an eraser
> jeans   keys   a magazine   matches   a mirror
> a pullover   shoes   a T-shirt   windows

A What are boots made of?
B They're made of leather. What's a computer made of?
A It's made of …

> **Materials**
> cotton   denim   glass   leather   metal   paper
> plastic   rubber   wood   wool

8 Pronunciation

🎧 Listen and repeat.

/eɪ/ waste	/e/ west
later	letter
pain	pen
paper	pepper
saint	sent
tale	tell
wait	wet

Now listen and write the words you hear.

9 Speaking

How have you changed since you became a teenager? Tell other students about your likes, dislikes, feelings, clothes, possessions and hobbies. Make notes about changes in their lives.

A I used to like the Spice Girls but I don't any more.
B I didn't use to like mushrooms but I do now.
A I used to be afraid of the dark, but I'm not now.
B I used to play the recorder but I don't any more.

10 Writing

Write about how you and other students have changed in the last few years. Use your notes from exercise 9.

6 THAT'S CLEVER!

3 The first car was invented by him

Past simple passive
Describing past processes

1 Opener

Tell each other what you know about Leonardo da Vinci.

2 Reading

Read and listen to the text.

Leonardo da Vinci
– ahead of his time

Leonardo da Vinci was not only a great artist, he was also a brilliant inventor. And believe it or not, the first car was invented by him over 500 years ago!

It's no secret that da Vinci drew plans for a car. Several attempts were made in the last century to build the vehicle, but without success. However, a team of computer designers, engineers and carpenters have finally put da Vinci's plans into practice. They spent eight months building a replica of da Vinci's car – and it works! The car, which was sketched by da Vinci in 1478, runs by clockwork.

'It was – or is – the world's first self-propelled vehicle. It is highly sophisticated, a work of genius – and Italian,' said Paolo Galuzzi, director of the Institute and Museum of the History of Science in Florence, where the model is on display.

'It is a very powerful machine,' said Professor Galuzzi. 'It could run into something and do serious damage.'

Da Vinci's other inventions

Flying machine He designed several flying machines, including a helicopter. The first successful powered flying machine was built and flown by Orville and Wilbur Wright in 1903.

Parachute In 1485, da Vinci sketched a design for a parachute. No one knows whether he ever tested a full-scale model. The first reported successful parachute jump was made in 1797.

Robot He produced what are thought to be the first ever designs for a human-like robot in 1495. The robot was designed to wave, sit up, move its head, and open and shut its mouth. The first robot, Steam Man, was created by John Brainerd in 1865.

Scuba diving He sketched an air chamber to allow a diver to swim underwater without connection to the surface. In 1943 the aqualung was invented by Jacques-Yves Cousteau and Emilie Gagnon.

3 Comprehension

Complete the questions with *What, When, Who* or *How many*.
Then match the questions with the answers.

1 _____ was the first car invented by?
2 _____ were several attempts made to build the vehicle?
3 _____ months were spent building the vehicle?
4 _____ was the car sketched by da Vinci?
5 _____ was built and flown in 1903?
6 _____ was the first successful parachute jump made?
7 _____ was the first robot created by?
8 _____ was invented in 1943?

a In 1797.
b In 1478.
c In the last century.
d Eight.
e John Brainerd.
f Leonardo da Vinci.
g The aqualung.
h The first real aeroplane.

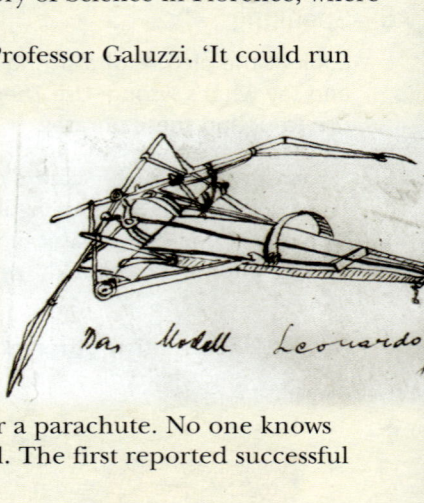

4 Grammar

Complete.

> **Past simple passive**
> The first robot _____ created in 1865.
> Several attempts _____ made in the last century.
> The car _____ sketched **by** da Vinci in 1478.
>
> We form the past simple passive with the past tense of _____ + past participle.
>
> ➡ Check the answers: Grammar Summary page 113

5 Grammar Practice

Complete with the past simple passive.

In a recent poll, the bicycle __1__ (vote) by BBC Radio listeners as their favourite invention of the last 150 years. The bicycle, which __2__ (invent) in Paris by Pierre Lallement in 1866, __3__ (choose) by 70% of voters. Atomic and nuclear bombs __4__ (vote) the least favourite inventions.

Listeners __5__ (invite) to nominate their favourite and least favourite inventions. Then a shortlist of ten 'best' and ten 'worst' inventions __6__ (draw) up for the poll. The computer, the light bulb and the World Wide Web __7__ (include) in the list of ten 'best' inventions. Plastic bags, mobile phones and car alarms __8__ (list) among the 'worst' inventions.

Interestingly, three inventions __9__ (select) for both lists: television, the telephone, and the internal combustion engine!

6 Speaking

Complete the quiz questions with the past simple passive. Then ask and answer the questions.

General Knowledge Quiz

1 When _____ the computer _____? (invent)
 A 1945   B 1965
2 When _____ the World Wide Web _____? (start)
 A 1989   B 1998
3 Who _____ *The Last Supper* and *Mona Lisa* _____ by? (paint)
 A Michelangelo   B Leonardo da Vinci
4 Who _____ *The Lord of the Rings* _____ by? (write)
 A JK Rowling   B JRR Tolkien
5 When _____ the Pyramids of Giza _____? (build)
 A Over 2,000 years ago.   B Over 3,000 years ago.
6 When _____ penicillin _____? (discover)
 A 1892   B 1928
7 Who _____ the *1812 Overture* _____ by? (compose)
 A Beethoven   B Tchaikovsky
8 Who _____ the Simpsons _____ by? (create)
 A Matt Groening   B Walt Disney

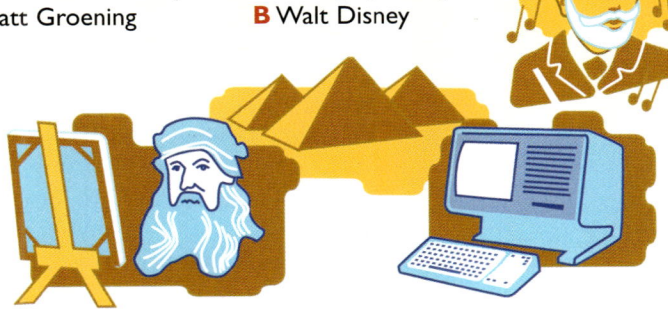

🎧 Now listen and check.

7 Vocabulary

Complete with *do* or *make*.

1 _____ an attempt
2 _____ damage
3 _____ a difference
4 _____ an exercise
5 _____ friends
6 _____ a list
7 _____ a mistake
8 _____ the shopping
9 _____ a sign
10 _____ sure
11 _____ the washing up
12 _____ some work

8 Pronunciation

Write the words in the correct column.

> artist   attempt   believe
> clockwork   compose   create
> damage   display   engine
> invent   machine   practice
> robot   surface

■.	.■
artist	*attempt*

🎧 Now listen and check. Repeat the words.

9 Speaking

Which of the inventions mentioned in this lesson do you think is the best? And which is the worst? Tell another student, giving reasons for your choices.

What do other students think? Have a class vote on the best and worst inventions.

10 Writing

What do you think is the best invention of all time? And what is the worst? Write a paragraph about each invention.

- Who was it invented by?
- When was it invented?
- Why do you think it is the best/worst invention?

6 THAT'S CLEVER!

4 Integrated Skills
Describing a process

Ancient Inventions

People often think that plastic surgery is a modern American invention, __1__. However, thousands of years before America was discovered by Columbus, Indian doctors did complicated plastic surgery. A medical textbook called the *Sushruta Samhita*, which was written in approximately 600 BC, gives detailed instructions for doing 'nose jobs' – __2__.

Brightly coloured cotton clothes were made in India four and a half thousand years ago. This was at a time when Europeans wore animal skins. Until cotton factories were developed in England 200 years ago, India supplied the world with cotton clothes.

Although we call them Arabic numbers, the numbers that we use today came from India and it was there that 'zero' was invented in AD 499. The Romans had counted using letters (M=1000, D=500, C=100, L=50, X=10, V=5 and I=1) __3__. For example, four was written IV, forty XXXX, four hundred CCCC and four thousand MMMM. However, in the new Indian system, using zero, the same numbers were written 4, 40, 400, 4,000.

Chocolate was invented over 2,500 years ago! The Mayans and Aztecs lived in parts of Mexico and central America from 600 BC __4__. They made a cold thick drink called *xocolatl* from the fruit of the tree. Although the Mayans and Aztecs loved chocolate, Europeans didn't discover it for another two thousand years. In 1519, the Spanish explorer Cortés visited Emperor Montezuma II of Mexico. To the explorer's great surprise, he found that Montezuma drank 50 cups of chocolate a day.

Paper and printing were Chinese inventions. Paper was invented in AD 105 by Cai Lun and the Chinese kept the process secret __5__. Although paper was introduced into Japan in AD 610, it didn't reach the West until much later. A hundred years after paper was first made, printing was invented in China – over a thousand years before it was invented in Europe. In China paper wasn't only used for books. Umbrellas, flags and toilet paper were made from it, __6__.

Hernán Cortés and Montezuma II

1 Opener
When and where do you think these things were invented?

   chocolate   cotton   paper   plastic surgery   printing

Reading

2 Read *Ancient Inventions* and check your answers to exercise 1. Then complete the text with phrases a–f.

a for more than five hundred years
b and grew *cacao* trees
c as well as the world's first paper money
d somehow connected with Hollywood
e and this made mathematics very difficult
f changing the shape of your nose

Now listen and check. Which words in the phrases helped you to complete the text?

3 Linking word: *although*

Find examples of *although* in the text. Then rewrite these sentences using *although* instead of *but*.

1 Paper was made Japan in AD 610, but it wasn't made in Europe until 1151.
2 Printing was invented in the 3rd century, but it didn't reach Europe until 1455.
3 The Mayans and Aztecs loved *xocolatl*, but the Spanish thought it tasted awful.
4 Leonardo da Vinci lived 500 years ago, but he designed the first car.
5 Krysta Morlan was only 16, but she invented the waterbike.
6 Louis Braille couldn't see, but he developed a reading system for the blind.

74

4 Listening

🎧 Listen to the description of how cotton was made and number the pictures to show the right order.

A   B   C   D   E   F

5 Speaking

Number these sentences to match the pictures in exercise 4 and use the pictures to tell each other how cotton was made.

- ☐ The white cotton was cleaned.
- ☐ The blue cloth was made into clothes.
- ☐ The cotton cloth was dyed deep blue.
- ☐ The cotton was spun so it could be used for making cloth.
- ☐ When it was ready, the cotton was picked.
- ☐ The cotton was made into cloth.

6 Writing

Complete this process description of how cotton was made.

> When it was ready …   Then …   When …
> After …   Then …   Finally, …

7 Learner Independence

Self assessment: look back over this unit, think about what you've learnt, and complete.

About me
I've learnt …
I used to … but now I …
I can …
I haven't managed to … yet.
I have difficulty in …

About the lessons
What I like best is …
The most interesting thing is …
I'm not keen on …
I don't enjoy …

8

Word creation: make 'people' nouns ending in *-er*, *-or* or *-ist* from these words.

> act   art   design   direct   engine   invent
> journal   novel   paint   profess   report
> run   science   tour   translate

-er	-or	-ist
designer	*actor*	*artist*

9 Phrasebook

🎧 Listen and repeat these useful expressions. Then find them in this unit.

> The idea was to …   Don't throw it away!
> in the first place   The possibilities are endless!
> Believe it or not …   It's no secret.   It works!

Now think of other situations where you could use each of the three exclamations.

Unit 6 Communication Activity
Student **A** page 108
Student **B** page 118

75

6 THAT'S CLEVER!
Inspiration Extra!

PROJECT History of Our Town File

Make a file about the history of your town, or an important town nearby.

1. Work in a group and make a list of what you know about your town: old buildings, important places, famous people who have lived there, changes (what it used to be like, how many people used to live there), new buildings and roads (and what used to be there before them). Then choose the most important facts to write about.

2. Find out more information about the town's history by asking local people and using the Internet or a library:

   > How old is it?
   > When is the first reference to the town? How many people lived there then and what did they do?
   > What was the town like 100 years ago?
   > Was it a market town, a port, or an industrial town with factories?
   > What changes have happened over the last 100 years?
   > What changes are planned for the future?

3. Work together and make a History of Our Town File. Read it carefully and correct any mistakes. Draw pictures or use photographs from magazines or newspapers. Show your History of Our Town File to the other groups.

POEM Changes: The Things We Used To Do

- Work in groups of three or four.
- Think about your own and your friends' lives a year ago. What changes have there been? For example, think about relationships, likes and dislikes, free time, family, holidays, music, sport and clothes.
- Now think of ways of completing these sentences:

  I used to … but now I …
  You used to … but now you …
  We used to … but now we …

  I used to like writing letters, but now I send text messages.
  You used to play snakes and ladders, but now you play computer games.
  We used to run to school, but now we walk slowly.

- Choose the best sets of three sentences and put them together to make a poem – it can be long or short.
- Give your poems to your teacher and listen. Can you guess which group wrote each poem?

SONG

Read and complete with these words. One word is used twice.

> game grown hearts own radio rain used

Brown-eyed Girl
Van Morrison

Hey, where did we go
Days when the __1__ came?
Down in the hollow
Playing a new __2__
Laughing and a-running, hey, hey
Skipping and a-jumping
In the misty morning fog
With our __3__ a-thumping and you
And you, my brown-eyed girl,
You, my brown-eyed girl.

Whatever happened to Tuesday and so slow
Going down the old mine
With a transistor __4__
Standing in the sunlight, laughing
Hiding behind a rainbow's wall
Slipping and a-sliding
All along the waterfall
With you, my brown-eyed girl,
You, my brown-eyed girl.

Do you remember when we __5__ to sing?
Sha la la la la la la la la la la dee da, just like that
Sha la la la la la la la la la dee da, la dee da

So hard to find my way
Now that I'm all on my __6__
I saw you just the other day
My, how you have __7__
Cast my memory back there, Lord
Sometimes I'm overcome thinking about
Laughing and a-running, hey, hey
Behind the stadium
With you, my brown-eyed girl,
You, my brown-eyed girl.

Do you remember when we __8__ to sing?
Sha la la la la la la la la la la dee da
Sha la la la la la la la la la dee da

Now listen and check.

UNIT 6

REVISION for more practice

LESSON 1

Look at exercise 2 on page 68 and find examples of the past perfect. Write five questions and answer them.

Had Ryan been fascinated by electronics as a child? Yes, he had.

LESSON 2

Write five sentences about what you used and didn't use to do when you were at primary school. Think about lessons, teachers, clothes, sports, homework, holidays, etc.

We didn't use to have English lessons.

LESSON 3

Complete with verbs in the past simple passive.

The first successful hot-air balloon __1__ (invent) in 1783. Air __2__ (heat) by a fire, the balloon __3__ (fill) with the hot air, and it took off. The passengers on the first hot-air balloon journey were three animals – a duck, a hen and a sheep __4__ (put) in the basket under the balloon. When the balloon __5__ (see) to be a success, the animals __6__ (follow) by people!

EXTENSION for language development

LESSON 1

Complete these sentences using the past perfect.
1. The school bus was completely empty because …
2. The DJ couldn't play any music because …
3. The man at the door had only one shoe because …
4. She didn't buy her boyfriend a present because …
5. She didn't get the text message because …

LESSON 2

Imagine you are a newspaper reporter. Write an interview with someone who used to be a big pop star a few years ago. But now they have no money and everyone has forgotten them.

Reporter Can you remember what it was like when you were number one?
Star Yes, it was great. Everyone used to like me and want to be my friend. We used to have all night parties, but now...

LESSON 3

Make your own general knowledge quiz and try it out on another student.
1. Who _____ (name of book) _____ by? (write)
2. When _____ (name of building) _____? (build)
3. Who _____ (name of song) _____ by? (sing)
4. When _____ (name of continent) _____? (discover)

YOUR CHOICE!

CONSTRUCTION Past simple active or passive?

Complete with the correct form of the verbs.
Although the ancient Greeks __1__ (know) about electrical forces, it wasn't until the 19th century that electricity __2__ (understand) properly. Then it __3__ (use) in practical ways and life __4__ (change) dramatically. Gas lamps and candles __5__ (replace) by electric light, electric trams __6__ (appear) on the streets, and lots of electrical appliances __7__ (invent). But one of the first electric irons, which __8__ (make) in 1889, __9__ (explode) and __10__ (kill) its inventor.

ACTION *I used to be … game*

- Work in a small group.
- In turn, imagine you are a famous person who is no longer alive. Don't say who you are, but tell the rest of the group one fact about yourself.
  I used to be a writer.
- The rest of the group asks *Yes/No* questions to find out who you used to be.
  A Did you use to live in the 19th century?
  B Did you use to live in England?

REFLECTION Past perfect

Match the examples a–f with language functions 1–3.
The past perfect is used …
1. to describe the earlier of two past events.
2. to talk about something that happened before a particular time in the past.
3. to explain why something happened.

a. They got lost because they hadn't taken a map.
b. The party had finished by midnight.
c. After I'd been to the gym, I had a shower.
d. She'd started working by the time she was 17.
e. When we'd done our homework, we watched TV.
f. He'd drunk lots of coffee, so he couldn't sleep.

INTERACTION *I'd never been so … before!*

- Work in a small group.
- Think of a dramatic event in your life, for example, when you were very excited, frightened, embarrassed or surprised.
- Make notes about what happened, when it happened, and why you felt the way you did.
- Tell each other about the event, ending:
  I'd never been so … before!

77

REVIEW UNITS 5–6

Grammar

1 Read and complete. For each number 1–12, choose word or phrase A, B or C.

Teen sleepwalks to top of crane

A teenage sleepwalker __1__ after she __2__ asleep on the arm of a 40-metre-high crane, police have __3__ reported.

Police and fire-fighters __4__ to a building site in south-east London after a passer-by __5__ the girl on the crane. A fire-fighter __6__ up and discovered the 15-year-old girl was fast asleep. He didn't want to wake her in case she panicked and fell off the crane. Luckily he __7__ the girl's mobile phone and called her parents. They then phoned their daughter to wake her up, and she __8__ safely down to the ground. The rescue operation lasted __9__ two hours.

Apparently the unnamed girl __10__ her home in the middle of the night and climbed the crane while she was asleep. An expert at the London Sleep Centre said, 'I've treated people who __11__ cars and ridden horses while asleep. One patient has even tried to fly a helicopter. But I've __12__ heard of a more unusual case than this.'

1	A rescued	B is rescued	C was rescued
2	A found	B was found	C were found
3	A ever	B just	C yet
4	A called	B was called	C were called
5	A had noticed	B has noticed	C did notice
6	A has climbed	B climbed	C was climbed
7	A found	B was found	C has found
8	A brought	B had brought	C was brought
9	A for	B since	C during
10	A leaves	B has left	C had left
11	A drive	B has driven	C have driven
12	A ever	B never	C yet

2 Rewrite the sentences using the present perfect with *just*.

The match began a minute ago.
The match has just begun.

1 The plane landed five minutes ago.
2 We saw the film last night.
3 It started raining a few seconds ago.
4 The students left school last month.
5 I bought some new trainers yesterday.
6 We heard the news half an hour ago.

3 Two students are going backpacking in Asia. Write sentences using the present perfect with *yet* and *already*.

buy the plane tickets ✓
They've already bought the plane tickets.

read all the guidebooks ✗
They haven't read all the guidebooks yet.

1 book somewhere to stay the first night ✗
2 apply for visas ✓
3 plan their route ✓
4 buy a phrasebook ✗
5 have the necessary vaccinations ✓
6 save up enough money ✓
7 pack their rucksacks ✗
8 organise travel insurance ✗

4 Ask and answer questions using the present perfect with *ever*.

Leo/try snowboarding ✗

> Has Leo ever tried snowboarding?
>> No, he hasn't.

1 Tiffany/go on a roller coaster ✓
2 Will/eaten lobster ✗
3 Anna/try bungee jumping ✓
4 Julie and Simon/visit Mexico ✗
5 Stella/win a race ✗
6 Ed and Colin/be on TV ✓

Now write sentences.

Leo has never tried snowboarding.

5 Complete with the present perfect or past simple.

A __1__ you ever __2__ (make) a parachute jump?
B No, I __3__ never __4__ (want) to. What about you?
A I __5__ (do) it last year.
B Really? __6__ you __7__ (enjoy) it?
A I __8__ (be) terrified before I __9__ (jump). But when my parachute __10__ (open) I __11__ (feel) great.
B Parachute jumping isn't for me – I __12__ (be) afraid of heights all my life!

6 Write sentences using the present perfect with *for* and *since*.

they/live in this town/1980
They've lived in this town since 1980.

1 he/have guitar lessons/six months
2 she/not/contact us/last Friday
3 I/be awake/6am
4 you/know each other/two weeks
5 my parents/be married/25 years
6 we/live here/I was born
7 you/not/go on holiday/ages
8 I/have a headache/yesterday

UNITS 5-6 REVIEW

7 Complete with the past perfect where possible. Otherwise use the past simple.

Chris Haas, 15, __1__ (invent) the Hands-On Basketball as a school project when he __2__ (be) nine. 'The idea __3__ (be) to make an invention to help people do something better,' he remembers. Chris's father __4__ (be) a basketball coach for many years before he __5__ (retire). 'I __6__ (know) how to shoot properly because my father __7__ (teach) me,' Chris says, 'so I __8__ (paint) hands on a basketball to show the other players how to hold it.' No one __9__ (think) of this before, and Chris __10__ (sell) his idea to a big company. He __11__ (not expect) to make a lot of money, but last year he __12__ (earn) $50,000 from his invention.

8 Think about life 300 years ago. Write sentences about what people used to do and didn't use to do.

travel by plane
They didn't use to travel by plane.

1 drive cars
2 travel by boat
3 cook food over a fire
4 buy frozen food
5 send emails
6 listen to the radio
7 read by candlelight
8 wash clothes by hand

9 Write sentences using the past simple passive.

vacuum cleaner/invent/Herbert Booth/1901
The vacuum cleaner was invented by Herbert Booth in 1901.

1 radium/discover/Marie and Pierre Curie/1898
2 first printed books/produce/China
3 electric light bulb/invent/Swan and Edison/1879
4 Mount Everest/first climb/Tenzing and Hillary/1953
5 mobile phones/first use/1978
6 London underground/open/1863
7 first colour photos/take/James Maxwell/1861
8 potatoes/bring/to Europe/the 16th century

Vocabulary

10 Complete with these words.

award   basket   cans   float   grateful
injuries   inspiration   kite   medal   mend

1 You can't fly a _____ if there's no wind.
2 A carpenter managed to _____ the broken chair.
3 We carried our picnic in a large _____.
4 Could I have two _____ of lemonade, please?
5 It's easier to _____ in the sea than in a freshwater pool.
6 Thank you, I'm extremely _____ for your help.
7 He had an motorbike accident, but his _____ weren't serious.
8 It must be wonderful to win an Olympic gold _____.
9 They say genius is one percent _____, and 99 percent hard work.
10 She was very proud to win an _____ for her first novel.

11 Match these words with their definitions.

blind   combine   deaf   foreigner   glad
recycle   reduce   simplify   sphere   vehicle

1 pleased, happy
2 bring or put together
3 something round, like a ball
4 unable to see
5 unable to hear
6 process waste so it can be used again
7 machine that travels on roads
8 opposite of *increase*
9 person from another country
10 make easier or less complicated

12 Match the words in list A with the words and phrases in list B.

A	B
1 become	a candle
2 do	into practice
3 earn	damage
4 light	of an idea
5 perform	a language
6 put	money
7 think	in a play
8 translate	underwater
9 swim	well-known

13 Find the odd word.

1 metal   plastic   rubber   tyre
2 cotton   leather   paper   wool
3 career   carpenter   engineer   farmer
4 finger   glove   hand   thumb
5 bottle   carton   can   drink
6 exciting   exhausting   including   surprising

PROGRESS CHECK

Now you can …
1 Talk about what has and hasn't happened
2 Talk about experiences
3 Talk about achievements
4 Describe events and things which are important to you
5 Describe a sequence of past events
6 Talk about past habits and states
7 Describe past processes

Look back at Units 5 and 6 and write an example for 1–6.

1 I haven't ridden a motorbike yet.

How good are you? Tick a box.
★★★ Fine ☐   ★★ OK ☐   ★ Not sure ☐

Not sure about something? Ask another student.

7 COMMUNICATION

1 He asked her not to go

ask/tell + object + infinitive
Reporting requests and commands

Animal Talk

'Calm down!' said Alex. 'Don't tell me to calm down!' replied Irene. Husband and wife? Brother and sister? No, Alex is an African grey parrot and Dr Irene Pepperburg has trained him to talk – he has a vocabulary of about 100 words. Alex can also count up to seven, and identify shapes, colours and materials. And he has a close relationship with Dr Pepperburg. When she had to leave Alex with the vet for an operation, he asked her not to go. 'Stop!' he screamed. 'I love you! Come back!'

Apes are also famous for learning human language. Koko, a gorilla who was taught sign language, has learnt more than 1,000 signs and can understand about 2,000 English words. She has even done an Internet 'chat'! But one of the most famous animal 'language learners' is Kanzi, a chimpanzee, who communicates by pressing symbols on a special keyboard.

Kanzi not only has a large vocabulary, he also makes up words, for example, 'finger bracelet' (ring) and 'white tiger' (zebra). And he responds to an enormous number of spoken commands and questions. In one test, the researcher, Dr Savage-Rumbaugh, asked him to wash a potato, and then she told him to turn off the water. She asked him to get a ball, and told him to take a red ball into the office. She told him to put a tomato in the fridge and to put a key in the fridge. Kanzi responded correctly to 74 per cent of 660 requests and instructions.

Kanzi is clearly a remarkable chimp. Once, Dr Savage-Rumbaugh's keys were stolen by another chimp at the research centre. She asked Kanzi to get them back for her. Kanzi went to talk to the guilty chimp, and brought back the stolen keys. And when he's relaxing, Kanzi likes watching TV – *Tarzan* is one of his favourite movies!

But can animals *really* learn and use language? If your parrot tells you not to be silly, it's probably because the parrot has often heard you say 'Don't be silly!'. And perhaps we should spend more time trying to understand how animals communicate with each other, instead of teaching them to communicate with us.

1 Opener

Look at the photos. What kind of bird is it? What kind of animal is it? And what do you think they can do?

2 Reading

Read and listen to *Animal Talk*.

3 Comprehension.

Complete with Alex, Kanzi or Koko.

1 _____ uses sign language.
2 _____ can speak.
3 _____ uses a keyboard.
4 _____ can say about 100 words.
5 _____ understands about 2,000 words.
6 _____ watches films on TV.
7 _____ can count.
8 _____ invents words.

4 Grammar

Complete.

Reported requests: ask + object + infinitive
'Could you wash the potato?'
→ She _____ him _____ wash the potato.
'Please don't go!'
→ He asked her _____ _____ go.

Reported commands: tell + object + infinitive
'Calm down!'
→ He _____ her _____ calm down.
'Don't be silly!'
→ The parrot told me _____ _____ be silly.

The verb *tell* is always followed by an object.

➡ Check the answers: Grammar Summary page 113

80

8 Pronunciation

🎧 Listen and repeat.

Linking
She had_to leave_Alex with_the vet for_an_operation.
She has_even done_an_Internet_chat!
He_also makes_up words, for_example, 'white_tiger'.
He responds_to_an_enormous_number …
She_asked_him to_get_a ball.
Can_animals_really learn_and_use language?

9 Vocabulary

Match the phrases 1–6 with their opposites a–f. How many of the phrasal verbs can you find in this lesson?

		Opposites	
1	Put it on.	a	Bring it back.
2	Pick it up.	b	Come back.
3	Go away.	c	Put it down.
4	Stand up.	d	Turn it off.
5	Take it away.	e	Take it off.
6	Turn it on.	f	Sit down.

Now look at the phrases with *it*. In each case, say what *it* could be.

Put it on.   *It could be a jacket.*
             It could be a cap.

5 Grammar Practice

Which of these sentences are requests, and which are commands? Match them with the reported requests and commands in *Animal Talk*.

1 'Put the tomato in the refrigerator.'
2 'Take the red ball into the office.'
3 'Can you get the ball?'
4 'Turn the water off.'
5 'Please would you get my keys back?'

6 Grammar Practice

Write sentences reporting the requests with *asked* and the commands with *told*.

Doctor: 'You should stop smoking, Mr Davies.'
The doctor told Mr Davies to stop smoking.

1 Teacher: 'Anya, could you clean the board, please?'
2 Mother: 'Children, go to bed!'
3 Leo: 'Mum, can you give me some money?'
4 Coach: 'Right, team, you must win the match.'
5 Fire-fighter: 'Please keep calm, everyone, and leave the building'.
6 Julie: 'Simon, would you carry my rucksack?'
7 Pilot: 'Passengers, fasten your seatbelts.'
8 Teacher: 'Sit down, everyone.'

10 Speaking

How often do your parents ask/tell you to do things? And how often do they ask/tell you *not* to do things? Tell another student, using these phrases to help you.

turn my music down   eat too quickly
do the washing-up   tidy my room
use the phone
help with the cooking/shopping/housework
come home late   wash the car
do my homework   play computer games
turn off the TV   put on/take off clothes
be rude   be quiet   have a haircut
get up   go to bed

7 Listening

🎧 Listen to a researcher talking to a chimp called Charlie, and look at these sentences. Make a note of the mistake in each sentence.

1 'Can you pick up the red box?'
2 'Don't eat the banana.'
3 'Take off my shoe.'
4 'Would you put the ball on the desk?'
5 'Could you open the window, please?'
6 'Please don't stand on the table.'

Now ask and answer.   *Did she ask Charlie to pick up the red box?*
                     No, she asked him to …

11 Writing

Write about things your parents asked/told you to do or not to do yesterday. Use the phrases in exercise 10 to help you.

They asked me to turn down my music.

7 COMMUNICATION

2 He said it didn't bother him

Reported statements: *say* and *tell*
Reporting what someone said

Who put @ in your email?

In English it is called simply 'at', but other languages have more interesting names. In South Africa it is 'monkey's tail'; in Denmark it is often 'pig's tail'; in France it is sometimes 'little snail'; in Greece it is 'little duck'; in Hungary it is 'worm'; in Poland it is sometimes 'little cat'; in Russia it is usually 'little dog', in Sweden it is 'elephant's trunk' and Turkish emailers call it simply 'ear'.

Today we talk to Ray Tomlinson, the man who invented @ and email.

Q: When and why did you invent email?
It was in 1971 and I'm not sure there was a real reason for inventing it. It was a fun thing to try out and probably took four to six hours to do. I can't remember exactly how long it took. Less than a day, spread over a week or two.

Q: How do you feel about spam and viruses?
I get annoyed when I get spam. It's a tough problem but we're going to solve it. So far the solutions aren't working – they either filter too much or not enough. We must find a better way to stop spam. Viruses are another problem and you usually get them from an email attachment. An ISP could throw away all emails with attachments, but then email wouldn't be any use. We'll have to find a solution.

Q: Does it bother you that you're not a household name – that most people don't know what you've done?
No, it doesn't bother me. Computer nerds know that I've done it. I get emails from people who say 'What you did is great. Why don't you do something about spam?' It's kind of nice that some people are interested in what I did – but it's not the centre of my life.

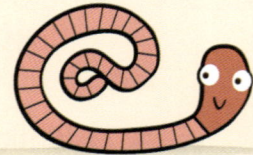

1 Opener

How often do you use the phone? … write letters? … send emails?

Which do you do most/least often?

2 Reading

Read and listen to *Who put @ in your email?*

3 Comprehension

True, false, or no information? Correct the false sentences.

1 Ray Tomlinson said he had invented the computer in 1971.
2 He said it was easy to invent email.
3 He told the interviewer that email was a tough problem.
4 He said that they were going to solve the problem of spam.
5 He said that solutions to spam were working.
6 He told the interviewer that he got lots of emails.
7 He said computer nerds didn't know that he had invented email.
8 Emails to Ray said what he had done was great.
9 Ray said it was nice that no one was interested in what he had done.

4 Grammar

Complete.

Reported statements

Direct speech	Reported speech
'I'm not sure.' →	He said (that) he wasn't sure.
'The solutions aren't working.' →	He said (that) the solutions weren't working.
'It doesn't bother me.' →	He said (that) it didn't bother him.
'It took four to six hours.' →	He said (that) it had taken four to six hours.
'I've done it.' →	He told her (that) he had done it.
'We're going to solve it.' →	He said (that) they were going to solve it.
'We must find a better way.' →	He told her (that) they had to find a better way.
'I can't remember.' →	He said (that) he couldn't remember.
'We'll have to find a solution.' →	He said (that) they would have to find a solution.

Direct speech	Reported speech
Present simple →	_____
Present continuous →	_____
Past simple →	_____
Present perfect →	_____
am/is/are going to →	_____
must →	_____
can →	_____
will →	_____

➡ Check the answers: Grammar Summary page 114

5 Grammar Practice

Match these reported statements with Ray's words from exercise 2.

1 Ray said that inventing email had been a fun thing to do.
2 He said he couldn't remember exactly how long it took to invent email.
3 He told the interviewer that he got annoyed when he got spam.
4 He said that they were going to find a way to solve the problem of spam.
5 He said that they had to find a better way to stop spam.
6 He told the interviewer it didn't bother him that he wasn't a household name.
7 He got emails from people who said that what he had done was great.

6 Grammar Practice

The interviewer also asked 'A lot of people say email has changed society – do you agree?' Write Ray's reply in reported speech.

1 'There isn't an easy answer.'
2 'Email has had an effect.'
3 'But I don't think people are different.'
4 'We must look at how they communicate.'
5 'Friendly people can still be friendly by email.'
6 'In the past people went to libraries.'
7 'In the future they will use the Internet.'
8 'Email and Internet use is going to increase enormously.'
9 'It's exciting because so much is happening.'

7 Vocabulary

Match these words with their definitions.

attachment   Internet   ISP   spam   virus

1 computer system which lets people worldwide exchange information
2 program which damages or destroys information on computers
3 Internet Service Provider
4 computer file sent with an email
5 'junk' emails sent to people who don't want them

8 Pronunciation

🎧 Listen and repeat.

/g/ dog	/k/ dock
pig	pick
dug	duck
bag	back
game	came
good	could

Now listen and write the words you hear.

9 Listening

🎧 Peter is having problems with his girlfriend, Stella. Look at what Stella said. Then listen and find out what actually happened.

What Stella said
'I'll meet you at 8.'
'The film begins at 8.30.'
'You can borrow my MP3 player.'
'I've left your birthday present at home.'
'I must get home early.'
'You didn't phone me.'

What happened
She didn't turn up until …
It started at …
She lent it to …
She hadn't …
She went out …
Her phone was …

Now tell each other what Stella said and what actually happened.

> She said she would meet him at 8, but she didn't turn up until 8.30.

10 Writing

When did you last hear good news about these topics?

Sport   Family   Education
Friends   Music

How did you hear the news? Did someone tell you face to face or on the phone? Did you hear the news on the radio or on TV? Did you read it in the newspaper, a letter or an email? Report what the person, programme, newspaper, letter or email said.

Last night it said on TV that my team had won the match.

7 COMMUNICATION

3 We asked how he had got the idea

Reported questions
Reporting what someone asked

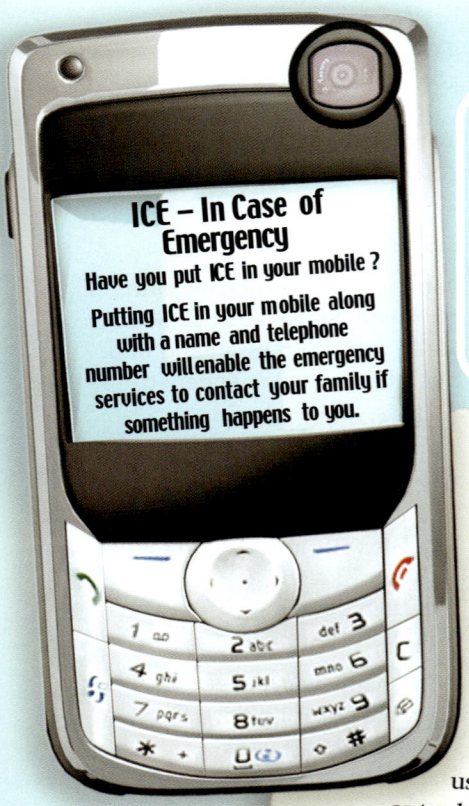

ICE – In Case of Emergency

Have you put ICE in your mobile?

Putting ICE in your mobile along with a name and telephone number will enable the emergency services to contact your family if something happens to you.

- Type ICE followed by a contact name (for example, ICE – Mum or ICE – David) and number into the address book of your mobile phone.
- Tell your ICE contact that their number is in your phone.

Paramedic Bob Brotchie hits the headlines

Bob, 41, the inventor of ICE, is the centre of media attention. We asked how he had got the idea for ICE. 'I was thinking about some difficult situations where people couldn't speak because of injury or illness. In these cases the police or paramedics usually go through the person's mobile phone to find out who they are. Now if someone has saved a contact number under ICE, all we have to do is go to 'I' and there it is.'

ICE is a simple and effective idea and has become very popular in Britain. We asked if it was catching on in other countries. 'It's still early days,' he said, 'but Australia and New Zealand are considering it. It's only just hit the USA but several states, including Texas, want to go ahead with it. I think Germany now has a similar scheme called IN, but I haven't had a chance to go into it yet.'

The media interest in ICE has been phenomenal and Bob has given dozens of TV and radio interviews. What kind of questions have they asked him? 'They asked how I became a paramedic, what other jobs I'd done, what the best part of my work was and what I'd done at the weekend! They also wanted to know if anyone had used ICE in an emergency yet.'

1 Opener

Who will your school contact in an emergency or if you have an accident?

2 Reading

Read and listen to *ICE – In Case of Emergency* and the newspaper article.

3 Comprehension

Find reported questions in the newspaper article to match these answers.

1. I worked on the air ambulance for three years and that was the peak of my career as a paramedic.
2. I was working for ambulance control, answering emergency phone calls, and wanted to find out more about what life was like on the road in an ambulance.
3. Yes, we know of at least one definite case.
4. I was at work at the ambulance station. Just an average weekend without any serious accidents.
5. Lots – I've been a hairdresser, and had lots of jobs in sales. I've run a fish and chip shop, and worked on market stalls and in warehouses.

4 Grammar

Complete.

Reported questions

Direct speech	Reported speech
'Is it catching on in other countries?' →	We asked **if** it **was** catching on in other countries.
'Has anyone used ICE in an emergency yet?' →	They wanted to know _____ anyone _____ _____ ICE in an emergency yet.
'How did you get the idea?' →	We asked _____ he _____ _____ the idea.
'What other jobs have you done?' →	They asked _____ other jobs he _____ _____.

In reported Yes/No questions, we use _____ before the reported question.
We don't use the auxiliary verb *do* in reported questions.

➡ Check the answers: Grammar Summary page 114

5 Grammar Practice

Match the direct questions 1–5 with the reported questions a–e.

1. Do you usually carry a mobile phone?
2. What is your mobile or home phone number?
3. Are you carrying a mobile phone at the moment?
4. Have you saved a contact number on a mobile under ICE?
5. When did you first hear about ICE?

a. I asked when he/she had first heard about ICE.
b. I asked if he/she was carrying a mobile phone at the moment.
c. I asked if he/she usually carried a mobile phone.
d. I asked if he/she had saved a contact number on a mobile under ICE.
e. I asked what his/her mobile phone number was.

Now ask another student the questions and write sentences reporting the questions and answers.

I asked Tina when she had first heard about ICE. She said she had heard about it on the radio.

6 Role Play

Role play an interview between a reporter and Bob Brotchie.

The reporter asked
– how long he had worked on the air ambulance.
– how often the air ambulance had gone to accidents.
– if he had enjoyed working on the air ambulance.
– if he could remember a particular accident.
– if the motorcyclist had been badly injured.
– what they had done.
– how long it had taken.
– if the motorcyclist had been OK.

Bob said
– he had worked on it for three years.
– it had gone to accidents up to five times a day.
– he had. It had been very stressful but it had saved lives.
– one morning they had rescued a motorcyclist.
– he had been. He had been in a crash with a car.
– they had flown him to hospital.
– he had been in the operating theatre in under an hour.
– he had lost a leg but they had saved his life.

> How long did you work on the air ambulance?
> I worked on it for three years.

Now listen and check.

7 Vocabulary

Match the phrasal verbs with their meanings. How many of the verbs can you find in this lesson?

1. go ahead with
2. go down
3. go into
4. go on
5. go through
6. go up

a. search
b. rise/increase
c. continue
d. find out more about
e. fall/become less
f. start

8 Pronunciation

🎧 Listen and write the words in the correct column.

attention   consider   definite
difficult   effective   injury
reporter   similar

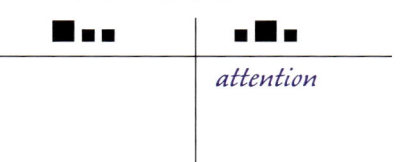

■ ▪ ▪	▪ ■ ▪
	attention

Now listen and check. Repeat the words.

9 Writing

Ask another student about what they did last night and note down the answers. Ask about:

Times	When did you …?
Homework	Did you …? What …?
People	Who did you …?
Food	What did you have …?
TV	Did you watch …?

Now write sentences reporting the questions and answers.

I asked Alex when he had gone to bed. He said he had gone to bed at eleven o'clock.

7 COMMUNICATION

4 Integrated Skills
Telling a story

1 Opener

Look at the newspaper headline and the photos. What do you think the newspaper story is about? Which of these words do you expect to find in it?

> coastguard   dinghy   emergency
> helicopter   illness   keyboard
> success   watertight   wave   vet

Reading

2 Read the newspaper story and answer the questions.

1. Where did Ken and Emily Booth capsize?
2. Why did their dinghy capsize?
3. How long did they spend trying to right the dinghy?
4. When did Emily remember her mobile?
5. How did they feel by then?
6. How far is Tokyo from Southampton?
7. How were the teenagers rescued?
8. What did the coastguard say anyone in trouble should do?

3 Find words in the story which mean:

1. small sailing boat *n*
2. turned over in the water *v*
3. closed so that water can't get in *adj*
4. opposite of failure *n*
5. something you can put things in *n*
6. person who helps people or ships in trouble *n*
7. opposite of danger *n*
8. get in touch with *v*
9. turn over a boat which has capsized *v*

4 Linking words: sequencing adverbs

Look at the text and find these words:

> after   then   later
> next   afterwards

Sequencing adverbs are like signposts. They help us to find our way through a story.

AMAZING RESCUE –
THANKS TO MOBILE PHONE

Two teenagers capsized in the sea off the south coast of England and called Japan on a mobile phone to ask for help.

Brother and sister Ken and Emily Booth were on a sailing holiday near Southampton. But because of huge waves their dinghy capsized and they were thrown into the sea.

Ken, 17, and Emily, 16, spent 30 minutes trying to right the capsized dinghy, but without success. They couldn't get back into the dinghy, and they couldn't attract the attention of passing ships. After they'd been in the water for about 40 minutes, the situation was getting serious, and they felt very cold. Then Emily remembered her mobile phone in its watertight container in her pocket and reached for it.

But she didn't think of dialling 999, the emergency number. Instead she phoned their father, who was 6,000 miles away in Tokyo on a business trip. Emily explained: 'I thought it would be quicker to phone someone I knew and tell them our position. I dialled Dad's number and he contacted the coastguard.'

About ten minutes later, after they had held on to the dinghy for nearly an hour, they heard a helicopter. Next, everything happened very quickly, and Ken and Emily were picked up and carried to safety.

Afterwards, the coastguard said that the teenagers were lucky to be alive and very, very lucky that the mobile had worked. 'Anyone in trouble should contact the coastguard direct on 999,' he added.

86

5 Listening

🎧 You are going to hear a radio news report which covers the same story as the newspaper. First, look at the questions in exercise 2 again.

Now listen and note down the answers from the radio news.

Speaking

6 Look at your answers to exercise 2 and exercise 5, and compare the newspaper and radio reports. Tell each other about the differences.

- A In the newspaper it said that Ken and Emily had capsized off the south coast of England.
- B It said on the radio that they'd capsized off the south coast of Britain.

7 Look at the newspaper story again and role play the conversation between a journalist and Emily.

Journalist	Emily
Ask Emily where she was when they capsized.	
	Reply.
Ask why the dinghy capsized.	
	Explain why.
Ask what they did when they fell into the sea.	
	Reply.
Ask why she didn't dial 999.	
	Explain why not.
Ask how they were rescued.	
	Describe what happened.
Ask how she felt after the rescue.	
	Reply.

8 Writing

Write your own news story about two people in an amazing rescue. Use sequencing adverbs to help readers find their way through the story. Use the newspaper story and these questions to help you.

- Who are the people and how old are they? Where are they from?
- Where were they and what were they doing when they got into trouble?
- What happened to them? Did they get lost or have an accident? Was someone injured?
- Who did they contact to ask for help? How did they make contact?
- What happened when help arrived? How were the people rescued?
- What did they say after the rescue?

Choose a headline for your story, and read or show it to other students in the class. Which rescue story is the most amazing?

Learner Independence

9 You can practise reading and listening to news stories in English on the Internet. You can also learn lots of new vocabulary! The BBC has an excellent site with news stories in simple English for young people at: http://news.bbc.co.uk/cbbcnews/hi/world/

10 Word creation: make nouns ending in -tion from these verbs and complete the sentences.

> attend   communicate   describe   inform
> invent   invite   operate   situate

1. Thanks to the _____ of mobile phones, it's easier to contact people.
2. People go to hospital if they need an _____.
3. Email and text messaging are useful means of _____.
4. I waved to attract her _____, but she didn't see me.
5. What's your address? I'll send you an _____ to my party.
6. You can find out lots of _____ on the World Wide Web.
7. It's important to keep calm in a dangerous or stressful _____.
8. Did you see the robbers? Can you give me a _____ of them?

11 Phrasebook

🎧 Listen and repeat these useful expressions. Then find them in this unit.

> Calm down!   I can't remember exactly.
> It doesn't bother me.
> Why don't you do something about …?
> It's still early days.   I haven't had a chance to …
> How did you get the idea?   … but without success
> It said on the radio that …

Now write a five-line dialogue using at least three of the expressions.

Unit 7 Communication Activity
Student **A** page 108
Student **B** page 118

7 COMMUNICATION

Inspiration Extra!

PROJECT News File

Make a file about how you and others get the news.

1. Work in a group and make a list of all the different ways in which you can get the news. For example, face to face, on the TV or radio, in newspapers and magazines, by phone, in a text message, by letter, by email, on a website or at a meeting.

2. Interview other students and find out how they usually get different kinds of news. Find out which TV programmes they watch, which radio programmes they listen to, which newspapers and magazines they read, and which websites they visit. Notice any similarities and differences.

Type of news	How do you usually get it?
School	*Morning assembly, noticeboard, gossip.*
Family	
Local	
Sports	
National	
World	

3. Work together and make a News File using the information from your interviews. Read it carefully and correct any mistakes. Draw pictures or use photographs from newspapers or magazines or the Internet to illustrate the different media. Show your News File to the other groups.

GAME Guess what they said

- Work in groups of four: A, B, C and D.
- Choose a topic from this list:
  TV Sport Weather Holidays Music Animals People
- A writes a question about the topic to B. B writes a reply.
- C and D ask A and B up to five questions to find out what A's question was and what B's answer was. Then a new topic is chosen and A and B, C and D change roles.

   C Did you ask if he had watched the news on TV last night?
   A Yes, I did.
   D Did you say that you had?
   B Yes, I did.

SKETCH Hotel Reception

Read and listen.

MANAGER Good evening, sir, can I help you?
GUEST Yes, I've booked a room for tonight.
MANAGER What's your surname?
GUEST Watt.
MANAGER I asked what your surname was.
GUEST My surname is Watt.
MANAGER Oh, right.
GUEST No, my surname isn't Wright – it's Watt. W-A-T-T.
MANAGER Yes, sir. And what's your first name?
GUEST No, I said Watt was my surname.
MANAGER Could you please tell me your first name?
GUEST Oh, I see! It's Richard.
MANAGER Thank you, Mr Watt. Address?
GUEST No, I don't want a dress. I want a room.
MANAGER Sir, I need to know where you live.
GUEST I live in the USA.
MANAGER Can you be more specific?
GUEST I live in a large apartment in Los Angeles.
MANAGER Mr Watt, please tell me your address.
GUEST Apartment 34, 281 West 47th Street, Los Angeles.
MANAGER Thank you, sir. Here's your key. You're in room 420.
GUEST For 20? But I booked a room for one!
MANAGER That's right, sir. Room 420 is a single room.
GUEST A single room for 20 people – this is a very strange hotel!
MANAGER Well, Mr Watt, we have some very strange guests!

Now act out the sketch in pairs.

UNIT 7

REVISION for more practice

LESSON 1

Write sentences about things your teacher asked/told you to do or not to do:
- in today's lesson.
- for homework.

She asked me to hand out the photocopies.

LESSON 2

Look at exercise 9 on page 83. Write sentences about what Stella said, and what actually happened.

She said she would meet him at 8, but she didn't turn up until 8.30.

LESSON 3

Write sentences reporting Peter's questions to Stella.

Peter's questions
Why didn't you phone me?
What are you doing this evening?
Will you have dinner with me?
Do you like Japanese food?
Have you ever tried sushi?
How often do you eat fish?

He asked why ...

EXTENSION for language development

LESSON 1

Write five requests beginning *Can/Could/Will/Would you ...?* and five instructions. Then exchange them with another student, and write sentences reporting your partner's requests and instructions.

Could you lend me your mobile phone?
Petra asked me to lend her my mobile phone.

LESSON 2

Complete these questions. Ask two other students the questions and write sentences reporting their answers.

What's your favourite ...?   What happened ...?
Do you like ...?   Have you ever ...?
Where are you going ...?

Adam said his favourite sport was basketball.

LESSON 3

Look at exercise 9 on page 85. Ask three students similar questions about last weekend and write sentences reporting the questions and answers.

I asked Barbara when she had gone to bed on Saturday. She said she had gone to bed at midnight.

YOUR CHOICE!

CONSTRUCTION Reported speech
Put the words in the right order.
1 window to the he her close asked
2 not I shout him to asked
3 told be teacher the to them quiet
4 worry she her weather didn't said bad that the
5 was I that taxi told waiting the them
6 to said we hurry you that had
7 time asked was she the what him
8 right wanted he the was answer it know if to

REFLECTION Reported speech
Match the examples a–j with language functions 1–4.
Reported speech is used to report:
1 Requests   3 Statements
2 Commands   4 Questions

a His father told him not to be late.
b She said he couldn't remember anything.
c He asked what her mobile number was.
d He said that there would be another bus soon.
e She asked her to buy some bread.
f He told the class to stop talking.
g I asked him not to bother.
h She said that she had won the competition.
i She told them it was going to be a great party.
j They wanted to know if he needed some help.

ACTION Blind walking game
- Work in pairs A and B. A closes his/her eyes or puts on a blindfold.
- B asks A to stand up, move around the room and sit down somewhere else, using *Can/Could/Will/Would you ... ?*
Can you take three steps forward?
Would you turn left?
- A must keep his/her eyes closed but can ask questions.
  A Sorry, what did you say?
  B I asked you to turn left.
- B mustn't touch A or let A bump into objects or other students.

INTERACTION Be your parent!
- Work in a small group. Choose to role play being either your father or mother.
- Ask two or three 'parents' in your group about their son/daughter. Ask what he/she is like at home and what they hope he/she will do in the future.
- In your role as your mother/father, report to the group what you learnt from the other 'parents'.
You said your son was always polite and helpful!

culture
GLOBAL ENGLISH

1
'We tell students you need two things to succeed: English and computers,' says Chetan Kumar, manager at the Euro Languages School in a busy suburb in Delhi, India. 'We teach English. For computers,' he points to a nearby Internet café, 'you can go next door.'

2
Within ten years, two billion people will be in English classes and about half the world, three billion people, will speak the language, a recent report suggests. As a 12-year-old from Sichuan in the south west of China said, 'If you can't speak English, it's like you're deaf and dumb.' About 100 million Chinese children are studying English, more than there are people living in Britain.

3
Students of English in China are also getting younger and younger. A growing number of parents are sending their children to English classes before they start primary school. For some mothers-to-be, even that's not early enough. Zhou Min, who introduces English programmes at the Beijing Broadcasting Station, says some pregnant women speak English to their unborn babies.

4
The new English speakers aren't just learning the language, they're changing it. New 'Englishes' are developing fast all over the world, from 'Japlish', the English used in Japanese advertisements, to 'Hinglish,' a mixture of Hindi and English ('Hungry kya?' 'Are you hungry?' a recent Indian ad for pizza asked).

1 Reading

Read the text and match these headings with paragraphs 1–7.

> New 'Englishes'   Starting very young
> A language school in India   Working in English
> Numbers of learners of English
> An English-only village   Computers

🎧 Now listen and check.

2 Vocabulary

Match these words with their definitions.

1 global *adj*   a scientific knowledge
2 technology *n*   b worldwide
3 dumb *adj*   c going to have a baby
4 pregnant *adj*   d laugh in a silly way
5 call centre *n*   e unable to speak
6 giggle *v*   f office where lots of people talk on the phone to customers

5

Why do so many people want English? In a word, jobs. In India, for example, you need English to work in a telephone call centre. At the new Toyota and Peugeot factory in the Czech Republic, English is the language in which the Japanese, French and Czech workers communicate. Jitka Přikrylová, director of a Prague English-language school, said 'The world has opened up for us, and English is its language.'

6

Technology also plays a huge role in English's global importance. Eighty percent of the electronically stored information in the world is in English; and sixty-six percent of the world's scientists read in it. 'It's very important to learn English because computer books are only in English,' says Umberto Duarte, a Uruguayan IT student learning English in London.

7

Schools are becoming more and more imaginative. Last August, South Korea set up the Gyeonggi English Village, where students do everything in English. In one class, student Chun Ho Sung, wearing a long black wig and playing the role of British film star Orlando Bloom, is interviewed. 'Do you think you are handsome?' asks the interviewer. Shyly, in broken English, Chun replies: 'Yes, I do. I am very handsome.' The other teenagers all start giggling.

3 Comprehension

Answer the questions with information from the box.

| How many? | 66   100 million   3 billion |
| Where? | The Czech Republic   China   India   South Korea |

According to the article:

1 How many people will speak English in ten years' time?
2 How many Chinese children are learning English?
3 Where do they speak 'Hinglish'?
4 In which country do women talk to their unborn children in English?
5 Where do people with different first languages use English as a working language?
6 What percentage of scientists read in English?
7 Which country has a village where learners can practise their English?

4 Speaking

Do you agree or disagree with these statements? Why?

- It's good that everyone is learning English so we can all communicate.
- The power of English is bad and it's killing other languages.
- People should learn other languages, not just English.
- The English language belongs to the world, not to the English.
- It's easier to learn a language if you start very young.
- I don't mind speaking with an accent – I'm me, not an English man or woman.
- In the last week I've visited a website in English and/or sent an email in English.

5 Writing

Write a paragraph giving your opinion about some of the statements in exercise 4.

8 NATURAL WORLD

1 They should have known

should(n't) have/ought to have
Criticising past actions

1 Opener

How much water have you used today?

2 Reading

Read and listen to *Water Facts* and *Water Disasters*.

3 Comprehension.

Match the questions with the answers. There are two wrong answers.

1. Why can we only use 1% of the world's fresh water?
2. How long can people survive without water?
3. Roughly how much more water does it take to produce beef than potatoes?
4. What did governments do in the 1990s about the future water shortage?
5. How many people have so far lost their homes in the Three Gorges project?
6. Why does Kate think the Chinese shouldn't have gone ahead with the dam?

a They take a long time to build and a lot of people to work on them.
b They started building more big dams.
c Because of its effect on the people and the countryside around it.
d For three days.
e Forty times.
f Because it is salt.
g A million.
h Because most of it is locked in snow and ice in the Arctic and Antarctic.

WATER FACTS

- 97.5% of the water on earth is salt water, which humans can't drink.
- Most fresh water can't be used either because it's frozen in the polar ice caps. So only 1% of the world's fresh water is available for use.
- Humans can only live for three days without water.
- The average amount of water needed to produce a kilo of potatoes is 1,000 litres, while it takes 42,500 litres to produce a kilo of beef.
- The average US citizen uses 500 litres of water a day, while the average citizen of the Gambia in West Africa uses 4.5 litres of water a day.
- Every year we take 200 billion cubic metres of water more out of the ground than is replaced by rainfall. (1 cubic metre = 908 litres)

Water Disasters

We interviewed environmental campaigner Kate Ellis about lessons we can learn from the past.

Q Why are you so concerned about water?
A Because it's essential to life. Water will be as important in the twenty-first century as oil was in the twentieth. By 2025 two-thirds of the world's population may face a shortage of water.
Q So what are governments doing about it?
A They've known about the problem for a long time. They started building more big dams to store water in the 1990s. But there have been many mistakes.
Q What kind of mistakes?
A Take China's Three Gorges dam, for example. It's the largest dam in the world. But the Chinese should have thought about the human cost – one million people have already had to leave their homes, and nearly two million will eventually be affected.
Q In other words, you think the Chinese shouldn't have gone ahead with the project.
A That's right. They ought to have thought about the human and environmental consequences of such a big dam.

4 Grammar

Complete.

> **should(n't) have/ought to have**
> The Chinese should _____ thought about the human cost.
> They _____ _____ gone ahead with the project.
> They _____ to _____ thought about the consequences.
>
> We can use *should have* or *ought to have* with the same meaning. The negative forms are *shouldn't have* and *oughtn't to have* (not *ought to haven't*).

➡ Check the answers: Grammar Summary page 114

5 Grammar Practice

Say what these people should and/or shouldn't have done to save water this week, using these phrases.

use a hosepipe   go to a public swimming pool
save the rainwater   turn off the tap
wash the car every day   have a bath
use a watering can   have a shower

6 Grammar Practice

Write sentences using *should have* and *shouldn't have*.

You forgot your father's birthday.
I shouldn't have forgotten my father's birthday.

1. You didn't make your bed this morning.
2. You didn't finish your homework before you went out.
3. You left your sports bag at school.
4. You were rude to the bus driver on the way home.
5. You didn't remember to bring your dictionary home.
6. You forgot to phone your teacher back.
7. You didn't help to clear the table after supper.
8. You came home after midnight.

7 Pronunciation

🎧 Listen and repeat.

/dʒ/ /ʃ/ /tʃ/

George shouldn't have watched the shark chew the ship – he should have jumped in shouting 'Jaws!' and punched it.

8 Speaking

Think about situations in your life when you did or didn't do things which you are not happy about now. Make notes under these headings and then tell another student about them.

Age *12*
Situation *Shop.*
What I did/didn't do
Saw a friend steal a CD but didn't tell anyone.
What I should/shouldn't have done
Told him to put the CD back.

> One day when I was 12 I was in a record shop. I saw one of my friends steal a CD but I didn't say anything. I should have told him to put the CD back.

9 Writing

Write two paragraphs about the situations in exercise 8, one paragraph about yourself and one about the student you talked to.

93

8 NATURAL WORLD

2 What would you do?

Second conditional
Talking about imaginary or unlikely situations
Giving advice

SURVIVAL QUESTIONNAIRE
What would you do to survive in these situations?

1 What would you do in the desert if you didn't have enough water?
- A I'd eat a lot because there's water in food.
- B I wouldn't eat, and I'd breathe through my nose.
- C I'd walk as fast as possible and look for an oasis.

2 What if you were outside in a thunderstorm and lightning was near?
- A If I were near a big tree, I'd stand under it for shelter.
- B I'd join other people and ask everyone to hold hands.
- C I'd take off all metal objects and crouch on the ground.

3 What would you do if you were out walking and met a bear?
- A I'd run away as fast as I could.
- B I wouldn't run, I'd back away slowly.
- C I'd climb up the nearest tree.

4 What would you do if you were in a forest fire?
- A I'd run uphill to get as high as I could.
- B I'd work out which way the wind was blowing, and run in the same direction.
- C I'd run away from the fire towards a wide road or a river.

5 What if you were in a boat on the edge of a waterfall?
- A I'd jump out of the boat and go over the waterfall feet first.
- B I'd jump out of the boat and dive over the waterfall.
- C I wouldn't jump, I'd stay in the boat and hold on tight.

Now turn to page 119 and find out your score.

1 Opener

Look at the pictures in the *Survival Questionnaire*. Which of these words do you expect to find in the questionnaire?

desert   fire   forest   ice   jungle   lightning   mountain
oasis   river   snow   thunderstorm   waterfall   wind

2 Reading

Read and answer the questionnaire. Then compare your answers with other students.

94

3 Listening

🎧 Listen and write down Jake's answers to the questionnaire. What's his score?

4 Grammar

Complete.

> **Second conditional**
> If + past simple, would(n't) …
>
> If I **met** a bear, I **would run** away as fast as I **could**.
> If I **were** near a big tree, I _____ _____ under it for shelter.
> If I _____ on the edge of a waterfall, I _____ n't _____ out of the boat.
> What _____ you _____ if you _____ n't _____ enough water?
> What _____ you _____ outside in a thunderstorm?
>
> We use the second conditional to talk about imaginary present or unlikely future situations.

➡ Check the answers: Grammar Summary page 114

5 Grammar Practice

Write sentences using the correct form of the verbs: past simple or would …

1. How (you/survive) if you (get) lost in the mountains?
2. If my mobile (work), I (dial) 999.
3. What (you/do) if the battery (be) flat?
4. If I (have) a mirror, I (try) to send signals.
5. (you/feel) scared if you (be) alone?
6. I (sing) rap songs if I (feel) scared.
7. What if you (have) to spend the night in the mountains?
8. If I (be) cold, I (make) a fire.

6 Speaking

Ask and answer questions about these imaginary situations. What would you say and do? How would you feel?

1. You meet an alien.
2. You're stuck in a lift.
3. You win a million dollars.
4. You lose your bag.
5. You see a ghost.
6. You meet your favourite star.

If I met an alien, I'd invite it home for tea.

7 Listening

🎧 Look at these phrases, and listen to the advice given to people with problems 1–6. Match the phrases with the problems.

> lie down   take more exercise   see a dentist
> go to the doctor   stop talking
> take a deep breath and count to 100
> go to bed later   drink a glass of water
> count sheep   eat lots of oranges
> drink hot lemon and honey   read a boring book
> take an aspirin

1. I've got hiccoughs.
2. I've got toothache.
3. I can't get to sleep at night.
4. I think I'm getting a cold.
5. I've got a headache.
6. I've got a cough and a sore throat.

Do you agree with the advice you heard? Give your advice in response to the problems using *If I were you, I'd/I wouldn't …* You can add your own ideas.

8 Pronunciation

Which of these words contain the sound /f/?

> cough   enough   ghost   hiccough
> high   laugh   lightning   night
> thought   through   tight   weight

🎧 Listen and check. Repeat the words.

9 Speaking

Imagine you were going backpacking with another student, and you could only take ten of these items with you. Which items would you take in your survival pack, and why?

> a box of matches   candles   a compass
> a digital camera   a first aid kit   insect spray
> a magnifying glass   a map   a mobile phone
> a needle and thread   a pencil and paper
> a penknife   plastic bags   a radio   safety pins
> a small mirror   a spoon   sun cream   sunglasses
> a torch   an umbrella   a water bottle   a whistle

> If we took a box of matches, we could light a fire.

Now tell other students which items you would take.

> We'd take a box of matches so we could light a fire.

10 Writing

A British friend of yours is going on a camping holiday in your country next week, and asks your advice about what to take. Write some helpful advice – and think about the weather!

If I were you, I'd take some insect spray. There are lots of mosquitoes at this time of the year.

8 NATURAL WORLD

3 You'd like to stay there, wouldn't you?

Question tags
Asking for agreement and checking

1 Opener

Match these living spaces with the photos.

cave   hotel   igloo   terraced house   tree house

2 Reading

Read and listen.

JAKE   What's all this, Tiff?
TIFFANY   It's a photographic exhibition about different kinds of places to live. You can see that, can't you?
JAKE   I mean – why have they chosen these particular places?
TIFFANY   This one's the world's biggest igloo. It says it's 40 metres round, 12 metres across and 5 metres high. It can hold 500 people! It's in a place called Puvirnituq in northern Canada.
JAKE   I get it – they're all special in some way. Oh, and I know what that one is – it's the smallest house in Britain. You didn't expect me to know that, did you?
TIFFANY   No, I didn't! And look! That tree house has been in the papers recently, hasn't it?
JAKE   I think it's in the north-east of England. It's the world's biggest tree house and it can hold 300 people! But what's that modern hotel doing here?
TIFFANY   Let's see. Oh yes. It's on Paradise Island in the Bahamas and it's got the world's most expensive hotel room. It's called the Bridge Suite and costs £14,000 a night! You'd like to stay there, wouldn't you?
JAKE   You must be joking – they wouldn't let someone like me in. But I rather like the Gamirasu Cave Hotel in Turkey …
TIFFANY   Yes, you are a bit of a caveman, aren't you?

96

3 Comprehension

True, false, or no information? Correct the false statements.

1. It was Tiffany's idea to visit the exhibition.
2. The exhibition was in London.
3. The igloo is special because it's in Puvirnituq.
4. The smallest house in Britain is in Conway in Wales.
5. Tiffany was surprised that Jake recognised the photo of the smallest house.
6. Jake has visited the tree house.
7. Tiffany thought that Jake would like to stay in the Bridge Suite.

4 Grammar

Complete.

> **Question tags**
> You can see that, _____ you?
> You'd like to stay there, _____ you?
> It's been in the papers, _____ it?
> You didn't expect me to know that, _____?
> Jake thinks it's in the north east, **doesn't** he?
> They went to the exhibition, **didn't** they?
>
> Affirmative statement → negative tag
> Negative statement → affirmative tag
>
> ➡ Check the answers: Grammar Summary page 114

5 Grammar Practice

Complete with these question tags.

can it   did she   didn't he   do you   doesn't he
hasn't it   weren't they   would he

1. It's got the world's most expensive hotel room, _____?
2. You don't know what that is, _____?
3. The photos were of special places, _____?
4. Jake asked Tiffany about the photos, _____?
5. Tiffany didn't expect Jake to know about the smallest house, _____?
6. Jake wouldn't like to stay in the Bridge Suite, _____?
7. Jake likes the cave hotel, _____?
8. The tree house can't hold 300 people, _____?

6 Pronunciation

🎧 Listen and check your answers to exercise 5. We use question tags with falling intonation to ask for agreement, and with rising intonation to check if something is true. Repeat the sentences. Which have rising intonation and which have falling intonation?

7 Speaking

Do the *Inspiration Quiz* without looking back in the book. Discuss your answers with another student using question tags. Then look back and check your answers.

INSPIRATION QUIZ

1. Where was Bethany Hamilton bitten by a shark?
2. Which singer did Martin Scorsese first hear when he was 16?
3. Who invented BookCrossing?
4. Who wrote *Sense and Sensibility*?
5. Who did Dorothy Sherry see at her home in 1978?
6. What was the big house in *Rebecca* called?
7. What did Kelly Homes win?
8. Who rode round the world on motorbikes?
9. What things did Leonardo da Vinci invent?
10. How many words can Alex the parrot say?
11. What does ICE stand for?
12. Where is the Three Gorges dam?

> It was on an island, wasn't it?
>
> It begins with H, doesn't it?

8 Writing

Write two paragraphs describing other people or places in *Inspiration 3*. Now read out your paragraphs but don't say the name of the person or place. Can the other students guess who or what it is?

It's a place in the Andes mountains where the Incas used to live. You walk along a long trail until you find the city high up on the edge of a mountain.

8 NATURAL WORLD

4 Integrated Skills
Describing a country

AUSTRALIA

1
Australia is the largest island, the smallest continent, and the sixth largest country in the world. Its total area is 7,686,900 square km – about the same size as the USA (excluding Hawaii and Alaska). Australia lies to the south of Asia, with the Indian Ocean to the west and the Pacific Ocean to the east. The population of Australia is 20 million and the capital city is Canberra, in the south-east of the country. The official language is English, and the currency is the Australian dollar.

2
The Aborigines have lived in Australia for about 50,000 years. In 1788, the British founded a prison colony on the east coast of Australia, and, as more Europeans arrived in Australia, the Aborigines were driven from their land. There are now only about 250,000 Aboriginal Australians, approximately 1% of the total population. The government is now making major efforts to preserve the Aboriginal culture. Over 70% of Australians live in cities or towns, mostly on the south-east and south-west coasts. The largest (and oldest) city is Sydney, with a population of 4.2 million.

3
Australia is famous for its 'outback', the hot dry land of the interior. About two-thirds of the country is rocky desert or semi-desert. On the eastern coastal plains there are areas of grasslands, largely watered by Australia's longest river, the Murray-Darling (3,696 km). Australia also has several mountain ranges; its highest mountain is Mount Kosciuszko (2,228 m) in the south-east. The island of Tasmania lies off the south-west coast of Australia and off the north-east coast is the Great Barrier Reef. This coral reef is over 2,000 km long, and is the largest living structure in the world.

4
Well-known Australian animals include the kangaroo, koala and platypus, and birds such as the emu and the 'laughing' kookaburra. The tropical rainforests in the north have a huge variety of birds, including the extraordinary cassowary (Australia's largest bird), crocodiles, large lizards – and snakes. And the Great Barrier Reef is home to hundreds of sharks and thousands of tropical fish.

5
Australia's major industry is mining (including coal, copper, gold and iron). Tourism is also an important industry, thanks to the climate, scenery and wildlife. Most of the country is too dry to grow crops, but some areas produce sugar cane, wheat, and grapes for wine. Australia is probably best-known for sheep-farming – huge numbers of sheep are raised for their wool and meat.

6
Australia's typical climate is warm, with lots of sunshine and little rain. Average temperatures in Sydney are 8 to 16°C in July and 18 to 26°C in January. Much of the Australian interior has a continental climate, with high temperatures during the day which drop considerably at night. There are often monsoons in the tropical north, and hurricanes and cyclones on the north-east and north-west coasts. But droughts are also common – more than 33% of the country has less than 26mm of rain a year.

1 Opener

Which of these words do you associate with Australia? Which do you associate with Canada? Which words refer to weather?

coral reef   cyclone   desert   drought
forest   grasslands   ice   monsoon
outback   prairie   rainforest   tundra

Reading

2 Read the guidebook description of Australia and match these headings with paragraphs 1–6.

Geography   Industry and agriculture
Key facts   The people   Weather   Wildlife

🎧 Now listen and check.

UNIT 8

3 Student A Ask Student B questions 1–8 about Australia.

Student B Answer the questions as quickly as possible.

1 How big is Australia?
2 What's its capital city?
3 How many Aborigines live there today?
4 What's the population of Sydney?
5 What's the highest mountain?
6 What's special about the Great Barrier Reef?
7 What's the most important industry?
8 What's Australia's typical climate like?

Now change roles. Ask and answer questions 9–16.

9 What's the population of Australia?
10 How long have the Aborigines lived there?
11 How many Australians live in cities and towns?
12 What's the longest river?
13 Where is Tasmania?
14 Name two Australian animals and two birds.
15 What kind of farming is Australia famous for?
16 Where are monsoons common?

4 Listening

🎧 Look at the factfile and listen to a description of Canada.

Student A   Listen and complete the notes in the yellow sections.

Student B   Listen and complete the notes in the blue sections.

CANADA FACTFILE

Area: _____ million square km   Population: _____
Capital: Ottawa   Official languages: English, _____
Currency: Canadian _____

Number of Native Canadians: _____
_____% of Canadians live in cities/towns.
_____% live within 200 km of US border.
Largest city: Toronto (_____ million)

_____ Canada: mainly forest, tundra, ice and snow
_____ Canada: Rocky Mountains
Highest mountain: Mount Logan (_____ m)
West-central Canada: prairie grassland
_____-central plains: major industrial areas
Most _____ river: St Lawrence
_____ river: Mackenzie (4,241 km)
Niagara Falls: _____ falls in the world
Also _____ lakes, over 60% of the world's lakes

Industry: _____, oil and gas, _____, motor vehicles, _____.
Agriculture: wheat, _____ and vegetables

Canadian wildlife: polar _____, moose, caribou, elk, brown bear, grizzly bear, several kinds of wild cat, _____ off east/west coasts
Over _____ different kinds of birds

_____ Canada: short hot summers, long cold winters
_____ and _____ coasts: warmer winters, cooler summers
Ottawa average temperatures: minus 15° to minus _____ °C in January; 15° to _____ °C in July
_____ Canada: extremely cold all year
West and south-east Canada: a lot of _____; other areas much drier.

5 Speaking

Students A and B work together. Use your notes from exercise 4 to tell each other about Canada.

If you could visit either Australia or Canada, which would you choose? Tell each other why.

6 Writing

Write a description of your country or a country which you are interested in. Use the text about Australia to help you.

7 Learner Independence

Where can you read or hear English outside school? Tick the chart, and add more headings if possible.

	Read	Hear
in shops		
in restaurants/cafés		
in hotels		
at the travel agent's		
in museums		
at the cinema		
on TV/on the radio		
on the Internet		
at the railway station		

Now compare your chart with another student. Give examples of things you can see/hear in English, for example:

notices and signs   brochures
announcements   news programmes

8 Word creation: complete the chart with adjectives ending in -al.

Noun	Adjective	Noun	Adjective
coast		industry	
continent		music	
electric		nature	
environment		office	
globe		tropics	

9 Phrasebook

🎧 Listen and repeat these useful expressions. Then find them in this unit.

In other words, …   What would you do?
What if …?   If I were you, I'd …
I've got hiccoughs.   I've got toothache.
I've got a headache.   I get it.   You must be joking.

Now think of three different ways to complete each of the three incomplete expressions.

> **Unit 8** Communication Activity
> Student **A** page 108
> Student **B** page 118

99

8 NATURAL WORLD
Inspiration *Extra!*

PROJECT Urban Survival File

Make a file giving advice to a visitor about how to survive in your town.

1. Work in a group and look at the Survival Questionnaire in Lesson 2. It deals with survival in the wild. But what about the urban jungle – survival in your town or a big city in your country? What would you do in difficult or dangerous situations?

2. Make notes to answer these questions:

   Are there places which are not safe for young people during the day or night? Why?
   What about crime – pickpockets, for example?
   How can you contact the police if you have a problem?
   What should you do if you have an accident?

3. Work together and make an Urban Survival File. Read it carefully and correct any mistakes. Draw pictures or use photographs from magazines or newspapers. Show your Urban Survival File to the other groups.

GAME Word Race

- Work in small groups.
- Choose a topic from this list. Then each write down as many words as you can about that topic in one minute.

  backpacking   buildings   places
  school   illness   water   weather

- Compare your results and make sure all the words are to do with the topic. Then check the meanings of the words other students have which you don't. The student with the most words wins.

LIMERICK

Read and listen.

There was a young woman called Mabel
Who wanted to dance on the table
'Don't know if I should
I would if I could
But I'm not sure if I'm able.'

SONG

Listen and complete with the missing words.

I Will Survive

First I was __1__
I was petrified
Kept thinking I could never live
Without you by my side
But I spent so many nights
Thinking how you did me wrong
And I grew __2__
And I learned how to get along
And so you're back
From outer space!
I just walked in to find you here
With that __3__ look upon your face
I should have changed that __4__ lock
I should have made you leave your key
If I'd known for just one second
You'd be back to bother me

Chorus
Go on now, go!
Walk out the door!
Just turn around now
'Cause you're not __5__ anymore
Weren't you the one
Who tried to hurt me with goodbye?
Did you think I'd crumble?
Did you think I'd lay down and die?
Oh no, not I!
I will survive
Oh, as long as I know how to love
I know I'll stay __6__
I've got all my life to live
I've got all my love to give
And I'll survive
I will survive
Hey, hey

It took all the strength I had
Not to fall apart
Kept trying hard to mend
The pieces of my __7__ heart
And I spent oh so many nights
Just feeling __8__ for myself
I used to cry
But now I hold my head up __9__
And you see me
Somebody __10__
I'm not that chained up little person
Still in love with you
And so you felt like dropping in
And you expect me to be __11__
Now I'm saving all my loving
For someone who's loving me

Chorus (twice)

100

UNIT 8

REVISION *for more practice*

LESSON 1

Your friend Max is always getting into trouble. This is what happened yesterday morning. Write sentences telling him what he should and shouldn't have done.

He was late for school because he missed the bus.
He missed the bus because he got up late.
He got up late because he didn't wake up on time.
He didn't wake up on time because he forgot to set his alarm clock.
He didn't remember to set it because he went to bed very late.

You shouldn't have been late for school. You ...

LESSON 2

Write sentences saying what you would feel and what you would do in these imaginary situations:

you're lost in a strange town
you're on a train and you've lost your ticket
you've revised for the wrong questions in an exam
you've chosen clothes in a shop but then find you don't have any money on you

If I were lost in a strange town, I would ...

LESSON 3

Add question tags to sentences 1–8 in exercise 3 on page 97.

1 *It was Tiffany's idea to visit the exhibition, wasn't it?*

EXTENSION *for language development*

LESSON 1

Think about situations where a friend or member of your family forgot something, or made a mistake, or did something wrong. Write sentences about what they should or shouldn't have done.

My friend Tim should have said sorry when he forgot to meet me.

LESSON 2

Imagine that you were head or director of your school for a day. Write sentences saying what things you would change and why.

First of all, I would pay the teachers a lot more because teaching us is hard work.

LESSON 3

Look back through *Inspiration 3*. Which lessons did you enjoy most and why? Which lessons were more difficult and why? Now work with another student and guess which lessons they enjoyed most or found more difficult and why.

> You really enjoyed the lesson about describing pictures, didn't you? I think it's because you like art.

YOUR CHOICE!

CONSTRUCTION Question tags

Complete with the correct question tag.
1 They enjoyed the exhibition, _____ _____ ?
2 She'd been a surfer for a long time, _____ _____ ?
3 He'd like to stay in a cave hotel, _____ _____ ?
4 She's been a runner for 12 years, _____ _____ ?
5 It's the best lesson in the book, _____ _____ ?
6 Koko understands 2,000 words, _____ she?
7 The researcher asked her to get the keys, _____ she?
8 He would run away, _____ _____ ?

REFLECTION Question tags

Match the beginnings of the rules with the endings.
1 In the present simple we make the tag
2 In the past simple we make the tag
3 When the main verb is *be* in the present and past simple we make the tag
4 In the present perfect and past perfect we make the tag

a with *is/isn't, are/aren't, was/wasn't* and *were/weren't*.
b with *do/does* or *don't/doesn't*.
c with *has/hasn't, have/haven't* and *had/hadn't*.
d with *did/didn't*.

ACTION Back to the board game

- Work in a small group.
- Student A stands with his/her back to the board. Student B chooses a word from this unit, writes it on the board so that the other students can see it, and tells student A the first letter of the word.
- Student A asks the other students up to ten *Yes/No* questions to find the word.
  Is it a noun?
  Is it an animal?
- If A guesses the word, he/she chooses the next word.

INTERACTION
If you were a ..., what ... would you be?

Ask each other questions using these words.

colour   animal   kind of food   car   sport   kind of music
TV programme   sound   country   month

A If you were a colour, what colour would you be?
B If I were a colour, I'd be green because …

101

REVIEW UNITS 7–8

Grammar

1 Read and complete. For each number 1–12, choose word or phrase A, B or C.

Teenager saves tourist in rainforest

How __1__ you survive if you were lost in the rainforest? A tourist who was lost for a week in the rainforest of Queensland, north-eastern Australia, said he __2__ on bananas and chewing gum.

Stuart Ridley was rescued __3__ a teenager on a helicopter tour had seen him flashing sunlight off a mirror from his camera. Ridley, 27, explained that he __4__ his car because he wanted a closer look at wildlife in the rainforest. But it was dark when he turned back, __5__ he couldn't find his car.

Reporters asked Ridley how he __6__ during his week in the rainforest. He __7__ them he had found plenty of water to drink – he was in the wettest part of Australia – but he had got very hungry. 'I only had six bananas and a packet of chewing gum in my rucksack.' And he was also concerned __8__ snakes – the Queensland rainforest is home to the taipan, one of the most dangerous snakes in the world.

Ridley saw helicopters flying overhead during the week but he couldn't __9__ their attention. Finally, a teenage helicopter passenger, Susie Ward, 15, saw the light from the mirror and asked the pilot __10__ back round the area.

When Ridley was picked up and flown to safety, he apologised for causing trouble. 'I __11__ have left my car', he said. He was very grateful to the teenager who spotted him from the helicopter. 'She probably saved my life, __12__ she?

1	A will	B would	C did
2	A live	B did live	C lived
3	A after	B by	C while
4	A would leave	B had left	C did leave
5	A so	B then	C because
6	A did survive	B survive	C had survived
7	A said	B told	C replied
8	A about	B because	C of
9	A pull	B make	C attract
10	A to fly	B flying	C fly
11	A should	B shouldn't	C oughtn't
12	A did	B had	C didn't

2 Write sentences reporting the requests with *asked* and the commands with *told*.

1 Mrs Evans said, 'Leo, will you tidy your room, please.'
2 The teacher said, 'Students, don't make so much noise.'
3 Julie said, 'Simon, you must take it easy.'
4 The researcher said, 'Kanzi, would you get my keys back?'
5 'Bethany, try it one more time,' said her father.
6 'Jake, please don't be late,' said Tiffany.
7 The police officer shouted 'Stop!' at the thief.
8 'Think of me as your friend,' said Adam to the contestants.

3 Report these statements.

'I'm going for a swim,' said Shane.
Shane said he was going for a swim.

1 'I'm not looking for a girlfriend,' said Leo.
2 'I want to change the world,' said Tiffany.
3 'I danced for five hours,' said Kate.
4 'I can't concentrate for long,' said Rob.
5 'We'll try to solve the mystery,' said Sherlock Holmes.
6 'I've never enjoyed myself so much,' said Kirsty.
7 'We must drive back to Manderley tonight,' said Max.
8 'I won't let success go to my head,' said Kelly.

4 Jake looked worried, so Tiffany asked him questions. Report her questions using *asked*.

'Are you all right?'
She asked if he was all right.

1 'What's the matter?'
2 'Where did you lose it?'
3 'How much money was in it?'
4 'Do you know the number of the bus?'
5 'Have you told the police?'
6 'Are you going to phone them?'
7 'Why aren't you more careful?'

5 Rewrite these sentences using *should/shouldn't have*.

He was wrong to drive so fast.
He shouldn't have driven so fast.

1 Why didn't you ask me to help you?
2 I was silly to stay out so late last night.
3 Why didn't the students work harder?
4 It was a bad idea for us to sail the dinghy in the storm.
5 You were wrong to read my diary.
6 Why didn't you phone the police?
7 The team ought to have won the match.
8 Why did I listen to you?

UNITS 7-8 REVIEW

6 Write sentences using the correct form of the verbs: past simple or *would*.

1. If I (have) toothache, I (go) to the dentist.
2. You (not get) hiccoughs if you (not eat) so quickly.
3. Where (you/live) if you (can) live anywhere?
4. If you (be) on a roller coaster, how (you/feel)?
5. If I (know) the answer, I (tell) you.
6. The singer (not perform) well if she (have) a sore throat.
7. If we (not have) water, we (die).
8. What (you/say) if your country (win) the World Cup?

7 Give advice to someone who can't sleep at night, using *If I were you, I'd/I wouldn't …* and these phrases.

1. drink coffee in the evening
2. buy a new bed
3. try to relax
4. eat cheese for supper
5. read ghost stories in bed
6. stop worrying about it

8 Complete with question tags.

1. Bob Brotchie invented ICE, _____?
2. It didn't take him long, _____?
3. You'd like to go to the party, _____?
4. You don't want to be late, _____?
5. It hasn't rained for ages, _____?
6. We waste a lot of water, _____?
7. Emus can't fly, _____?
8. Chimpanzees have got tails, _____?

Vocabulary

9 Complete with these words.

> agriculture attachment beef breath
> currency emergency honey shelter
> shortage snail solution tight

1. I can't walk in these shoes – they're too _____.
2. You can't use a hosepipe because there's a _____ of water.
3. Regular rainfall is essential for successful _____.
4. Don't worry – I have the _____ to your problem!
5. I received the email, but I couldn't open the _____.
6. Please hurry up, you're as slow as a _____.
7. If you have a sore throat, try drinking hot lemon and _____.
8. Take a deep _____ and calm down.
9. It was raining hard, so we stood in a shop doorway for _____.
10. When you go abroad, you often need to buy foreign _____.
11. In the UK, you dial 999 to contact the _____ services.
12. Roast _____ is a traditional English meal.

10 Match these words with their definitions.

> bracelet consequence cool a dozen dumb
> igloo peak plain safety trunk

1. opposite of *danger*
2. large flat area of land
3. living space made of ice
4. piece of jewellery worn on the arm
5. highest point
6. elephant's nose
7. opposite of *warm*
8. unable to speak
9. twelve
10. result

11 Match the verbs in list A with the words and phrases in list B.

	A	B
1	attract	your bed
2	clear	your shoes
3	fasten	the tap
4	hold	attention
5	keep	the table
6	make	calm
7	take off	hands
8	turn off	your seatbelt

12 Find the odd word.

1. gorilla lizard tiger zebra
2. candle match torch whistle
3. aspirin dentist doctor vet
4. lake oasis prairie waterfall
5. coal copper gold iron
6. cyclone hurricane monsoon sunshine

PROGRESS CHECK

Now you can …

1. Report requests and commands
2. Report what someone said
3. Report what someone asked
4. Criticise past actions
5. Talk about imaginary or unlikely situations
6. Give advice
7. Ask for agreement and check

Look back at Units 7 and 8 and write an example for 1–7.

1 My mother told me to wash my hands.

How good are you? Tick a box.

★★★ Fine ☐   ★★ OK ☐   ★ Not sure ☐

Not sure about something? Have a look at the Grammar Summary.

CONGRATULATIONS!

You've finished *Inspiration 3*. Well done! Now take some time to reflect on what you've achieved.

★ Grammar

You've revised and extended the grammar which you already knew and you've met and practised new grammar points. Turn to the Grammar Summary on page 109 and see how much you've covered.

★ Vocabulary

The Word List on page 120 lists all the new words in *Inspiration 3* as well as groups of words by topic. On the Contents pages you can find all the vocabulary areas you have covered. Choose some of the areas (eg Films, Leisure activities) and write a list of all the words you can remember for each one.

But you've learnt more than grammar and vocabulary. In *Inspiration 3* you've also learnt to communicate.

★ Communication

You can …
Describe what people usually do and what they're doing now
Talk about past events and how you felt about them
Interview people about important past events in their lives
Express your opinions, and agree or disagree with other views
Say what your plans and hopes are
Describe how something works
Describe a favourite picture and say what it means to you
Talk about what is or isn't against the law
Give advice to people with problems
Describe what your senses tell you
Predict the future
Make promises and offers
Say whether things have happened or not
Interview people about their experiences
Interview people about things they did last year
Describe past habits
Carry out a survey
Describe how something is made
Say what people asked or told you to do
Report an interview
Express regrets about the past
Say what you would do in imaginary situations
Ask for agreement and check that something is true

What else can you do?

You've also developed other language skills.

★ Writing

You can write …
A personal profile
A diary entry
A short news article
A description of an important past event
A short film review
A short book review
A description of a picture
A poem
Definitions of words
Predictions about the future
An email about a journey
A process description
A news story about a rescue
A report of an interview
Advice on what to do
Descriptions of people and places
A description of a country

What else can you write?

★ Reading

You can read …
A questionnaire
A diary entry
An interview
A sketch
Descriptions of films
An article about a TV reality show
A quiz
A magazine article about favourite pictures
A newspaper story about unusual laws
A website problem page
An article about international aid
Descriptions of great novels
An article about the 'return' of the dead
A story
A newspaper article about a journey
An article about extreme sports
An online diary about a journey
Poems and limericks
A magazine article about inventions
An article about recycling
An article about animals learning language
An article about emergencies
A magazine article about English around the world
An article about water
A guidebook description of a country

What else can you read?

★ Listening

You can listen to and understand …
An interview about personal details
A phone conversation
Descriptions of past events
A song
A TV game show
A conversation about laws in the UK
A story
A conversation about a magazine article
A description of a journey
A description of a process
Instructions
An interview about emergencies
A radio news report
A description of a country

What else can you listen to and understand?

You've also developed another very important skill.

★ Learner Independence

You have learnt …
How to keep a Learning Diary
How to keep a personal phrasebook
Ways to create words using prefixes and suffixes
Phrases you can use to ask questions in class
How to discuss classroom rights and responsibilities
How to guess the meanings of words
How to make adjectives from nouns and nouns from verbs
How to assess your own progress
Ways of using the Internet to improve your language skills
How to use resources for practising English out of school

How do you feel?

Have a class discussion about your English lessons and *Inspiration 3*.

Talk about
- Three things you liked about the lessons
- Three things you liked about the Student's Book and the Workbook
- Three things that you learnt (apart from English!)
- Activities and exercises you would like to do more often
- Activities and exercises you would like to do less often
- Something you would like to change
- What you would like to do in your English lessons next year

Now write a letter to your teacher giving your opinions.

COMMUNICATION ACTIVITIES
STUDENT A

UNIT 1

Read the text. Then ask Student B questions to complete it. Answer Student B's questions.

> What was John Ferreira doing?

ANIMAL ATTACKS
Believe it or not – all these stories are true!

Californian John Ferreira was ___1___ (what/do?) with friends one afternoon when he saw a great white shark. It was ___2___ (what/do?) straight towards the friends, and there wasn't time to get back to the beach. When the shark's huge jaws opened, John pushed his surfboard into its mouth. The shark's jaws closed on it and didn't open again. Meanwhile John and his friends swam ___3___ (where?).

It was a quiet Saturday in Baton Rouge, Louisiana. Maddie Mix was driving ___4___ (where?) when suddenly 10,000 bees attacked her car. The bees covered the car and it was hard for Maddie to ___5___ (what/do?). She noticed that she was passing a garage which had a car wash. Quickly Maddie drove ___6___ (where?) and the bees flew away.

In ___7___ (when?), Rodney Fluery of Mountain, California, and his dog Randy had a lucky escape. Rodney and Randy were walking near his house when the dog suddenly ___8___ (what/do?). Something was moving in the grass in front of them. It was a ___9___ (what?) – one of the most dangerous snakes in the USA. The snake came closer and then attacked the dog. But Rodney was quicker than the snake. He ___10___ (what/do) the snake and bit its neck. Soon the snake was dead and Rodney and Randy were safe.

UNIT 2

Describe the painting and ask questions about Student B's painting. Work together to find as many differences as possible between the two paintings.

106

STUDENT A

UNIT 3

Two people are discussing nuclear power. The sentences in the box are one person's part of the debate. But the sentences are not in the right order.

NUCLEAR POWER, NO THANKS

☐ Let's start with the situation today. We have to do something about global warming – the world is getting hotter and hotter.

☐ But wind and wave power won't give us all the energy we need. Anyway, the fact is that nuclear power is here now, and we must use it and build more power stations.

☐ I can't believe that it's 40%. And the other thing about nuclear power is that it's safe.

☐ That's right and we don't need to look far for other ways of producing energy. Nuclear power works and it doesn't produce the greenhouse gases that cause global warming.

Work with Student B to put the debate in the right order. Don't look at Student B's sentences. You begin the debate: 'Let's start with the situation today …'

UNIT 4

Give definitions of these words to Student B, but don't say the word.

> Number 1. It's a holiday people have after they get married.

1. honeymoon
2. superstition
3. lucky charm
4. library
5. tunnel
6. frequently

Now listen to Student B's definitions of these words. If you guess the word write it down, but don't say it.

7. _ _ r _ s _ _ p _
8. _ r _ _ s _
9. _ u _ t _ _
10. i _ _ t _ _ c _ _ _
11. _ a _ _ _ r
12. _ _ b _ l _ _ c _

Then check your answers with Student B.

UNIT 5

Tiffany and three of her friends are going to Spain on holiday tomorrow. Ask Student B questions to complete the chart.

A Has Tiffany packed her bag?
B Yes, she's already packed it.
A Has Tiffany found her passport?
B No, she hasn't found it yet.

	Tiffany	Pam	Kate	Jane
pack her bag		✗	✓	
find her passport			✗	✓
buy a phrasebook	✓	✓		
check her ticket	✗			✓
decide what clothes to take		✗	✓	
buy a book to read	✓			✗
say goodbye to her boyfriend			✓	✗
see the weather forecast	✓	✓		

Now look at the chart and answer Student B's questions.

B Has Tiffany bought a phrasebook?
A Yes, she's already bought one.
B Has Tiffany checked her ticket?
A No, she hasn't checked it yet.

107

STUDENT A

UNIT 6

Read the instructions and complete the chart. Then read the instructions to Student B.

1. Write today's date in the top left hand corner.
2. Below today's date write the first month of the year.
3. In the bottom right hand corner write your teacher's name.
4. Above the teacher's name write the number of days in a year.
5. On the right of the first month of the year write teenage inventor Gina's surname.
6. Between Gina's surname and the number of days in a year write Braille's first name.
7. In the top right hand corner write the number of days in April.
8. Below Gina's surname write the number of hours in a day.
9. In the bottom left-hand corner write the year da Vinci designed the car.
10. On the right of today's date write the name of your school.
11. Between the number of hours in a day and your teacher's name write the sixth month of the year.
12. On the left of the number of days in April write the name of the inventor of paper.

Now listen to Student B's instructions and complete this chart.

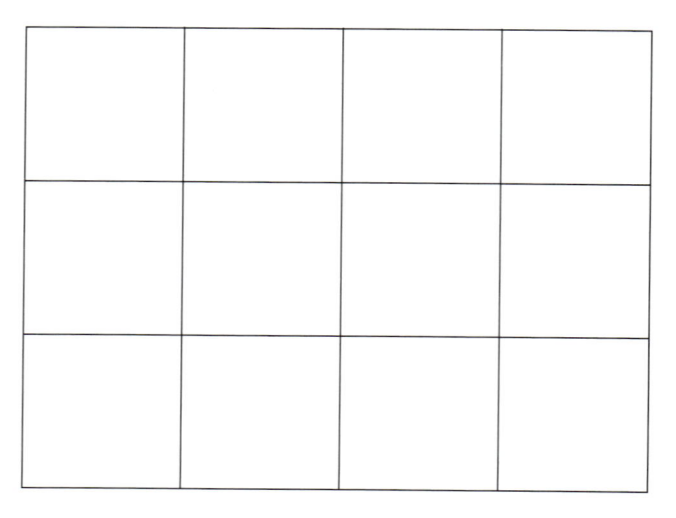

Now compare your charts.

UNIT 7

Describe these creatures to Student B without saying their names.

Now listen to Student B's descriptions of five creatures. What are they?

UNIT 8

Student B has the missing words from this crossword. You have Student B's missing words. Don't say the words! Take turns to ask each other for clues and try to complete the crossword.

A What's 1 down?
B Australia is one.

B What's 1 across?
A It's a kind of metal.

Crossword (filled entries):
- 1 across: COPPER
- 5 down: LIGHT
- 7 across: TAKE
- 8 across: TORCH
- 9 across: NOISY
- 10 across: SIGN
- 11 down: (part of SIGN)
- 13 across: NEEDLE
- 14 down: (part of NEEDLE)
- 15 across: MIRROR

108

GRAMMAR SUMMARY

Present simple and present continuous
UNIT 1 LESSON 1

- We use the present simple to talk about states, routines, timetables and regular actions:
  He lives in Manchester.
  All the girls like older boys.
  At weekends, I listen to music.
  We go to clubs every Saturday night.
  He doesn't want a girlfriend.
  Do you have a girlfriend?

- We also use the present simple to talk about what people do in their jobs and occupations:
  What do you do? (= What's your job?)
  I'm a teacher.
  He's a politician.

- We use the present continuous to talk about temporary events and what is happening now.
  He's learning Spanish.
  We're destroying the planet.
  I'm not looking for a girlfriend.
  What are you reading at the moment?

- We can also use the present continuous to talk about future arrangements, and we often say the time and/or place:
  What are you doing at half term?
  I'm spending a week in New York.
  See also Unit 4 Lesson 2.

- We form the present continuous with *am/is/are* + present participle (*-ing* form).

- **Spelling:** verb + *-ing*
  Most verbs add *-ing*:
     learn – learn**ing**   read – read**ing**
  Verbs ending in *-e* drop the *-e* and add *-ing*:
     writ**e** – writ**ing**   mak**e** – mak**ing**
  But we don't make a change after *be* or *-ee*:
     be – be**ing**   see – see**ing**
  Other verbs:
     get – ge**tt**ing   swim – swi**mm**ing   run – ru**nn**ing
     put – pu**tt**ing   sit – si**tt**ing   travel – trave**ll**ing

Adverbial phrases of frequency
UNIT 1 LESSON 1

How often?	
every	day
	night
once a	week
twice a	month
three times a	year

- We use adverbial phrases of frequency to answer the question: *How often …?* They usually go at the end of the sentence:
  She goes to parties every Friday night.
  I go to the cinema once or twice a month.

Past simple
UNIT 1 LESSONS 2 AND 3

- There are two past simple forms of *be*: *was* and *were*:
  This was our holiday.
  We were really excited.
  I wasn't good enough.
  Was she also on the phone home?

- **Regular verbs**
  Spelling: affirmative forms of regular verbs
  Most verbs add *-ed*:
     want – want**ed**   call – call**ed**
  Verbs ending in *-e* add *-d*:
     apologise – apologise**d**   like – like**d**
  Verbs ending in a consonant and *-y* drop the *-y* and add *-ied*:
     cr**y** – cr**ied**   worr**y** – worr**ied**
  But we don't drop the *-y* after a vowel:
     pla**y** – pla**yed**   enjo**y** – enjo**yed**

- **Irregular verbs**
  There is a complete list of all the irregular verbs in *Inspiration 3* on page 127.

- **Regular** and **irregular** verbs both form the negative and questions in the same way.
  It didn't bother me.
  It didn't mean anything to me.
  Why did I hate every minute of it?
  Did she feel the same as me?

Past simple and past continuous
UNIT 1 LESSON 3

- We use the past simple to describe a completed event or a short action at a particular time in the past:
  The attack happened so fast.
  I didn't scream.

                              Past simple
                                   ↓
  ──▶
                              Past continuous

- We use the past continuous to describe a longer activity, to give the background to an event in the past simple. The event in the past simple often 'interrupts' the past continuous activity.
  She was waiting for the next big wave when she saw the shark.
  She asked everyone 'When can I surf again?' while she was recovering in hospital.
  What was she thinking when the shark attacked?

- We often use *when* and *while* to link past events.
  When a wave came, I caught it.
  While he was swimming, he heard a splash.
  See also Linking words on page 115.

- We form the past continuous with *was/were* + present participle (*-ing* form).

109

GRAMMAR SUMMARY

Verb + gerund
UNIT 2 LESSON 1

- A gerund (*-ing* form) is a noun formed from a verb. We can use a gerund after these verbs:
  avoid enjoy go (+ activity) hate can't help keep like love mind risk can't stand start stop
  He can't avoid meeting the monsters.
  You can't help laughing.
  Zombies keep attacking people.
  She risks losing her life.
  They start fighting to save the world.
- We can also use a gerund after prepositions:
  Bob gave **up** being a superhero.
  He's fed up **with** living a normal life.
  They dream **of** winning the competition.
  They are incredibly good **at** spelling.
  Can they succeed **in** rescuing her?
  I feel **like** buying a DVD.
  I'm not keen **on** watching musicals.

so/nor + auxiliary verbs
UNIT 2 LESSON 1

Agreeing
I love …	So do I.
I'm scared of …	So am I.
I don't mind …	Nor do I.
I can't stand …	Nor can I.

- We use *so* + auxiliary verb to agree with affirmative statements.
- We use *nor* + auxiliary verb to agree with negative statements.

Verb + infinitive
UNIT 2 LESSON 2

- We can use *to* + infinitive after these verbs:
  agree ask decide expect help hope know how learn manage mean need offer pretend promise refuse seem teach tell want would like
- These verbs **always** take an object before the infinitive:
  teach tell
  I can teach **you** to dance.
  He told **us** to try new dance steps.
- These verbs **never** take an object before the infinitive:
  agree decide hope know how learn manage offer pretend refuse seem
  I hope to help you.
  They learn to sing.
  Most contestants manage to do it.
  Don't pretend to be a poet.
  Don't refuse to experiment.

- These verbs **often** take an object before the infinitive:
  ask expect help mean need promise want would like
  I expect **you** to practise hard.
  I expect to be on time.
  We can help **you** to develop your talents.
  We can help to cook supper.
  I promised **her** to work hard.
  Promise to work together.
  I want **you** to listen carefully.
  I want to go home.
  I'd like **you** to visit me.
  I'd like to welcome you.
- See also Unit 7 Lesson 1.

Present simple passive
UNIT 2 LESSON 3

- We use the passive to focus on the action rather than the agent (the person or thing that performs the action):
  The book is registered at www.bookcrossing.com.
  You are invited to pick it up.
  Each book is labelled.
- When we want to refer to the agent, we use *by* + noun:
  The books are found by other people.
  The website is visited by thousands of members.
- We form the present simple passive with the present tense of *be* + past participle. There is a complete list of all the irregular past participles in *Inspiration 3* on page 127.
- See also Unit 6 Lesson 3.

must and can't
UNIT 3 LESSON 1

- We use *must* and *can't* to make logical deductions.
- We use *must* to show that we are sure that something is true:
  It must be you because your answers match the profile.
  You must be joking!
- We use *can't* to show that we are sure that something is untrue:
  It can't be Colin because he prefers meat.
  You can't be serious.
- We don't use *mustn't* to make deductions.
- See also Unit 3 Lesson 2.

could, may and might
UNIT 3 LESSON 1

- We use *could*, *may* and *might* to show we think something is possibly true:
  Jack could be at home. He may be at the gym.
  He might be away. (Less likely)

110

GRAMMAR SUMMARY

must and mustn't/can't have to and don't have to
UNIT 3 LESSON 2

- We can use both *must* and *have to* to express present and future obligation, often when talking about rules:
  You must/You have to = *It's obligatory*.
  You must stay awake in a cheese factory.
  They have to avoid the police.
  Everyone has to obey the law.
- We often use *must* instead of *have to* to show we feel strongly about something:
  You must stop smoking.
- We can use *mustn't* and *can't* to express present and future prohibition: You mustn't/You can't = *It's not allowed*.
  You mustn't fall asleep.
  You can't take a lion to the cinema.
- You can = *It's allowed*.
- We use *don't have to* to express lack of obligation:
  You don't have to = *It's not necessary*.
  Americans don't have to worry.
- The past tense of both *must* and *have to* is *had to*:
  The students had to plan their journey carefully.
- See also Unit 3 Lesson 1.

Reflexive pronouns
UNIT 3 LESSON 2

myself	ourselves
yourself	yourselves
himself/herself/itself	themselves

- We use a reflexive pronoun when the subject and the object are the same:
  He enjoys himself. (NOT *He enjoys him.*)
- We often use reflexive pronouns after these verbs and phrases:
  behave enjoy express find help hurt
  look after take care of
- Reflexive pronouns aren't usually used after:
  feel get up hurry remember wake up worry
- We also use reflexive pronouns for emphasis:
  Do it yourself!

should/ought to and shouldn't had better
UNIT 3 LESSON 3

- We can use *should/ought to* and *shouldn't* to give advice and warnings:
  You should try to ignore them.
  You ought to accept her apology.
  They shouldn't copy your work.
  What should I do?
- *should* and *ought to* have the same meaning. They are not as strong as *must* and *have to*.
- There is no *to* between *should* and the main verb; *ought* is followed by *to* + infinitive.
- The negative form *oughtn't to* is less common than *shouldn't*:
  They oughtn't to copy your work.
- We can use *had better* instead of *should* when something is important **now**:
  You'd better tell your friends and family.
  You'd better not tell her any more secrets!

Adjective + infinitive
UNIT 3 LESSON 3

- We can use *to* + infinitive after these adjectives:
  difficult easy good hard helpful illegal
  important (im)possible lucky nice normal
  pleased rude silly wrong
  I think it's difficult to keep a secret.
  It's normal to feel nervous about exams.
  We were lucky to get away from the shark.
  Pleased to meet you!

Verbs of perception + present participle can/could + verbs of perception
UNIT 4 LESSON 1

- We use the present participle after *see, watch, notice, hear, listen to, smell* and *feel* to talk about a continuous activity:
  People see Elvis walk**ing** out of a café.
  They hear him singing.
  I saw him biting his nails.
- We often use **can/could** before *see, hear, smell, taste,* and *feel*:
  I can feel him holding my hand.
  I could hear birds singing.
  Cats can't taste sugar.

111

GRAMMAR SUMMARY

will/won't, shall and going to
UNIT 4 LESSON 2

- We can use *will* and *won't* (*will not*) to say what we hope or predict for the future:
  I'll have seven years' bad luck.
  I hope we won't see any ghosts.
- We also use *will* and *won't* for offers, promises, and decisions made at the time of speaking:
  I'll lend you my lucky charm.
  I'll read out your horoscope.
  I'll keep my fingers crossed!
  Never mind – I'll buy another mirror.
- We can also use *Shall I …?* to make offers:
  Shall I read out your horoscope?
  Shall I help you to revise this evening?
- We use *going to* + infinitive to talk about future plans and intentions:
  I'm going to stay at home all day.
  Are you going to go out?
  I'm not going to worry about it.
- We also use *going to* + infinitive to predict the future from present evidence which suggests that something is very likely to happen:
  I can hear footsteps – we're going to see the ghost!
- There is sometimes very little difference in meaning between *going to* + infinitive (plans and intentions) and the present continuous (future arrangements):
  He's going to see the dentist tomorrow.
  (Plan: He probably has an appointment.)
  He's seeing the dentist tomorrow.
  (Arrangement: He has an appointment.)
  We often use the present continuous to avoid the phrase *going to go*:
  Are you going (to go) out later?

First conditional
UNIT 4 LESSON 3

- We use the first conditional to talk about the possible future when discussing the consequences of actions or events:
  If you fly in a small plane, you'll feel better about going up in a big one.
  If you press that button, you'll talk to Matt.
  If you listen carefully, I'll tell you what to do.
- We often leave out the conditional verb when the meaning is clear:
  What (will you do) if you can't sleep tonight?
- First conditional sentences have this structure:
  If + present simple, future simple
- The *if* clause can also follow the main clause:
  Future simple *if* + present simple
  You'll talk to Matt if you press that button.

Present perfect
UNIT 5 LESSONS 1, 2 AND 3

- We can use the present perfect to talk about recent completed actions or events:
  Now they've found the boat.
  Rebecca has won.
  We don't say the exact time of the action or event, but we can refer to an unfinished period of time, for example *all day, today, this week/month/year*.
  I haven't seen her today.
  Have you had fun this week?
- We can use the present perfect with *just* to talk about very recent events:
  They've just arrived in Kazakhstan.
- We use the present perfect with *already* to emphasise that something has happened:
  They've already travelled across Europe.
- We use the present perfect with *yet* to show that we expect something to happen; *yet* goes at the end of negative statements and questions:
  They haven't completed a quarter of their journey yet.
  Have they crossed Asia yet?
- We can also use the present perfect, often with *ever/never*, to talk about experiences in the time up to now.
  ever = at any time. It is used mainly in questions:
  Have you ever wondered what it's like?
  Have you ever wanted to ski off a mountain?
  ever is also used in affirmative statements after superlatives:
  It's the most exciting thing I've ever done.
  never = at no time. It is used mainly in statements:
  I've never tried anything like it.
  I've never enjoyed myself so much.
- We also use the present perfect with *for* and *since* to talk about the unfinished past.
- We use *for* + a period of time to say how long something has lasted:
  I've been a full-time runner for 12 years.
  Simon has had a bad headache for a couple of days.
- We use *since* + a specific point in time to say when something started:
  I've wanted to win a gold medal since I was 14.
  My family have supported me since I started running.
  We've been here since 9am.
- We form the present perfect with *have/has* + past participle.
- For regular verbs the past participle is the same as the past tense: *work, worked, worked*.
- For some irregular verbs the past participle is the same as the past tense, but for many it is different: *be, was/were, been*. There is a complete list of all the irregular verbs in *Inspiration 3* on page 127.
- The past participle of *go* can be *gone* or *been* (= gone and returned):
  He's gone to Rio. = He's in Rio now.
  He's been to Rio. = He's visited Rio but he's not there now.

GRAMMAR SUMMARY

Present perfect and past simple
UNIT 5 LESSONS 2 AND 3

- We can use the present perfect to talk about an indefinite time in the past:
  Kite surfing has recently become very popular worldwide.
- We use the past simple to talk about a specific time in the past:
  Kite surfing started in France in the 1980s.
- We use the present perfect with *for* and *since* to talk about the unfinished past:
  I've been at home for three hours.
  I've been at home since 4pm.
- We can express the same ideas using the past simple:
  I came home three hours ago.
  I came home at 4pm.

Past perfect
UNIT 6 LESSON 1

```
     Past perfect      Past simple
          ↓                ↓              NOW
|—————————————————————————————————————|
```

- We use the past perfect to describe the earlier of two past events, to make the order of events clear. We use the past simple for the more recent event:
  She had spent a lot of time in hospital and needed to do exercises.
- If the order of events is clear, we don't need to use the past perfect for the earlier event:
  Soon after she (had) started school, she made a kind of paper.
  But compare these sentences:
  The train left when I reached the station.
  (I saw the train.)
  The train had left when I reached the station.
  (I didn't see the train.)
- We often use the past perfect with *because* to explain why something happened:
  He was OK because he had put his helmet on properly.
- We often use the past perfect with time phrases beginning *by, by the time, since*:
  By the age of 12, she had invented a safer bicycle helmet.
  Ryan had won awards by the time he was 16.
  Louis Braille had been blind since the age of three.
- We form the past perfect with *had* + past participle.
- Contractions of *had*: *I'd/you'd/he'd/she'd/we'd/they'd*

used to + infinitive
UNIT 6 LESSON 2

- We can use *used to* when we talk about past habits and states:
  I used to be a car tyre.
  We used to mend our clothes.
  We didn't use to buy so much.
  Why did we use to buy fewer shoes?
- For present habits and states, we use the present simple:
  He walks to school every day. (NOT *He uses to walk …*)

Past simple passive
UNIT 6 LESSON 3

- We use the past simple passive to focus on a past action rather than the agent:
  The first robot was created in 1865.
  Several attempts were made in the last century.
- When we want to refer to the agent, we use *by* + noun:
  *The car was sketched **by** da Vinci in 1478.*
- We form the past simple passive with *was/were* + past participle.
- See also Unit 2 Lesson 3.

ask/tell + object + infinitive
UNIT 7 LESSON 1

- We can use *ask* + object + infinitive to report requests:
  'Could you wash the potato?'
  → *She asked him to wash the potato.*
  'Please don't go!'
  → *He asked her not to go.*
- We can use *tell* + object + infinitive to report commands and instructions:
  'Calm down!'
  → *He told her to calm down.*
  'Don't be silly!'
  → *The parrot told me not to be silly.*
- See also Unit 2 Lesson 2.

113

GRAMMAR SUMMARY

Reported statements and questions
UNIT 7 LESSONS 2 AND 3

- Tenses, pronouns and possessive adjectives usually change in reported speech.
- **Reported statements: say and tell**
  'I'm not sure.'
  → He said (that) he wasn't sure.
  'The solutions aren't working.'
  → He said (that) the solutions weren't working.
  'It doesn't bother me.'
  → He said (that) it didn't bother him.
  'It took four to six hours.'
  → He said (that) it had taken four to six hours.
  'I've done it.'
  → He told her (that) he had done it.
  'We're going to solve it.'
  → He said (that) they were going to solve it.
  'We must find a better way.'
  → He told her (that) they had to find a better way.
  'I can't remember.'
  → He said (that) he couldn't remember.
  'We'll have to find a solution.'
  → He said (that) they would have to find a solution.
- **Reported questions**
  Reported Yes/No questions: we use *if* before the reported question.
  Reported Wh- questions: we use the question word before the reported question.
  'Is it catching on in other countries?'
  → We asked if it was catching on in other countries.
  'Has anyone used ICE in an emergency yet?'
  → They wanted to know if anyone had used ICE in an emergency yet.
  'How did you get the idea?'
  → We asked how he (had) got the idea.
  'What other jobs have you done?'
  → They asked what other jobs he had done.
  The subject–verb order in reported questions is the same as in statements.
- In reported speech, verbs in the present usually change into the past, and verbs in the past usually change into the past perfect:

Direct speech	Reported speech
Present simple	→ Past simple
Present continuous	→ Past continuous
Past simple	→ Past perfect
Present perfect	→ Past perfect
am/is/are going to	→ was/were going to
must	→ had to
can	→ could
will	→ would

- Time phrases and other reference words also usually change in reported speech:

today	→ that day
tonight	→ that night
tomorrow	→ the next/following day
yesterday	→ the day before
now	→ then
here	→ there
this	→ that/the

should(n't) have/ought to have
UNIT 8 LESSON 1

- We can use *should(n't) have* and *ought to have* to criticise past actions, and to express regret about things people have or haven't done:
  The Chinese should have thought about the human cost.
  They shouldn't have gone ahead with the project.
  They ought to have thought about the consequences.
- *should have* and *ought to have* have the same meaning. The negative form *oughtn't to have* (NOT *ought to haven't*) is less common than *shouldn't have*.

Second conditional
UNIT 8 LESSON 2

- We use the second conditional to talk about imaginary present or unlikely future situations:
  If I met a bear, I would run away as fast as I could.
  If I were near a big tree, I would stand under it for shelter.
  If I were on the edge of a waterfall, I wouldn't jump out of the boat.
  What would you do if you didn't have enough water?
  Note the use of *were* instead of *was* in second conditional sentences.
- We often leave out the conditional verb when the meaning is clear:
  What (would you do) if you were outside in a thunderstorm?
- We use *If I were you, I'd/I wouldn't ...* to give advice:
  If I were you, I'd take some insect spray.
- Second conditional sentences have this structure:
  If + past simple, would(n't) ...
- The *if* clause can also follow the main clause:
  would(n't) ... if + past simple
  I'd take some insect spray if I were you.
- Contractions of *would*: I'd/you'd/he'd/she'd/we'd/they'd

Question tags
UNIT 8 LESSON 3

- We can use question tags with **falling** intonation to ask for agreement when we are sure about something:
  You can see that, can't you?
  You'd like to stay there, wouldn't you?
  You didn't expect me to know that, did you?
  Jake thinks it's in the north-east, doesn't he?
  They went to the exhibition, didn't they?
- We can use question tags with **rising** intonation to check if something is true:
  It's been in the papers, hasn't it?
  The tree house can't hold 300 people, can it?
- When the statement in the first part of the sentence is affirmative, the question tag is negative.
- When the statement in the first part of the sentence is negative, the question tag is affirmative.

Linking words

- We use **and** to connect two similar ideas:
  The beach life was fantastic and the parties lasted all night.
- We use **or** to connect two alternative ideas:
  Which do you prefer: fish or meat?
- We use **but** and **however** to connect two contrasting ideas:
  I wasn't hurt, but I was really embarrassed.
  77% of teens do not know the price of a bottle of milk. However, 66% know how much the Apple iPod Mini costs.
- We can also use **although** to connect two contrasting ideas:
  Although I wasn't hurt, I was really embarrassed.
- We use **because** to talk about reason or cause:
  The city was invisible because it was covered in cloud.
- We use **so** to talk about consequence or result:
  The city was covered in cloud, so it was invisible.
- We use **which** or **that** to refer to things:
  There's a photo which/that means a lot to me.
- We use **who** or **that** to refer to people:
  She's a woman who/that has feelings.
- We use these adverbs to sequence events in narratives:
  first   next   then   after that   afterwards   later   finally
- We use **while** and **when** to link activities or events that happen at the same time:
  While/When he was swimming, he heard a splash.
  We have to use *when* for short actions; *while* suggests longer background events:
  When a wave came, I caught it. (NOT *While a wave came …*)
- **until** means *up to the time when*:
  I laughed until I cried.

COMMUNICATION ACTIVITIES
STUDENT B

UNIT 1

Read the text. Then ask Student A questions to complete it. Answer Student A's questions.

> What did John Ferreira see?

ANIMAL ATTACKS
Believe it or not – all these stories are true!

Californian John Ferreira was surfing with friends one afternoon when he saw a ___1___ (what?). It was swimming straight towards the friends and there wasn't time to get back to the beach. When the shark's huge jaws opened, John pushed ___2___ (what?) into its mouth. The shark's jaws closed on it and didn't open again. Meanwhile John and his friend swam back to the beach.

It was a quiet ___3___ (what day?) in Baton Rouge, Louisiana. Maddie Mix was driving home when suddenly ___4___ (how many?) bees attacked her car. The bees covered the car and it was hard for Maddie to see. She noticed that she was passing ___5___ (what?) which had a car wash. Quickly Maddie drove into the car wash and the bees ___6___ (what/do?).

In 1971, Rodney Fluery of Mountain, California, and his dog Randy had a lucky escape. Rodney and Randy were ___7___ (what/do?) near his house when the dog suddenly stopped. Something was moving ___8___ (where?) in front of them. It was a rattlesnake – one of the most dangerous snakes in the USA. The snake came closer and then ___9___ (what/do?) the dog. But Rodney was quicker than the snake. He picked up the snake and bit ___10___ (what?). Soon the snake was dead and Rodney and Randy were safe.

UNIT 2

Describe the painting and ask questions about Student A's painting. Work together to find as many differences as possible between the two paintings.

STUDENT B

UNIT 3

Two people are discussing nuclear power. The sentences in the box are one person's part of the debate. But the sentences are not in the right order.

NUCLEAR POWER, NO THANKS

☐ I completely disagree. We should close nuclear power stations and not build any more. Nuclear power stations produce dangerous waste. We have to find better ways of producing energy – or learn to use less energy.

☐ Safe? You must be joking. Don't you remember the nuclear accident at Chernobyl? We must use wind and wave power to get energy.

☐ Actually, you're wrong – nuclear power stations do produce greenhouse gases, about 40% of the gases produced by other power stations.

☐ I agree and global warming is caused by burning oil, coal and gas for energy. We should look for other ways of producing energy.

Work with Student A to put the debate in the right order. Don't look at Student A's sentences. Student A begins the debate.

UNIT 4

Listen to Student A's definitions of these words. If you guess the word write it down, but don't say it.

1 _ _ n _ _ m _ o _
2 _ u _ _ _ s _ _ _ i _ _
3 _ u _ k _ _ h _ _ _
4 _ i _ _ _ _ y
5 _ u _ n _ _
6 f _ _ q _ _ n _ _ _

Then check your answers with Student A.

Now give definitions of these words to Student A, but don't say the word.

> Number 7. It makes predictions about your life.

7 horoscope
8 bruise
9 button
10 instructor
11 ladder
12 ambulance

UNIT 5

Tiffany and three of her friends are going to Spain on holiday tomorrow. Look at the chart and answer Student A's questions.

A Has Tiffany packed her bag?
B Yes, she's already packed it.
A Has Tiffany found her passport?
B No, she hasn't found it yet.

	Tiffany	Pam	Kate	Jane
pack her bag	✓			✗
find her passport	✗	✓		
buy a phrasebook			✗	✗
check her ticket		✓	✗	
decide what clothes to take	✓			✗
buy a book to read		✗	✓	
say goodbye to her boyfriend	✗	✗		
see the weather forecast			✗	✓

Now ask Student A questions to complete the chart.

B Has Tiffany bought a phrasebook?
A Yes, she's already bought one.
B Has Tiffany checked her ticket?
A No, she hasn't checked it yet.

117

STUDENT B

UNIT 6

Read the instructions and complete the chart.

1. Write the number of days in the week in the top right hand corner.
2. In the bottom left hand corner write the name of this book.
3. Above the name of this book write the surname of the waterbike inventor.
4. On the left of the number of days in the week write the last month of the year.
5. Below the last month of the year write the year the bicycle was invented.
6. Between the surname of the waterbike inventor and the year the bicycle was invented write the number of seconds in a minute.
7. On the right of the name of this book write the date of Christmas in your country.
8. In the bottom right hand corner write the year da Vinci designed a robot.
9. Above the year da Vinci designed a robot write the colours of your country's flag.
10. In the top left hand corner write the name of your school's headteacher.
11. On the right of the date of Christmas, write the year 'zero' was invented.
12. Between the name of your headteacher and the last month of the year write the number of students in the class.

Then listen to Student A's instructions and complete this chart.

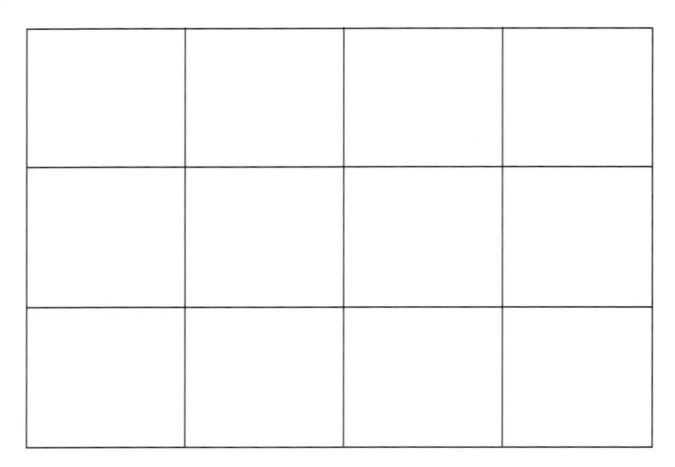

Now read your instructions to Student A.

Then compare your charts.

UNIT 7

Listen to Student A's descriptions of five creatures. What are they?

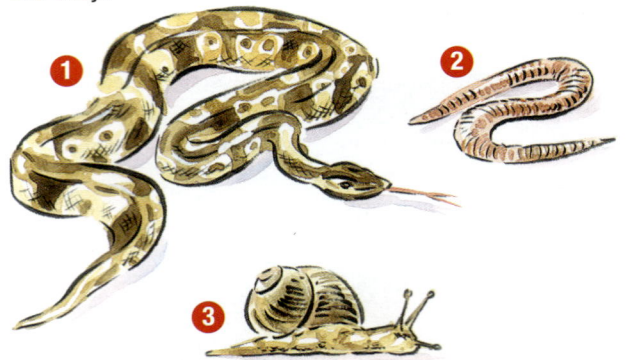

Now describe these creatures to Student A without saying their names.

UNIT 8

Student A has the missing words from this crossword. You have Student A's missing words. Don't say the words! Take turns to ask each other for clues and try to complete the crossword.

A What's 1 down?
B Australia is one.

B What's 1 across?
A It's a kind of metal.

¹C	²P	³E		⁴O	I	⁵L
O		E	M	⁶C		
N		N	U	R		
⁷T		K		⁸O		
I		N		P		
⁹N		I		¹⁰S	¹¹I	
E		F		¹²B		G
¹³N		E	¹⁴D	E		L
T			A	A		O
		¹⁵M		R		O

118

Unit 4 Lesson 2
How superstitious are you?
Questionnaire scores

Mostly As
You're quite superstitious, aren't you! You aren't alone. But try not to let superstitions worry you, because things can go wrong when you worry.

Mostly Bs
You aren't very superstitious and you don't expect bad luck. But you do give in to superstition sometimes, just for fun.

Mostly Cs
You are very rational and down-to-earth. You don't take any notice of superstitions and you don't believe in the supernatural.

Unit 8 Lesson 2
Survival Questionnaire
Questionnaire answers

1. A ✗ If you ate a lot, you'd use up the water in your body.
   B ✓ This would be the best way to avoid losing water.
   C ✗ If you walked as fast as possible, you'd lose water through sweating.

2. A ✗ If lightning hit the tree, you'd be in trouble.
   B ✗ Very bad idea. You should keep away from other people.
   C ✓ This would be the safest thing to do.

3. A ✗ If you ran away, the bear would probably run after you, and bears can run faster than people.
   B ✓ This would be the best way to escape the bear.
   C ✗ Bears can climb trees too.

4. A ✗ If you ran uphill you'd be in more danger because fire travels faster uphill.
   B ✗ This wouldn't be a good idea if the wind was blowing towards the fire.
   C ✓ This would be the best way to escape the fire.

5. A ✓ If you went over the waterfall feet first, you'd be more likely to survive.
   B ✗ If you dived over the waterfall, you could hit your head at the bottom.
   C ✗ If you stayed in the boat, you could be trapped or injured by it.

Score one point for each correct answer.

Scores

1–2 If I were you, I wouldn't leave home!
3–4 I wouldn't feel safe travelling with you!
5 You should survive most dangerous situations.
6 Who are you – James Bond?!

WORD LIST

(adj) = adjective
(adv) = adverb
(conj) = conjunction
(n) = noun
(pron) = pronoun
(v) = verb
(AmE) = American English
(TS) = tapescript

Unit 1

accent (n)	/ˈæksənt/
ambition (n)	/æmˈbɪʃn/
apartment (n) (AmE)	/əˈpɑːtmənt/
apologise (v)	/əˈpɒlədʒaɪz/
attack (n & v)	/əˈtæk/
bite off	/baɪt ˈɒf/
boots (n pl)	/buːts/
bother (v)	/ˈbɒðə/
brakes (n pl)	/breɪks/
bright (colour) (adj)	/braɪt/
Canada	/ˈkænədə/
care (about) (v)	/keə/
championship (n)	/ˈtʃæmpiənʃɪp/
cheer (v)	/tʃɪə/
close (adj)	/kləʊs/
college (n)	/ˈkɒlɪdʒ/
come out (sun) (TS)	/kʌm ˈaʊt/
completely (adv)	/kəmˈpliːtli/
cool (adj)	/kuːl/
cousin (n)	/ˈkʌzn/
crash (v)	/kræʃ/
crime (n)	/kraɪm/
do the dishes	/duː ðə ˈdɪʃɪz/
drugs (n pl)	/drʌgz/
either (adv)	/ˈaɪðə/
energy (n)	/ˈenədʒi/
engine (n)	/ˈendʒɪn/
environment (n)	/ɪnˈvaɪrənmənt/
experience (n)	/ɪkˈspɪəriəns/
fall asleep	/fɔːl əˈsliːp/
fall off	/fɔːl ˈɒf/
fleece (n)	/fliːs/
freedom (n)	/ˈfriːdəm/
friendship (n)	/ˈfrendʃɪp/
funfair (n)	/ˈfʌnfeə/
grow up	/grəʊ ˈʌp/
half term (n)	/hɑːf ˈtɜːm/
Hawaii	/həˈwaɪi/
helmet (n)	/ˈhelmɪt/
home game (n)	/ˈhəʊm geɪm/
human (adj)	/ˈhjuːmən/
in the open	/ɪn ði ˈəʊpn/
incredible (adj)	/ɪnˈkredɪbl/
inspire (v)	/ɪnˈspaɪə/
jaw (n)	/dʒɔː/
kick (n)	/kɪk/
Latin America	/ˌlætɪn əˈmerɪkə/
leave someone alone	/ˌliːv sʌmwʌn əˈləʊn/
look forward to	/lʊk ˈfɔːwəd tə/
mate (n)	/meɪt/
memory (n)	/ˈmemri/
mile (n)	/maɪl/
miss (miss someone) (v)	/mɪs/
mixture (n)	/ˈmɪkstʃə/
motorbike (n)	/ˈməʊtəbaɪk/
musical (adj)	/ˈmjuːzɪkl/
pain (n)	/peɪn/
personal (adj)	/ˈpɜːsnəl/
pier (n)	/pɪə/
politician (n)	/ˌpɒlɪˈtɪʃn/
politics (n)	/ˈpɒlɪtɪks/
power (n)	/paʊə/
professional (adj)	/prəˈfeʃnəl/
punch (v)	/pʌntʃ/
range (n)	/reɪndʒ/
recover (v)	/rɪˈkʌvə/
ride (funfair) (n)	/raɪd/
root (n)	/ruːt/
rubbish (n)	/ˈrʌbɪʃ/
score (v)	/skɔː/
scream (v)	/skriːm/
sense (n)	/sens/
shape (n)	/ʃeɪp/
shock (n)	/ʃɒk/
skates (n pl)	/skeɪts/
store (n) (AmE)	/stɔː/
strength (n)	/streŋθ/
suburb (n)	/ˈsʌbɜːb/
take part (in)	/teɪk ˈpɑːt/
tears (n pl)	/tɪəz/
train (v)	/treɪn/
trendy (adj)	/ˈtrendi/
truth (n)	/truːθ/
turn (= become) (v)	/tɜːn/
vivid (adj)	/ˈvɪvɪd/
warning (n)	/ˈwɔːnɪŋ/
wolf (n)	/wʊlf/

FEELINGS

angry (adj)	/ˈæŋgri/
bored (adj)	/bɔːd/
cheerful (adj)	/ˈtʃɪəfl/
depressed (adj)	/dɪˈprest/
embarrassed (adj)	/ɪmˈbærəst/
excited (adj)	/ɪkˈsaɪtɪd/
fed up (adj)	/fed ˈʌp/
frightened (adj)	/ˈfraɪtnd/
happiness (n)	/ˈhæpɪnəs/
happy (adj)	/ˈhæpi/
lonely (adj)	/ˈləʊnli/
miserable (adj)	/ˈmɪzrəbl/
nervous (adj)	/ˈnɜːvəs/
pleased (adj)	/pliːzd/
sad (adj)	/sæd/
scared (adj)	/skeəd/
terrified (adj)	/ˈterɪfaɪd/
tired (adj)	/ˈtaɪəd/
worried (adj)	/ˈwʌrɪd/

LANGUAGE LEARNING

break (a rule) (v)	/breɪk/
communicate (v)	/kəˈmjuːnɪkeɪt/
coursebook (n)	/ˈkɔːsbʊk/
discussion (n)	/dɪsˈkʌʃn/
examination (n)	/ɪgˌzæmɪˈneɪʃn/
get things wrong	/ˌget θɪŋz ˈrɒŋ/
grammar (n)	/ˈgræmə/
group work (n)	/ˈgruːp wɜːk/
learn by heart	/ˌlɜːn baɪ ˈhɑːt/
learner (n)	/ˈlɜːnə/
organised (adj)	/ˈɔːgənaɪzd/
pair work (n)	/ˈpeə wɜːk/
phrase (n)	/freɪz/
rule (n)	/ruːl/

MUSIC

blues (n)	/bluːz/
country and western (n)	/ˌkʌntri ənd ˈwestən/
drumbeat (n)	/ˈdrʌmbiːt/
folk (n)	/fəʊk/
guitar (n)	/gɪˈtɑː/
mandolin (n)	/ˈmændəlɪn/
rock and roll (n)	/ˌrɒk ən ˈrəʊl/

WATER (1)

lake (n)	/leɪk/
Pacific Ocean	/pəˌsɪfɪk ˈəʊʃn/
splash (n)	/splæʃ/
surf (n & v)	/sɜːf/
surfboard (n)	/ˈsɜːfbɔːd/
surfer (n)	/ˈsɜːfə/
wave (n)	/weɪv/

PHRASAL VERBS WITH GET

get away	/get əˈweɪ/
get back	/get ˈbæk/
get on (well)	/get ˈɒn/
get to	/get tʊ/
get together	/get təˈgeðə/
get up	/get ˈʌp/

PREFIXES DIS- and UN-

(dis)agree (v)	/ˌ(dɪs)əˈgriː/
(dis)appear (v)	/ˌ(dɪs)əˈpɪə/
(un)comfortable (adj)	/ˌ(ʌn)ˈkʌmftəbl/
(un)friendly (adj)	/ˌ(ʌn)ˈfrendli/
(un)happy (adj)	/ˌ(ʌn)ˈhæpi/
(un)lucky (adj)	/ˌ(ʌn)ˈlʌki/
(un)popular (adj)	/ˌ(ʌn)ˈpɒpjələ/
(un)usual (adj)	/ˌ(ʌn)ˈjuːʒʊəl/

CULTURE Identity

although (conj)	/ɔːlˈðəʊ/
belong (v)	/bɪˈlɒŋ/
border (n)	/ˈbɔːdə/
citizen (n)	/ˈsɪtɪzn/
confusing (adj)	/kənˈfjuːzɪŋ/
criticise (v)	/ˈkrɪtɪsaɪz/
dignity (n)	/ˈdɪgnɪti/
economic (adj)	/ˌekəˈnɒmɪk/
fact (n)	/fækt/
identify (v)	/aɪˈdentɪfaɪ/
identity (n)	/aɪˈdentəti/
marks (n pl)	/mɑːks/
nobody (pron)	/ˈnəʊbɒdi/
Pakistani	/ˌpækɪˈstɑːni/
particular (adj)	/pəˈtɪkjələ/
Pole (n)	/pəʊl/
proud (adj)	/praʊd/
religion (n)	/rɪˈlɪdʒn/
soul (n)	/səʊl/
typically (adv)	/ˈtɪpɪkli/

COUNTRIES (1)

Austria	/ˈɒstriə/
Bosnia	/ˈbɒzniə/
Colombia	/kəˈlʌmbiə/
Great Britain	/ˌgreɪt ˈbrɪtn/
Northern Ireland	/ˌnɔːðən ˈaɪələnd/
Pakistan	/ˌpækɪˈstɑːn/
Palestine	/ˈpæləstaɪn/

Unit 2

a great deal	/ə ˌgreɪt ˈdiːl/
account (n)	/əˈkaʊnt/
attend (v)	/əˈtend/
avoid (v)	/əˈvɔɪd/
background (n)	/ˈbækgraʊnd/
bench (n)	/bentʃ/
Best of luck!	/ˌbest əv ˈlʌk/
character (n)	/ˈkærɪktə/
chop (v)	/tʃɒp/
comment (n)	/ˈkɒment/
cover (n)	/ˈkʌvə/

curse (n)	/kɜːs/
cut down	/kʌt 'daʊn/
depend (on) (v)	/dɪ'pend/
dream (of) (v)	/driːm/
enormous (adj)	/ɪ'nɔːməs/
enthusiastic (adj)	/ɪnθjuːzi'æstɪk/
expect (v)	/ɪk'spekt/
experiment (v)	/ɪk'sperɪmənt/
expression (n)	/ɪk'spreʃn/
final (n)	/faɪnl/
finder (n)	/faɪndə/
fit (v)	/fɪt/
globe (n)	/gləʊb/
goal (n)	/gəʊl/
Greek	/griːk/
hard drive (n)	/hɑːd draɪv/
heated (adj)	/hiːtɪd/
in particular	/ɪn pə'tɪkjələ/
in return	/ɪn rɪ'tɜːn/
increasing (adj)	/ɪn'kriːsɪŋ/
incredibly (adv)	/ɪn'kredɪbli/
investigate (v)	/ɪn'vestɪgeɪt/
keen (on) (adj)	/kiːn/
keep (doing something) (v)	/kiːp/
kidnap (v)	/kɪdnæp/
label (n)	/leɪbl/
lie (on)	/laɪ/
low (adj)	/ləʊ/
manage (v)	/mænɪdʒ/
meeting (n)	/miːtɪŋ/
micro-processor (n)	/ˌmaɪkrəʊ'prəʊsesə/
monster (n)	/mɒnstə/
normal (adj)	/nɔːml/
note (n)	/nəʊt/
obey (v)	/ə'beɪ/
paperback (n)	/peɪpəbæk/
pearl (n)	/pɜːl/
pine tree (n)	/paɪn triː/
poet (n)	/pəʊɪt/
pretend (v)	/prɪ'tend/
produce (v)	/prə'djuːs/
pulp (n)	/pʌlp/
realistic (adj)	/rɪə'lɪstɪk/
register (v)	/redʒɪstə/
relaxed (adj)	/rɪ'lækst/
remind (v)	/rɪ'maɪnd/
remove (v)	/rɪ'muːv/
report back	/rɪˌpɔːt 'bæk/
reporter (n)	/rɪ'pɔːtə/
risk (v)	/rɪsk/
robot (n)	/rəʊbɒt/
rollers (n pl)	/rəʊləz/
secret (adj)	/siːkrət/
spelling (n)	/spelɪŋ/
style (n)	/staɪl/
succeed (v)	/sək'siːd/
suffer (v)	/sʌfə/
sunset (n)	/sʌnset/
superhero (n)	/suːpəˌhɪərəʊ/
take out	/teɪk 'aʊt/
talent (n)	/tælənt/
tell the truth	/tel ðə 'truːθ/
try out	/traɪ 'aʊt/
turn into	/tɜːn 'ɪntʊ/
unique (adj)	/juː'niːk/
virtual (adj)	/vɜːtʃʊəl/
volcanic (adj)	/vɒl'kænɪk/
wonder (v)	/wʌndə/
wood (n)	/wʊd/
worker (n)	/wɜːkə/
yoga (n)	/jəʊgə/
zombie (n)	/zɒmbi/

COUNTRIES (2)

Costa Rica	/ˌkɒstə 'riːkə/
Kenya	/kenjə/
Malaysia	/mə'leɪziə/
Singapore	/sɪŋə'pɔː/
Vietnam	/vieti'næm/

FILMS

action film (n)	/ækʃn fɪlm/
animation (n)	/ænɪ'meɪʃn/
comedy (n)	/kɒmədi/
documentary (n)	/dɒkjʊ'mentri/
drama (n)	/drɑːmə/
horror film (n)	/hɒrə fɪlm/
musical (n)	/mjuːzɪkl/
romantic film (n)	/rəʊ'mæntɪk fɪlm/
science fiction film (n)	/ˌsaɪəns 'fɪkʃn fɪlm/

OPINIONS

awful (adj)	/ɔːfl/
boring (adj)	/bɔːrɪŋ/
brilliant (adj)	/brɪliənt/
disappointing (adj)	/dɪsə'pɔɪntɪŋ/
excellent (adj)	/eksələnt/
exciting (adj)	/ɪk'saɪtɪŋ/
funny (adj)	/fʌni/
interesting (adj)	/ɪntrəstɪŋ/
scary (adj)	/skeəri/
silly (adj)	/sɪli/
terrible (adj)	/terɪbl/
terrific (adj)	/tə'rɪfɪk/
thrilling (adj)	/θrɪlɪŋ/

PERFORMANCE/DANCE

ballet (n)	/bæleɪ/
breakdancing (n)	/breɪkdɑːnsɪŋ/
choreographer (n)	/kɒri'ɒgrəfə/
coach (n)	/kəʊtʃ/
music business (n)	/mjuːzɪk bɪznɪs/
partner (n)	/pɑːtnə/
salsa (n)	/sælsə/
step (n)	/step/
trainer (person) (n)	/treɪnə/

PHRASAL VERBS WITH UP

come up with	/kʌm 'ʌp wɪð/
give up	/gɪv 'ʌp/
grow up	/grəʊ 'ʌp/
look up	/lʊk 'ʌp/
pick up	/pɪk 'ʌp/
set up	/set 'ʌp/
stand up	/stænd 'ʌp/
turn up	/tɜːn 'ʌp/

ADJECTIVE SUFFIXES -FUL and -LESS

careful	/keəfl/
careless	/keələs/
colourful	/kʌləfl/
colourless	/kʌlələs/
hopeful	/həʊpfl/
hopeless	/həʊpləs/
painful	/peɪnfl/
painless	/peɪnləs/
successful	/sək'sesfl/
truthful	/truːθfl/

REVIEW UNITS 1–2

bring up	/brɪŋ 'ʌp/
cost (n)	/kɒst/
embarrassing (adj)	/ɪm'bærəsɪŋ/
in the red	/ɪn ðə 'red/
price (n)	/praɪs/
result (n)	/rɪ'zʌlt/
simple (adj)	/sɪmpl/
survey (n)	/sɜːveɪ/
three-quarters (n pl)	/θriː 'kwɔːtəz/
two-thirds (n pl)	/tuː 'θɜːdz/

Unit 3

aim (v)	/eɪm/
airline (n)	/eəlaɪn/
annual (adj)	/ænjuəl/
apology (n)	/ə'pɒlədʒi/
army (n)	/ɑːmi/
as long as	/əz 'lɒŋ əz/
boil (v)	/bɔɪl/
broken (adj)	/brəʊkn/
bully (v)	/bʊli/
bullying (n)	/bʊliɪŋ/
carpet (n)	/kɑːpɪt/
cheat (v)	/tʃiːt/
cause (v)	/kɔːz/
cigar (n)	/sɪ'gɑː/
climate (n)	/klaɪmət/
concentrate (v)	/kɒnsəntreɪt/
dirty (adj)	/dɜːti/
disease (n)	/dɪ'ziːz/
drinking water (n)	/drɪŋkɪŋ wɔːtə/
electricity (n)	/ɪlek'trɪsəti/
factory (n)	/fæktri/
fair (adj)	/feə/
farmer (n)	/fɑːmə/
fault (n)	/fɒlt/
firmly (adv)	/fɜːmli/
floor (n)	/flɔː/
for long	/fə 'lɒŋ/
get married	/get 'mærɪd/
greenhouse gas (n)	/griːnhaʊs gæs/
guilty (adj)	/gɪlti/
heating (n)	/hiːtɪŋ/
host (n)	/həʊst/
I beg your pardon?	/aɪ beg jɔː ˌpɑːdn/
ignore (v)	/ɪg'nɔː/
in advance	/ɪn əd'vɑːns/
intend (v)	/ɪn'tend/
interrupt (v)	/ɪntə'rʌpt/
keep a secret	/ˌkiːp ə 'siːkrət/
lighted (adj)	/laɪtɪd/
likely (adj)	/laɪkli/
limit (v)	/lɪmɪt/
lottery ticket (n)	/lɒtəri tɪkɪt/
make a difference	/meɪk ə 'dɪfrəns/
mask (n)	/mɑːsk/
motor boat (n)	/məʊtəbəʊt/
nasty (adj)	/nɑːsti/
nicely (adv)	/naɪsli/
on standby	/ɒn 'stændbaɪ/
panic (v)	/pænɪk/
part-time (adj)	/pɑːt taɪm/
poor (adj)	/pɔː/
profile (n)	/prəʊfaɪl/
promise (n)	/prɒmɪs/
purpose (n)	/pɜːpəs/
refrigerator (n)	/rɪ'frɪdʒəreɪtə/
respect (n & v)	/rɪ'spekt/
responsible (adj)	/rɪ'spɒnsɪbl/
revision (n)	/rɪ'vɪʒn/
run (v)	/rʌn/
safety (n)	/seɪfti/
sand (n)	/sænd/
secretly (adv)	/siːkrətli/
stay awake	/steɪ ə'weɪk/
string (n)	/strɪŋ/
switch off	/swɪtʃ 'ɒf/
take a break	/teɪk ə 'breɪk/
take control	/teɪk kən'trəʊl/
take time	/teɪk taɪm/
tell lies	/tel 'laɪz/
texting (n)	/tekstɪŋ/
treat (v)	/triːt/
turn down (heating)	/tɜːn 'daʊn/
upset (adj)	/ʌp'set/
vacation (n)	/və'keɪʃn/
vacuum cleaner (n)	/vækjuəm kliːnə/
viewer (n)	/vjuːə/
weapon (n)	/wepn/
whale-hunting (n)	/weɪl hʌntɪŋ/

WORD LIST

FOOD
chilli sauce (n)	/ˈtʃɪli ˈsɔːs/
coconut (n)	/ˈkəʊkənʌt/
lemon (n)	/ˈlemən/
lobster (n)	/ˈlɒbstə/
melon (n)	/ˈmelən/
prawn (n)	/prɔːn/
salt (n)	/sɒlt/
spaghetti (n)	/spəˈgeti/
sugar (n)	/ˈʃʊgə/
tomato sauce (n)	/təˌmɑːtəʊ ˈsɔːs/
tuna steak (n)	/ˈtʃuːnə steɪk/

LAWS
against the law	/əˌgenst ðə ˈlɔː/
arrest (v)	/əˈrest/
break a law	/ˌbreɪk ə ˈlɔː/
forbidden (adj)	/fəˈbɪdn/
illegal (adj)	/ɪˈliːgl/
law-breaking (adj)	/ˈlɔːbreɪkɪŋ/
No entry.	/nəʊ ˈentri/
visa (n)	/ˈviːzə/

POLITICS
aid (n)	/eɪd/
developing world (n)	/dɪˌveləpɪŋ ˈwɜːld/
education (n)	/ˌedjuˈkeɪʃn/
election (n)	/ɪˈlekʃn/
the EU (European Union)	/ði iː ˈjuː/
government (n)	/ˈgʌvnmənt/
human rights (n pl)	/ˌhjuːmən ˈraɪts/
poverty (n)	/ˈpɒvəti/
trade (n)	/treɪd/

PHRASAL VERBS WITH *DOWN*
calm down	/ˌkɑːm ˈdaʊn/
let down	/ˌlet ˈdaʊn/
lie down	/ˌlaɪ ˈdaʊn/
sit down	/ˌsɪt ˈdaʊn/
slow down	/ˌsləʊ ˈdaʊn/
turn down	/ˌtɜːn ˈdaʊn/
write down	/ˌraɪt ˈdaʊn/

ADJECTIVE PREFIXES *IL-*, *IN-* and *IM-*
(il)legal	/(ɪ)ˈliːgl/
(il)logical	/(ɪ)ˈlɒdʒɪkl/
(im)perfect	/(ɪm)ˈpɜːfɪkt/
(im)polite	/(ɪm)pəˈlaɪt/
(im)possible	/(ɪm)ˈpɒsəbl/
(in)correct	/(ɪn)kəˈrekt/
(in)credible	/(ɪn)ˈkredɪbl/
(in)visible	/(ɪn)ˈvɪzɪbl/

CULTURE Great Novels
ankle (n)	/ˈæŋkl/
author (n)	/ˈɔːθə/
bald (adj)	/bɒld/
belt (n)	/belt/
cab (n)	/kæb/
collar (n)	/ˈkɒlə/
cry (= shout) (v)	/kraɪ/
detective (n)	/dɪˈtektɪv/
doorway (n)	/ˈdɔːweɪ/
dramatic (adj)	/drəˈmætɪk/
enemy (n)	/ˈenəmi/
excitedly (adv)	/ɪkˈsaɪtɪdli/
fall in love	/ˌfɔːl ɪn ˈlʌv/
gentleman (n)	/ˈdʒentlmən/
ground (n)	/graʊnd/
handkerchief (n)	/ˈhæŋkətʃɪf/
handsome (adj)	/ˈhænsəm/
heavily (adv)	/ˈhevɪli/
heroine (n)	/ˈherəʊɪn/
knock (v)	/nɒk/
let go	/let ˈgəʊ/
lifetime (n)	/ˈlaɪftaɪm/
literature (n)	/ˈlɪtrətʃə/
master (n)	/ˈmɑːstə/
memorable (adj)	/ˈmemrəbl/
mystery (n)	/ˈmɪstəri/
nearby (adv)	/nɪəˈbaɪ/
owner (n)	/ˈəʊnə/
push (v)	/pʊʃ/
remain (v)	/rɪˈmeɪn/
safely (adv)	/ˈseɪfli/
servant (n) (TS)	/ˈsɜːvənt/
shelter (v)	/ˈʃeltə/
shorthand (n)	/ˈʃɔːthænd/
silk (adj)	/sɪlk/
slip (v)	/slɪp/
solve (v)	/sɒlv/
turban (n)	/ˈtɜːbən/
unknown (adj)	/ʌnˈnəʊn/
unlike (prep)	/ʌnˈlaɪk/
villain (n)	/ˈvɪlən/
well-educated (adj)	/ˌwelˈedjʊkeɪtɪd/

Unit 4
adore (v)	/əˈdɔː/
afterwards (adv)	/ˈɑːftəwədz/
anger (n)	/ˈæŋgə/
bang (v)	/bæŋ/
bright (light) (adj)	/braɪt/
bruise (n)	/bruːz/
button (n)	/ˈbʌtn/
calculator (n)	/ˈkælkjʊleɪtə/
chance (n)	/tʃɑːns/
cheek (n)	/tʃiːk/
clap (v)	/klæp/
confess (v)	/kənˈfes/
confidence (n)	/ˈkɒnfɪdəns/
control (v)	/kənˈtrəʊl/
crash (computer) (v)	/kræʃ/
curly (adj)	/ˈkɜːli/
dare (v)	/deə/
down-to-earth (adj)	/ˌdaʊn tu ˈɜːθ/
drop (v)	/drɒp/
drown (v)	/draʊn/
fancy dress ball (n)	/ˌfænsi ˈdres bɔːl/
fine (n)	/faɪn/
flashy (adj)	/ˈflæʃi/
footstep (n)	/ˈfʊtstep/
forward (adv)	/ˈfɔːwəd/
get over	/get ˈəʊvə/
give in	/gɪv ˈɪn/
give someone a lift	/ˌgɪv ˌsʌmwʌn ə ˈlɪft/
heights (n pl)	/haɪts/
honeymoon (n)	/ˈhʌnimuːn/
however (conj)	/haʊˈevə/
inquest (n)	/ˈɪŋkwest/
It makes no difference.	/ɪt ˌmeɪks nəʊ ˈdɪfrəns/
It's up to you.	/ɪts ˌʌp tə ˈjuː/
juggle (v)	/ˈdʒʌgl/
keep in touch	/ˌkiːp ɪn ˈtʌtʃ/
kite (n)	/kaɪt/
knob (n)	/nɒb/
ladder (n)	/ˈlædə/
lorry (n) (TS)	/ˈlɒri/
nail (= fingernail) (n)	/neɪl/
notice (v)	/ˈnəʊtɪs/
presence (n)	/ˈprezəns/
press (v)	/pres/
prove (v)	/pruːv/
put on (clothes)	/pʊt ˈɒn/
rational (adj)	/ˈræʃnəl/
registration number (n)	/ˌredʒɪˈstreɪʃn ˌnʌmbə/
reply (v)	/rɪˈplaɪ/
role (n)	/rəʊl/
rough (adj)	/rʌf/
steady (adj)	/ˈstedi/
suicide (n)	/ˈsuːɪsaɪd/
take no notice	/ˌteɪk nəʊ ˈnəʊtɪs/
take over	/ˌteɪk ˈəʊvə/
trouble (v) (TS)	/ˈtrʌbl/
tunnel (n)	/ˈtʌnl/
turn off (the lights)	/ˌtɜːn ˈɒf/
unconscious (adj)	/ʌnˈkɒnʃəs/
verdict (n)	/ˈvɜːdɪkt/
wig (n)	/wɪg/

ADVERBS
absolutely	/ˈæbsəluːtli/
accidentally	/ˌæksɪˈdentli/
frequently	/ˈfriːkwəntli/
fully	/ˈfʊli/
gently	/ˈdʒentli/
impatiently	/ɪmˈpeɪʃntli/

FLIGHT
airfield (n)	/ˈeəfiːld/
control tower (n)	/kənˈtrəʊl ˌtaʊə/
controls (n pl)	/kənˈtrəʊlz/
instruments (n pl)	/ˈɪnstrəmənts/
land (v)	/lænd/
runway (n)	/ˈrʌnweɪ/
take off	/ˌteɪk ˈɒf/
throttle (n)	/ˈθrɒtl/

OCCUPATIONS
diver (n)	/ˈdaɪvə/
housekeeper (n)	/ˈhaʊskiːpə/
instructor (n)	/ɪnˈstrʌktə/
investigator (n)	/ɪnˈvestɪgeɪtə/
painter (n)	/ˈpeɪntə/

SUPERSTITION
haunted (adj)	/ˈhɔːntɪd/
horoscope (n)	/ˈhɒrəskəʊp/
lucky charm (n)	/ˌlʌki ˈtʃɑːm/
prediction (n)	/prɪˈdɪkʃn/
psychic (adj)	/ˈsaɪkɪk/
supernatural (n)	/ˌsuːpəˈnætʃrəl/
superstition (n)	/ˌsuːpəˈstɪʃn/
superstitious (n)	/ˌsuːpəˈstɪʃəs/
Touch wood. (n)	/ˌtʌtʃ ˈwʊd/

PHRASAL VERBS WITH *OUT*
find out	/ˌfaɪnd ˈaʊt/
go out	/ˌgəʊ ˈaʊt/
hold out	/ˌhəʊld ˈaʊt/
look out	/ˌlʊk ˈaʊt/
read out	/ˌriːd ˈaʊt/
take out	/ˌteɪk ˈaʊt/
try out	/ˌtraɪ ˈaʊt/

REVIEW UNITS 3–4
aircraft (n)	/ˈeəkrɑːft/
(un)necessary (adj)	/(ʌn)ˈnesəsəri/
object (n)	/ˈɒbdʒɪkt/
tidy (adj)	/ˈtaɪdi/

Unit 5
achieve (v)	/əˈtʃiːv/
advertising (adj)	/ˈædvətaɪzɪŋ/
apparently (adv)	/əˈpærəntli/
apply (for) (v)	/əˈplaɪ/
beef (n)	/biːf/
bouncy (adj)	/ˈbaʊnsi/
career (n)	/kəˈrɪə/
challenging (adj)	/ˈtʃæləndʒɪŋ/
champion (n)	/ˈtʃæmpiən/
combine (v)	/kəmˈbaɪn/
contain (v)	/kənˈteɪn/

122

WORD LIST

dream (n)	/driːm/
edge (n)	/edʒ/
exhausting (adj)	/ɪɡˈzɔːstɪŋ/
face (v)	/feɪs/
fail (v)	/feɪl/
float (v)	/fləʊt/
fortunately (adv)	/ˈfɔːtʃənətli/
freshwater (adj)	/ˈfreʃwɔːtə/
giant (adj)	/ˈdʒaɪənt/
glad (adj)	/ɡlæd/
grateful (adj)	/ˈɡreɪtfl/
guinea pig (n)	/ˈɡɪni pɪɡ/
hug (n)	/hʌɡ/
imagine (v)	/ɪˈmædʒɪn/
interviewer (n)	/ˈɪntəvjuːə/
line (n)	/laɪn/
litre (n)	/ˈliːtə/
llama (n)	/ˈlɑːmə/
magic (adj)	/ˈmædʒɪk/
medal (n)	/ˈmedl/
overwhelming (adj)	/ˌəʊvəˈwelmɪŋ/
pair (n)	/peə/
rise (v)	/raɪz/
roast (adj)	/rəʊst/
roll (v)	/rəʊl/
roller coaster (n)	/ˈrəʊlə ˌkəʊstə/
ruins (n pl)	/ˈruːɪnz/
runner (n)	/ˈrʌnə/
shore (n)	/ʃɔː/
speed (v)	/spiːd/
sphere (n)	/sfɪə/
steep (adj)	/stiːp/
steer (v)	/stɪə/
stone (n)	/stəʊn/
strap (v)	/stræp/
support (v)	/səˈpɔːt/
take up	/teɪk ˈʌp/
uncontrollably (adv)	/ˌʌnkənˈtrəʊləbli/
ups and downs (n)	/ˌʌps ən ˈdaʊnz/
valuable (adj)	/ˈvæljʊbl/
well-paid (adj)	/ˈwelpeɪd/
whizz (v)	/wɪz/
worth (adj)	/wɜːθ/

COUNTRIES (4)

Alaska	/əˈlæskə/
Argentina	/ˌɑːdʒənˈtiːnə/
Chile	/ˈtʃɪli/
the Czech Republic	/ðə ˌtʃek rɪˈpʌblɪk/
Ecuador	/ˈekwədɔː/
Kazakhstan	/ˌkæzəkˈstɑːn/
Mongolia	/mɒŋˈɡəʊliə/
Peru	/pəˈruː/
Slovakia	/sləˈvækiə/
Ukraine	/juːˈkreɪn/
Uruguay	/ˈjʊərəɡwaɪ/
Venezuela	/ˌvenəzˈweɪlə/

HEALTH

altitude sickness (n)	/ˈæltɪtjuːd ˌsɪknəs/
first aid (n)	/ˌfɜːst ˈeɪd/
have an accident	/ˌhæv ən ˈæksɪdənt/
headache (n)	/ˈhedeɪk/
injury (n)	/ˈɪndʒəri/

SPORT

bungee jumping (n)	/ˈbʌndʒi dʒʌmpɪŋ/
ice hockey (n)	/ˈaɪs hɒki/
kite surfing (n)	/ˈkaɪt sɜːfɪŋ/
paragliding (n)	/ˈpærəɡlaɪdɪŋ/
paraskiing (n)	/ˈpærəskiːɪŋ/
sailing (n)	/ˈseɪlɪŋ/
skiing (n)	/ˈskiːɪŋ/
snowboarding (n)	/ˈsnəʊbɔːdɪŋ/
sphereing (n)	/ˈsfɪərɪŋ/
water-skiing (n)	/ˈwɔːtəskiːɪŋ/
zorbing (n)	/ˈzɔːbɪŋ/

TRAVEL

hostel (n)	/ˈhɒstl/
motorcycle (n)	/ˈməʊtəsaɪkl/
route (n)	/ruːt/
trail (n)	/treɪl/
travel (n)	/ˈtrævl/
trek (n)	/trek/

NOUN SUFFIX -ITY

activity (n)	/ækˈtɪvəti/
electricity (n)	/ɪlekˈtrɪsəti/
nationality (n)	/ˌnæʃəˈnæləti/
popularity (n)	/ˌpɒpjəˈlærəti/
possibility (n)	/ˌpɒsəˈbɪləti/
reality (n)	/riˈæləti/
responsibility (n)	/rɪsˌpɒnsəˈbɪləti/
speciality (n)	/ˌspeʃiˈæləti/

CULTURE Your holiday, their home

afford (v)	/əˈfɔːd/
bargain (n)	/ˈbɑːɡɪn/
bikini (n)	/bɪˈkiːni/
culture (n)	/ˈkʌltʃə/
distance (n)	/ˈdɪstəns/
dress (v)	/dres/
free (=without paying) (adv)	/friː/
import (v)	/ɪmˈpɔːt/
in favour of	/ɪn ˈfeɪvə əv/
increase (v)	/ɪnˈkriːs/
local (person) (n)	/ˈləʊkl/
millionaire (n)	/ˌmɪljəˈneə/
offend (v)	/əˈfend/
preach (v)	/priːtʃ/
private (adj)	/ˈpraɪvət/
reduce (v)	/rɪˈdjuːs/
resort (n)	/rɪˈzɔːt/
tap (water tap) (n)	/tæp/
turn on (a tap)	/tɜːn ˈɒn/

Unit 6

ad (= advertisement) (n)	/æd/
advantage (n)	/ədˈvɑːntɪdʒ/
appliance (n)	/əˈplaɪəns/
Arabic	/ˈærəbɪk/
attempt (n)	/əˈtemt/
blind (adj)	/blaɪnd/
bottle top (n)	/ˈbɒtl tɒp/
brick (n)	/brɪk/
broccoli (n)	/ˈbrɒkəli/
brush (n)	/brʌʃ/
campaign (n)	/kæmˈpeɪn/
cards (play cards) (n pl)	/kɑːdz/
carpenter (n)	/ˈkɑːpɪntə/
chamber (n)	/ˈtʃeɪmbə/
clockwork	/ˈklɒkwɜːk/
complicated (adj)	/ˈkɒmplɪkeɪtɪd/
compose (v)	/kəmˈpəʊz/
connect (v)	/kəˈnekt/
connection (n)	/kəˈnekʃn/
construct (v)	/kənˈstrʌkt/
consume (v)	/kənˈsjuːm/
countless (adj)	/ˈkaʊntləs/
deaf (adj)	/def/
design (n)	/dɪˈzaɪn/
detailed (adj)	/ˈdiːteɪld/
disabled (adj)	/dɪsˈeɪbld/
dot (n)	/dɒt/
dye (n)	/daɪ/
electrical (adj)	/ɪˈlektrɪkl/
electronics (n)	/ɪlekˈtrɒnɪks/
endless (adj)	/ˈendləs/
explode (v)	/ɪksˈpləʊd/
flag (n)	/flæɡ/
force (n)	/fɔːs/
full-scale (adj)	/ˈfʊlskeɪl/
genius (n)	/ˈdʒiːniəs/
glove (n)	/ɡlʌv/
heat (v)	/hiːt/
hen (n)	/hen/
imaginative (adj)	/ɪˈmædʒɪnətɪv/
in the first place	/ˌɪn ðə ˈfɜːst pleɪs/
inspiration (n)	/ˌɪnspəˈreɪʃn/
introduce (v)	/ˌɪntrəˈdjuːs/
lamp (n)	/læmp/
list (v)	/lɪst/
material (n)	/məˈtɪəriəl/
medical (adj)	/ˈmedɪkl/
mend (v)	/mend/
nominate (v)	/ˈnɒmɪneɪt/
not only … but also (conj)	/nɒt ˈəʊnli… bət ˈɔːlsəʊ/
on display	/ɒn dɪsˈpleɪ/
operation (n)	/ˌɒpəˈreɪʃn/
pick (v)	/pɪk/
poll (n)	/pəʊl/
powered (adj)	/ˈpaʊəd/
powerful (adj)	/ˈpaʊəfl/
practical (adj)	/ˈpræktɪkl/
printer (n)	/ˈprɪntə/
process (n)	/ˈprəʊses/
product (n)	/ˈprɒdʌkt/
put into practice	/ˌpʊt ɪntə ˈpræktɪs/
pyramid (n)	/ˈpɪrəmɪd/
raised (adj)	/reɪzd/
recorder (instrument) (n)	/rɪˈkɔːdə/
recycle (v)	/riːˈsaɪkl/
recycled (adj)	/riːˈsaɪkld/
replace (v)	/rɪˈpleɪs/
reported (adj)	/rɪˈpɔːtɪd/
resource (n)	/rɪˈzɔːs/
run into	/rʌn ˈɪntə/
self-propelled (adj)	/ˌselfprəˈpeld/
shortlist (n)	/ˈʃɔːtlɪst/
shut (v)	/ʃʌt/
sign language (n)	/ˈsaɪn læŋɡwɪdʒ/
simplify (v)	/ˈsɪmplɪfaɪ/
sketch (v)	/sketʃ/
skins (n pl)	/skɪnz/
soldier (n)	/ˈsəʊldʒə/
sophisticated (adj)	/səˈfɪstɪkeɪtɪd/
spin (v)	/spɪn/
stylish (adj)	/ˈstaɪlɪʃ/
supply (v)	/səˈplaɪ/
surface (n)	/ˈsɜːfɪs/
system (n)	/ˈsɪstəm/
test (v)	/test/
throw away	/θrəʊ əˈweɪ/
tram (n)	/træm/
tyre (n)	/taɪə/
vehicle (n)	/ˈviːɪkl/
war (n)	/wɔː/
waste (n)	/weɪst/
wear out	/weə ˈaʊt/
workout (n)	/ˈwɜːkaʊt/
yoghurt (n)	/ˈjɒɡət/

ADVERBS

approximately (adv)	/əˈprɒksɪmətli/
dramatically (adv)	/drəˈmætɪkli/
entirely (adv)	/ɪnˈtaɪəli/
highly (adv)	/ˈhaɪli/
interestingly (adv)	/ˈɪntrəstɪŋli/

CONTAINERS

bag (n)	/bæɡ/
basket (n)	/ˈbɑːskɪt/
bottle (n)	/ˈbɒtl/
can (n)	/kæn/
carton (n)	/ˈkɑːtn/
pencil case (n)	/ˈpensl keɪs/
pot (n)	/pɒt/

123

WORD LIST

INVENTIONS and DISCOVERIES
aqualung (n)	/ˈækwəlʌŋ/
atomic bomb (n)	/əˌtɒmɪk ˈbɒm/
bicycle (n)	/ˈbaɪsɪkl/
Braille	/breɪl/
car alarm (n)	/ˈkɑː əˌlɑːm/
computer (n)	/kəmˈpjuːtə/
helicopter (n)	/ˈhelɪkɒptə/
internal combustion engine (n)	/ɪnˌtɜːnl kəmˈbʌstʃn ˌendʒɪn/
invention (n)	/ɪnˈvenʃn/
iron (n)	/aɪən/
light bulb (n)	/laɪt bʌlb/
mobile phone (n)	/ˌməʊbaɪl ˈfəʊn/
nuclear bomb (n)	/ˌnjuːklɪə ˈbɒm/
parachute (n)	/ˈpærəʃuːt/
penicillin (n)	/ˌpenəˈsɪlɪn/
plastic surgery (n)	/ˌplæstɪk ˈsɜːdʒəri/
printing (n)	/ˈprɪntɪŋ/
robot (n) (repeat)	/ˈrəʊbɒt/
telephone (n)	/ˈteləfəʊn/
television (n)	/ˈtelɪvɪʒn/
World Wide Web (n)	/ˌwɜːld waɪd ˈweb/

MATERIALS
cotton (n & adj)	/ˈkɒtn/
denim (n & adj)	/ˈdenɪm/
glass (n & adj)	/glɑːs/
leather (n & adj)	/ˈleðə/
metal (n & adj)	/ˈmetl/
paper (n & adj)	/ˈpeɪpə/
plastic (n & adj)	/ˈplæstɪk/
rubber (n & adj)	/ˈrʌbə/
wood (n & adj)	/wʊd/
wool (n & adj)	/wʊl/

PHRASES WITH DO
do damage	/ˌduː ˈdæmɪdʒ/
do an exercise	/ˌduː ən ˈeksəsaɪz/
do the shopping	/ˌduː ðə ˈʃɒpɪŋ/
do the washing up	/ˌduː ðə wɒʃɪŋ ˈʌp/
do some work	/ˌduː səm ˈwɜːk/

PHRASES WITH MAKE
make an attempt	/ˌmeɪk ən əˈtemt/
make a difference	/ˌmeɪk ə ˈdɪfrəns/
make friends	/ˌmeɪk ˈfrendz/
make a list	/ˌmeɪk ə ˈlɪst/
make a mistake	/ˌmeɪk ə mɪˈsteɪk/
make a sign	/ˌmeɪk ə ˈsaɪn/
make sure	/ˌmeɪk ˈʃʊə/

NOUN SUFFIX -OR
actor	/ˈæktə/
director	/dəˈrektə, daɪˈrektə/
emperor	/ˈempərə/
inventor	/ɪnˈventə/
professor	/prəˈfesə/
translator	/trænsˈleɪtə/

NOUN SUFFIX -ER
designer	/dɪˈzaɪnə/
engineer	/endʒɪˈnɪə/
eraser	/ɪˈreɪzə/
explorer	/ɪkˈsplɔːrə/
listener	/ˈlɪsnə/
painter	/ˈpeɪntə/
recycler	/riːˈsaɪklə/
reporter	/rɪˈpɔːtə/
ruler	/ˈruːlə/
runner	/ˈrʌnə/
supporter	/səˈpɔːtə/

NOUN SUFFIX -IST
artist	/ˈɑːtɪst/
journalist	/ˈdʒɜːnəlɪst/
novelist	/ˈnɒvəlɪst/
scientist	/ˈsaɪəntɪst/
tourist	/ˈtʊərɪst/

REVIEW UNITS 5–6
case (n)	/keɪs/
company (n)	/ˈkʌmpəni/
crane (n)	/kreɪn/
earn (v)	/ɜːn/
passer-by (n)	/ˈpɑːsəbaɪ/
shoot (baseball) (v)	/ʃuːt/
sleepwalker (n)	/ˈsliːpwɔːkə/
unnamed (adj)	/ʌnˈneɪmd/
vaccination (n)	/ˌvæksɪˈneɪʃn/

Unit 7

attract attention	/əˌtrækt əˈtenʃn/
average (adj)	/ˈævərɪdʒ/
bracelet (n)	/ˈbreɪslət/
bring back	/brɪŋ ˈbæk/
capsize (v)	/kæpˈsaɪz/
catch on	/kætʃ ˈɒn/
command (n)	/kəˈmɑːnd/
consider (v)	/kənˈsɪdə/
contact (v)	/ˈkɒntækt/
container (n)	/kənˈteɪnə/
correctly (adv)	/kəˈrektli/
definite (adj)	/ˈdefənət/
dial (v)	/ˈdaɪəl/
dinghy (n)	/ˈdɪŋi/
direct (adv)	/dɪˈrekt, daɪˈrekt/
dozen (n)	/ˈdʌzn/
effect (n)	/ɪˈfekt/
effective (adj)	/ɪˈfektɪv/
enable (v)	/ɪˈneɪbl/
enormously (adv)	/ɪˈnɔːməsli/
hold on	/həʊld ˈɒn/
household name (n)	/ˌhaʊshəʊld ˈneɪm/
Hungary	/ˈhʌŋɡəri/
in case of	/ɪn ˈkeɪs əv/
in trouble	/ɪn ˈtrʌbl/
It's early days.	/ɪts ˈɜːli deɪz/
junk (n)	/dʒʌŋk/
keyboard (n)	/ˈkiːbɔːd/
make up (= invent)	/meɪk ˈʌp/
media (n)	/ˈmiːdiə/
nerd (n)	/nɜːd/
peak (n)	/piːk/
phenomenal (adj)	/fəˈnɒmənəl/
relationship (n)	/rɪˈleɪʃnʃɪp/
remarkable (adj)	/rɪˈmɑːkəbl/
request (n)	/rɪˈkwest/
research centre (n)	/rɪˈsɜːtʃ ˌsentə/
researcher (n)	/rɪˈsɜːtʃə/
respond (v)	/rɪˈspɒnd/
right (v)	/raɪt/
run (v)	/rʌn/
sales (n pl)	/seɪlz/
scheme (n)	/skiːm/
serious (adj)	/ˈsɪəriəs/
similar (adj)	/ˈsɪmɪlə/
single room (n)	/ˌsɪŋɡl ˈruːm/
specific (adj)	/spəˈsɪfɪk/
spread (v)	/spred/
state (n)	/steɪt/
stressful (adj)	/ˈstresfl/
symbol (n)	/ˈsɪmbl/
tail (n)	/teɪl/
take off (clothes)	/teɪk ˈɒf/
tough (adj)	/tʌf/
trunk (n)	/trʌŋk/
Turkish	/ˈtɜːkɪʃ/
type (v)	/taɪp/
warehouse (n)	/ˈweəhaʊs/
watertight (adj)	/ˈwɔːtətaɪt/

ANIMALS (1)
ape (n)	/eɪp/
cat (n)	/kæt/
chimpanzee (n)	/ˌtʃɪmpænˈziː/
dog (n)	/dɒɡ/
duck (n)	/dʌk/
elephant (n)	/ˈelɪfənt/
gorilla (n)	/ɡəˈrɪlə/
monkey (n)	/ˈmʌŋki/
parrot (n)	/ˈpærət/
pig (n)	/pɪɡ/
snail (n)	/sneɪl/
tiger (n)	/ˈtaɪɡə/
worm (n)	/wɜːm/
zebra (n)	/ˈzebrə/

EMAIL
attachment (n)	/əˈtætʃmənt/
filter (v)	/ˈfɪltə/
Internet (n)	/ˈɪntənet/
ISP (Internet Service Provider) (n)	/aɪ es ˈpiː/
spam (n)	/spæm/
virus (n)	/ˈvaɪrəs/

MEDICAL and EMERGENCY SERVICES
air ambulance (n)	/ˌeə ˈæmbjələns/
ambulance control (n)	/ˈæmbjələns kənˌtrəʊl/
coastguard (n)	/ˈkəʊstɡɑːd/
emergency services (n pl)	/ɪˈmɜːdʒənsi ˌsɜːvɪsɪz/
paramedic (n)	/ˌpærəˈmedɪk/
save someone's life	/ˌseɪv sʌmwʌnz ˈlaɪf/
vet (n)	/vet/

PHRASAL VERBS WITH GO
go ahead with	/ɡəʊ əˈhed wɪð/
go down	/ɡəʊ ˈdaʊn/
go into	/ɡəʊ ˈɪntə/
go on	/ɡəʊ ˈɒn/
go through	/ɡəʊ ˈθruː/
go up	/ɡəʊ ˈʌp/

NOUN SUFFIX -TION
attention	/əˈtenʃn/
communication	/kəˌmjuːnɪˈkeɪʃn/
description	/dɪsˈkrɪpʃn/
information	/ˌɪnfəˈmeɪʃn/
instruction	/ɪnˈstrʌkʃn/
invention	/ɪnˈvenʃn/
invitation	/ˌɪnvɪˈteɪʃn/
operation	/ˌɒpəˈreɪʃn/
position	/pəˈzɪʃn/
situation	/ˌsɪtʃuˈeɪʃn/
solution	/səˈluːʃn/

CULTURE Global English
broken English	/ˌbrəʊkn ˈɪŋɡlɪʃ/
call centre (n)	/ˈkɔːl ˌsentə/
dumb (adj)	/dʌm/
electronically (adv)	/ɪlekˈtrɒnɪkli/
giggle (v)	/ˈɡɪɡl/
global (adj)	/ˈɡləʊbl/
growing (adj)	/ˈɡrəʊɪŋ/
Hindi	/ˈhɪndi/
importance (n)	/ɪmˈpɔːtəns/
Internet café (n)	/ˌɪntənet ˈkæfeɪ/
manager (n)	/ˈmænɪdʒə/
mother-to-be (n)	/ˌmʌðə tə ˈbiː/
next door (adv)	/neks ˈdɔː/

pregnant (adj)	/ˈpregnənt/
report (n)	/rɪˈpɔːt/
shyly (adv)	/ˈʃaɪli/
speaker (n)	/ˈspiːkə/
stored (adj)	/stɔːd/
technology (n)	/tekˈnɒlədʒi/
unborn (adj)	/ʌnˈbɔːn/

Unit 8

Aboriginal (adj)	/æbəˈrɪdʒɪnəl/
Aborigine (n)	/æbəˈrɪdʒəni/
affect (v)	/əˈfekt/
amount (n)	/əˈmaʊnt/
announcement (n)	/əˈnaʊnsmənt/
aspirin (n)	/ˈæsprɪn/
available (adj)	/əˈveɪləbl/
back away	/bæk əˈweɪ/
breathe (v)	/briːð/
brochure (n)	/ˈbrəʊʃə/
colony (n)	/ˈkɒləni/
concerned (adj)	/kənˈsɜːnd/
consequence (n)	/ˈkɒnsɪkwəns/
considerably (adv)	/kənˈsɪdərəbli/
count sheep	/kaʊnt ˈʃiːp/
crouch (v)	/kraʊtʃ/
cubic metre (n)	/ˌkjuːbɪk ˈmiːtə/
currency (n)	/ˈkʌrənsi/
dentist (n)	/ˈdentɪst/
dollar (n)	/ˈdɒlə/
drive (from) (v)	/draɪv/
eastern (adj)	/ˈiːstən/
effort (n)	/ˈefət/
essential (adj)	/ɪˈsentʃl/
exhibition (n)	/eksˈbɪʃn/
Gambia	/ˈgæmbɪə/
hold hands	/həʊld ˈhændz/
honey (n)	/ˈhʌni/
in other words	/ɪn ˌʌðə ˈwɜːdz/
lock (v)	/lɒk/
native (adj)	/ˈneɪtɪv/
notice (n)	/ˈnəʊtɪs/
photographic (adj)	/fəʊtəˈgræfɪk/
preserve (v)	/prɪˈzɜːv/
raise (v)	/reɪz/
shelter (n)	/ˈʃeltə/
shortage (n)	/ˈʃɔːtɪdʒ/
signal (n)	/ˈsɪgnəl/
store (v)	/stɔː/
structure (n)	/ˈstrʌktʃə/
survive (v)	/səˈvaɪv/
take a deep breath	/teɪk ə ˌdiːp ˈbreθ/
tight (adv)	/taɪt/
use (n)	/juːs/
variety (n)	/vəˈraɪəti/
work out	/wɜːk ˈaʊt/

ANIMALS (2)

brown bear (n)	/braʊn ˈbeə/
caribou (n)	/ˈkærɪbuː/
cassowary (n)	/ˈkæsəwəri/
crocodile (n)	/ˈkrɒkədaɪl/
elk (n)	/elk/
emu (n)	/ˈiːmjuː/
grizzly bear (n)	/ˌgrɪzli ˈbeə/
kangaroo (n)	/ˈkæŋgəruː/
koala (n)	/kəˈwɑːlə/
kookaburra (n)	/ˈkʊkəbʌrə/
lizard (n)	/ˈlɪzəd/
moose (n)	/muːs/
platypus (n)	/ˈplætɪpəs/
polar bear (n)	/ˌpəʊlə ˈbeə/
shark (n)	/ʃɑːk/
sheep (n)	/ʃiːp/
snake (n)	/sneɪk/
whale (n)	/weɪl/
wildlife (n)	/ˈwaɪldlaɪf/

GEOGRAPHICAL FEATURES

coral reef (n)	/ˌkɒrəl ˈriːf/
desert (v)	/ˈdezət/
falls (n pl)	/fɔːlz/
forest (n)	/ˈfɒrɪst/
grassland (n)	/ˈgrɑːslænd/
Great Barrier Reef (n)	/ˌgreɪt bærɪə ˈriːf/
Indian Ocean	/ˌɪndɪən ˈəʊʃn/
interior (n)	/ɪnˈtɪərɪə/
jungle (n)	/ˈdʒʌŋgl/
mountain range (n)	/ˈmaʊntɪn reɪndʒ/
oasis (n)	/əʊˈeɪsɪs/
outback (n)	/ˈaʊtbæk/
plain (n)	/pleɪn/
polar ice cap (n)	/ˌpəʊlə ˈaɪs kæp/
prairie (n)	/ˈpreəri/
rainforest (n)	/ˈreɪnfɒrɪst/
river (n)	/ˈrɪvə/
rocky (adj)	/ˈrɒki/
scenery (n)	/ˈsiːnəri/
semi-desert (n)	/ˈsemidezət/
tundra (n)	/ˈtʌndrə/
waterfall (n)	/ˈwɔːtəfɔːl/

ILLNESSES and AILMENTS

cold (n)	/kəʊld/
cough (n)	/kɒf/
headache (n)	/ˈhedeɪk/
hiccoughs (n pl)	/ˈhɪkʌps/
sore throat (n)	/sɔː ˈθrəʊt/
toothache (n)	/ˈtuːθeɪk/

INDUSTRY and AGRICULTURE

agriculture (n)	/ˈægrɪkʌltʃə/
coal (n)	/kəʊl/
copper (n)	/ˈkɒpə/
crops (n pl)	/krɒps/
industry (n)	/ˈɪndəstri/
iron (n)	/ˈaɪən/
mining (n)	/ˈmaɪnɪŋ/
oil (n)	/ɔɪl/
motor vehicle (n)	/ˈməʊtə viːɪkl/
sheep farming (n)	/ˈʃiːp fɑːmɪŋ/
sugar cane (n)	/ˈʃʊgə keɪn/
wheat (n)	/wiːt/

LIVING SPACES

cave (n)	/keɪv/
hotel (n)	/həʊˈtel/
igloo (n)	/ˈɪgluː/
terraced house (n)	/ˌterəst ˈhaʊs/
tree house (n)	/ˈtriː haʊs/

SURVIVAL KIT

candle (n)	/ˈkændl/
compass (n)	/ˈkʌmpəs/
first aid kit (n)	/ˌfɜːst ˈeɪd kɪt/
insect spray (n)	/ˈɪnsekt spreɪ/
magnifying glass (n)	/ˈmægnɪfaɪɪŋ ˌglɑːs/
map (n)	/mæp/
matches (n pl)	/ˈmætʃɪz/
mirror (n)	/ˈmɪrə/
needle and thread	/ˌniːdl ən ˈθred/
penknife (n)	/ˈpennaɪf/
safety pin (n)	/ˈseɪfti pɪn/
sun cream (n)	/ˈsʌn kriːm/
torch (n)	/tɔːtʃ/
whistle (n)	/ˈwɪsl/

WATER (2)

dam (n)	/dæm/
fresh water (n)	/ˌfreʃ ˈwɔːtə/
frozen (adj)	/ˈfrəʊzn/
hosepipe (n)	/ˈhəʊzpaɪp/
rainwater (n)	/ˈreɪnwɔːtə/
salt water (n)	/ˈsɒlt ˈwɔːtə/
water (v)	/ˈwɔːtə/
watering can (n)	/ˈwɔːtərɪŋ kæn/

WEATHER and CLIMATE

continental (adj)	/ˌkɒntrɪˈnentl/
cyclone (n)	/ˈsaɪkləʊn/
drought (n)	/draʊt/
hurricane (n)	/ˈhʌrɪkən/
ice (n)	/aɪs/
lightning (n)	/ˈlaɪtnɪŋ/
minus (temperature) (adj)	/ˈmaɪnəs/
monsoon (n)	/mɒnˈsuːn/
rainfall (n)	/ˈreɪnfɔːl/
snow (n)	/snəʊ/
sunshine (n)	/ˈsʌnʃaɪn/
temperature (n)	/ˈtemprɪtʃə/
thunderstorm (n)	/ˈθʌndəstɔːm/
tropical (adj)	/ˈtrɒpɪkl/
wind (n)	/wɪnd/

ADJECTIVE SUFFIX -AL

coastal	/ˈkəʊstl/
continental	/ˌkɒntrɪˈnentl/
electrical	/ɪˈlektrɪkl/
environmental	/ɪnvaɪərənˈmentl/
global	/ˈgləʊbl/
industrial	/ɪnˈdʌstrɪəl/
musical	/ˈmjuːzɪkl/
natural	/ˈnætʃrəl/
official	/əˈfɪʃl/
tropical	/ˈtrɒpɪkl/
typical	/ˈtɪpɪkl/

Review Units 7–8

overhead (adv)	/ˌəʊvəˈhed/
plenty (pron)	/ˈplenti/
spot (v)	/spɒt/
sunlight (n)	/ˈsʌnlaɪt/
taipan (n)	/ˈtaɪpæn/
waste (v)	/weɪst/

PRONUNCIATION GUIDE

Vowels

/ɑː/	arm, large
/æ/	cap, bad
/aɪ/	ride, fly
/aɪə/	diary, science
/aʊ/	how, mouth
/aʊə/	our, shower
/e/	bed, head
/eɪ/	day, grey
/eə/	hair, there
/ɪ/	give, did
/i/	happy, honeymoon
/iː/	we, heat
/ɪə/	ear, here
/ɒ/	not, watch
/əʊ/	cold, boat
/ɔː/	door, talk
/ɔɪ/	point, boy
/ʊ/	foot, could
/u/	annual
/uː/	two, food
/ʊə/	sure, tourist
/ɜː/	bird, heard
/ʌ/	fun, come
/ə/	mother, actor

Consonants

/b/	bag, rubbish
/d/	desk, cold
/f/	fill, laugh
/g/	girl, big
/h/	hand, home
/j/	yes, young
/k/	cook, back
/l/	like, fill
/m/	mean, climb
/n/	new, want
/p/	park, happy
/r/	ring, borrow
/s/	say, this
/t/	town, city
/v/	very, live
/w/	water, away
/z/	zoo, his
/ʃ/	shop, machine
/ʒ/	usually, television
/ŋ/	thank, doing
/tʃ/	cheese, picture
/θ/	thing, north
/ð/	that, clothes
/dʒ/	jeans, bridge

IRREGULAR VERBS

Infinitive	Past simple	Past participle
be	was, were	been
become	became	become
begin	began	begun
bet	bet	bet
bite	bit	bitten
blow	blew	blown
break	broke	broken
bring	brought	brought
broadcast	broadcast	broadcast
build	built	built
burn	burnt/burned	burnt/burned
buy	bought	bought
catch	caught	caught
choose	chose	chosen
come	came	come
cost	cost	cost
cut	cut	cut
dig	dug	dug
do	did	done
draw	drew	drawn
dream	dreamt/dreamed	dreamt/dreamed
drink	drank	drunk
drive	drove	driven
eat	ate	eaten
fall	fell	fallen
feed	fed	fed
feel	felt	felt
fight	fought	fought
find	found	found
fly	flew	flown
forbid	forbad(e)	forbidden
forget	forgot	forgotten
freeze	froze	frozen
get	got	got
give	gave	given
go	went	gone/been
grow	grew	grown
have	had	had
hear	heard	heard
hide	hid	hidden
hit	hit	hit
hold	held	held
hurt	hurt	hurt
keep	kept	kept
know	knew	known
lay	laid	laid
learn	learnt/learned	learnt/learned
leave	left	left
lend	lent	lent
let	let	let

Infinitive	Past simple	Past participle
lie	lay	lain
light	lit	lit
lose	lost	lost
make	made	made
mean	meant	meant
meet	met	met
pay	paid	paid
put	put	put
read /riːd/	read /red/	read /red/
rewrite	rewrote	rewritten
ride	rode	ridden
ring	rang	rung
rise	rose	risen
run	ran	run
say	said	said
see	saw	seen
sell	sold	sold
send	sent	sent
set	set	set
shake	shook	shaken
shine	shone	shone
shoot	shot	shot
show	showed	shown
shut	shut	shut
sing	sang	sung
sink	sank	sunk
sit	sat	sat
sleep	slept	slept
smell	smelt/smelled	smelt/smelled
speak	spoke	spoken
speed	sped	sped
spell	spelt/spelled	spelt/spelled
spend	spent	spent
spin	spun/span	spun
spread	spread	spread
stand	stood	stood
steal	stole	stolen
stick	stuck	stuck
swim	swam	swum
take	took	taken
teach	taught	taught
tell	told	told
think	thought	thought
throw	threw	thrown
understand	understood	understood
wake	woke	woken
wear	wore	worn
win	won	won
write	wrote	written

Macmillan Education
Between Towns Road, Oxford OX4 3PP
A division of Macmillan Publishers Limited
Companies and representatives throughout the world

ISBN 978-1-4050-2945-2

Text © Judy Garton-Sprenger and Philip Prowse 2006
Design and illustration © Macmillan Publishers 2006

The rights of Judy Garton-Sprenger and Philip Prowse to be identified as authors of this work have been asserted by them in accordance with the Copyright, Designs and Patents Act 1988.

First published 2006

All rights reserved; no part of this publication may be reproduced, stored in a retrieval system, transmitted in any form, or by any means, electronic, mechanical, photocopying, recording, or otherwise, without the prior written permission of the publishers.

Designed by Giles Davies Design Ltd
Illustrated by Hemesh Alles pp47, 48, 50, 51, 71; John Batten p75; Mark Duffin pp68, 84, 98; Tim Kahane pp25, 73; Peter Lubach pp 34, 35, 69, 106; Gillian Martin p45; Julian Mosedale pp46, 87, 95; Mark Ruffle pp49, 82, 93(b); Martin Sanders p52; Kate Sheppard pp16, 40, 64, 88; Simon Smith p94; Nadine Wickenden p93(a); Gary Wing pp 108, 119
Cover design by Sue Ayres
Cover photographs with kind permission of: Getty Images, Photodisc and Photolibrary.

Authors' acknowledgements
The authors would like to thank all the team at Macmillan Education in the UK and world-wide for everything they have done to help create *Inspiration*.

We are most grateful to Carl Robinson (Publisher, Secondary Europe) for initiating and overseeing the whole project so effectively and with such enthusiasm, Dulcie Booth (Commissioning Editor) for her energy, total commitment and attention to detail, Giles Davies (Design) for his imagination and creativity, and Sue Bale (Publishing Director) for all her support. We would also like to thank Julie Brett (Editorial Manager), Deirdre Gyenes (Managing Designer), Candice Renault (Photo Research), Hazel Barrett and Pauline Dooler (Permissions), Sue F. Jones and Marion Simon (Workbook Editors) and Xanthe Sturt-Taylor (Teacher's Book Editor) for their great contribution and professionalism. Our thanks are also due to Amanda Bailey and Susannah McKee for writing the excellent Teacher's Book. Jan Bell deserves more than thanks for the flair and organisational skills she brought to the superb Inspiration Builder (Teacher's Resource Pack).

We would also like to thank James Richardson for his usual great skill in producing the recorded material and the actors who appear on the recordings and bring the book to life.

We owe an enormous debt of gratitude to teenage students and their teachers in many different countries who welcomed us into their classrooms and contributed so much to the formation of Inspiration. In particular we would like to thank teachers and classes in Argentina, Greece, Italy, Poland, Spain, Switzerland, Turkey and Uruguay. We are equally indebted to all those participants on teacher training courses in Europe, South America and elsewhere from whom we have learnt so much, in particular British Council courses in the UK and overseas, and courses at the University of Durham and NILE in Norwich.

Many individuals attended focus groups and commented on syllabus and materials, and we would like to express our great thanks to all of them, in particular Ursula Bader, Anna Bialas, Maria Birkenmajer, Paolo Jacomelli, Sue F. Jones, Antonia Köppel, Annemarie Kortleven, Malgorzata Lombarowicz, Agnieszka Mulak, Urzula Nowak, Katarzyna Pietraga, Peach Richmond, Marta Rosińska, Jean Rüdiger-Harper, Karl Russi, Ursula Schauer, Grzegorz Spiewak, Adam Trim, Maya Tsiperson, Paul Weibel, Ewa Zemanek, and Halina Zgutka.

We are grateful for permission to reprint the following copyright material:
Extract from Soul Surfer by Bethany Hamilton with Sheryl Berk and Rick Bundschuh (Pocket Books, an imprint of Simon & Schuster UK Ltd, 2004), copyright © Bethany Hamilton 2004, reprinted by permission of the publishers. Extract from 'Feel Like Going Home' Director Interview with Martin Scorsese taken from www.snappermusic.com/theblues/aboutfilms/scorseseinterview.html, reprinted by permission of Vulcan Productions Inc. Extracts from 'Global Truths', first published in Bulb Magazine issue No: 2, reprinted by permission of the publisher. *You've Got A Friend* Words and Music by Carole King copyright © Screen Gems-EMI Music Inc, USA 1971, reprinted by permission of EMI Music Publishing Ltd, London, WD2H 0QY and International Music Publications Ltd. All Rights Reserved. Extract from 'British teens milk parents for money – but do they know the cost of a pint of the white stuff?' taken from ICM Polls, reprinted by permission of the publisher. Extract from ELVIS SPEAKS FROM THE BEYOND and other celebrity GHOST STOIRES by Hans Holzer (Dorset Press, a division of Barnes & Noble Inc.), by arrangement with Hans Holzer, 1993), copyright © Hans Holzer 1993, reprinted by permission of the author.

Celebrate the Future Hand in Hand Words by Cheryl Berman Music by Ira Antelis copyright © Wonderland Music Company Incorporated 2003, administered and reprinted by permission of Warner/Chappell Music Ltd, London, W6 8BS. All Rights Reserved. Short quote by Kirsty Jones, reprinted by permission of the author. Article about Kelly Holmes, reprinted by permission of Jane Cowmeadow Agency on behalf of Kelly Holmes. Extract about Gina Gallant, reprinted by permission of the author. Benjamin Zephaniah 'The Tourists Are Coming' taken from Wicked World (Penguin Books, 2000), copyright © Benjamin Zephaniah 2000, reprinted by permission of PFD (www.pfd.co.uk), on behalf of Benjamin Zephaniah. Quote taken from 'Imaginative recycling' by Oliver Heath taken from www.foe.co.uk, reprinted by permission of Friends of the Earth (England Wales & N. Ireland). Extract from 'She's a lovely little car – one owner, 526 years old, runs like clockwork' by Georgina Littlejohn first published in The London Metro 26.04.04, reprinted by permission of Solo Syndication Ltd. *Brown-eyed Girl* Words and Music by Van Morrison copyright © Web IV Music Incorporated, USA/Universal Music Publishing Limited 1967, reprinted by permission of Music Sales Limited. All Rights Reserved. International Copyright Secured. Extracts from 'A Conversation With The Inventor of Email' by Sharon Gaudin copyright © Sharon Gaudin 2002, taken from www.itmanagement.earthweb.com. Extract from 'Not the Queen's English' by Carla Power copyright © Newsweek Inc 2005, first published in Newsweek International 07.03.05, reprinted by permission of the publisher. *I Will Survive* Words and Music by Dino Fekaris & Freddie Perren copyright © Perren-Vibes Music Company/PolyGram International Publishing Incorporated, USA/Universal Music Publishing Limited 1978, reprinted by permission of Music Sales Limited. All Rights Reserved. International Copyright Secured.

Although we have tried to trace and contact copyright holders before publication, in some cases this has not been possible. If contacted we will be pleased to rectify any errors or omissions at the earliest opportunity

The authors and publishers would like to thank the following photographs for permission to reproduce their photographic material:

Action Plus Sports Images p58(1, 2, 4), Alamy/ Rex Butcher/ Jon Arnold Images pp10-11, Alamy/ Sally and Richard Greenhill p90(b), Alamy/ Simon Grosset p86(l), Alamy/ Dallas and John Heaton p67r, Alamy/ Ute Klaphake p6(tl), Alamy/ Hana Lijima/ Arcaid p96(mr), Alamy/ Dennis MacDonald p15(a), Alamy/ Polzer p96(b), Alamy/ Jiri Rezac p90(t), Alamy/ Royalty Free p15(b), p70(5), Alamy/ Christa Stadtler p10, Alamy/ Edd Westmacott p30(b); Andes Press Agency/ Carlos Reyes-Manzo p92(t); BBN p82; Bridgeman Art Library p26(B), p72(tr), p107; British Library p74r; Corbis/ China Photos/ Reuters p92(b), Corbis/ Jon Feingersh p36, Corbis/ Rick Friedman p81, p97, Corbis/ Charles Gupton p40, Corbis/ Gary Hershorn p60(1), Corbis/ Historical Picture Archive p74(l), Corbis/ Douglas Kirkland p88(l), p97, Corbis/ Serge Krouglikoff p22(tc), Corbis/ Michael Prince p22(bc), Corbis/ Royalty Free p30(t), p61, Corbis/ Setboun p86r, Corbis/ Paul Steel p66(l), Corbis/ Tom Stewart p15c, p63, Corbis/ Lucilio Studio, Inc. p16r, Corbis/ Ron Watts p88r; Isabelle Dubois p96(igloo); Gamirasu Cave Hotel/Süleyman Çakır/ www.gamirasu.com p96(ml); Getty Images/ Giuseppe Cacace p72(l), Getty Images/ Peter Cade p84, Getty Images/ Frank Driggs Collection p14(b), Getty images p72(br), p96(t), Getty Images/ Three Lions p76, Getty Images/ Brad Wilson p78; Great Ape Trust of Iowa p80; Noah Hamilton p12; Impact Photos/ Mark Henley p93; Imperial War Museum p26C; Lebrecht Music and Arts p14(m); Lonely Planet Images/ Grant Dixon p62(b), Lonely Planet Images/ Eric L. Wheater p62(t); Ewan Mc Gregor and Charley Boorman/ Time Warner Books UK/ Photography by Russ Malkin p56; Kathy Morlan/ Massachussets Institue of Technology p68(tr); Movie Store Collection Ltd. P14(t); The National Museum of Art, Architecture and Design, Oslo/ Munch Museum/ Munch-Ellingsen Group, Bono, Oslo, DACS, London 2006 p26(A); Oxford Cartographers pp18-19; Photolibrary.com/ Aflo Foto Agency p16(l), Photolibrary.com/ Mauritius Die Bildagentur Gmbh p22(b), Photolibrary.com/ Steve Turner p98(t); Redferns Music Picture Library/ Michael Ochs p44; Remarkable Pencils UK p70(1,4,6); Réunion des Musées Nationaux/ Hervé Lewandowski p106; Reuters/ Sherwin Crasto p91; Rex Features p28(t); Ronald Grant Archive p20(t,br, bl), p21(b,t), p28(b); Royalty Free/ BananaStock p6(tr), p6(Paolo), p7(Alex), p7(Alicia), p22(t), p23(t, b), p92(m), pp104-105, Royalty Free/ Corbis p98(m, b) p102, Royalty Free/ DigitalVision p13, Royalty Free/ Getty Images p100, p107, Royalty Free/ Image Source p6(br), Royalty Free/ Image State p64r, Royalty Free/ Photodisc p64(l, m), Royalty free/ Stockbyte p32; Ryan Patterson/ National Institute on Deafness and other Communication Disorders p68(bl); Still Pictures/ Hjalte Tin p38; Zorb Ltd, www.zorb.com p58(3). BookCrossing logo with courtesy of www.BookCrossing.com. Photography of Gina Gallant and her team courtesy of Gina Gallant p68(tl).

Commissioned photography by Dean Ryan (pp8, 11, 32, 70 and 96) and David Tolley (pp24 and 33).

We also wish to thank Nikki Legg (pp11 and 96), James Kirtland (p96), Andrew Moore (p8), Adam Leary, Laila Belyazid, Oscar Spigolon, Claudia Mba and Phillippa Nichol (p32).

Printed and bound in Spain by Edelvives
2010 2009 2008 2007
10 9 8 7 6 5 4 3